# THE PSYCHOLOGY OF RELIGIOUS DOUBT

# The Psychology of Religious Doubt

by Philip M. Helfaer

Beacon Press  *Boston*

Copyright © 1972 by Philip M. Helfaer
Library of Congress catalog card number: 72–75539
International Standard Book Number: 0–8070–1134–7
Beacon Press books are published under the auspices
of the Unitarian Universalist Association
Published simultaneously in Canada by Saunders of Toronto, Ltd.
Printed in the United States of America
9   8   7   6   5   4   3   2

*For*
*my mother, Emily L. Helfaer,*
*and*
*my father, Bertram M. Helfaer*

# Contents

## PART THREE

# The Resolution of Pervasive Doubt

PART FOUR

## The Liberal Context

# Acknowledgments

It is a pleasure to have this public opportunity to acknowledge and express my appreciation of those people who helped me in the work reported herein and who in the end made it possible. Most of this book was originally presented as a doctoral dissertation in the Department of Social Relations at Harvard University. To Dr. Daniel J. Levinson, Dr. Robert N. Bellah, and Dr. Arthur S. Couch, then in that department, I wish to express my gratitude and thanks. They were unstinting in their giving to me and to the work, helped and supported in ways too numerous to mention, and above all were always *there*. Without them the work would not have been completed. My gratitude to Dr. Myron R. Sharaf for his help and support in the later stages of the work is equally great and for similar reasons. I also wish to express here my indebtedness to Dr. Henry A. Murray who early on encouraged the development of my work. It is my hope that this book embodies to some degree the meanings and values he imparted to psychological investigation.

Other close friends also gave in large measure and contributed in various ways and at different times, and I wish to thank them: Mr. and Mrs. Darrell L. Brown (for the serenity of The Vale); Dr. Bertram J. Cohler; Dr. JoAnne Melman; Dr. Marion Sanders; and Dr. Carter C. Umbarger.

Dr. Donald R. Cutler and Mr. Jeremy Cott, editors at Beacon Press, facilitated the work, and to them, my thanks.

I am grateful to the following instructors and officials of divinity schools for their interest and for allowing the pursuit of the research in their classrooms: Dr. John Brush and Dr. Harvey Cox of Andover Newton Theological School; Dean Walter Muelder and Dr. Earl Kent Brown of Boston University School of Theology; Dean Benjamin Hersey and Mr. Richard Waka of Crane Theological School; Dr. James Forrester, president of

Gordon Divinity School, and Dr. William N. Kerr of Gordon; Dr. John Burkholder and Dr. Herbert Richardson of Harvard Divinity School.

The studies reported in this book would not exist without the cooperation of the theological students who worked with me and gave very much of themselves. I wish to take this opportunity to express again my thanks and appreciation to Chelly and Pale, Electon and Mudge, and Briting and Joel; and to Eyman and Strindge, and to Cliff, Jameson, Sal, and Girth.

Finally, to BoKwan Chen, throughout much of the course of the work, companion in good times and hard, my thanks.

During some of the time I worked on this research I was supported by Public Health Service Predoctoral Fellowship number 5 F1 MH-17, 170-02, and at a later time by NIMH Post Doctoral Training Program in the Social Sciences, grant number T1-MH-10593, sponsored by Dr. Myron R. Sharaf. A Sigma Xi Grant-in-aid of Research helped defer costs involved in transcribing taped interviews.

# Preface

Today there are many signs of a resurgence of interest in religion —in forms traditional to America, in forms traditionally Eastern, and also in nontraditional forms represented by involvements with hallucinogens, communes, and other social trends. Perhaps in these politically dark times this is a sign of light. For if there are to be new social and political forms, individual psychic life must change also. I would hope that this work contributes in a small way to understanding the nature and sources of such change.

The religious beliefs discussed herein are mainly traditional Protestant ones. I hope the reader will understand that these beliefs, while of interest and importance in themselves, are also only one kind of vehicle for universal human concerns—faith and doubt, hope and despair, meaning and meaninglessness, wholeness and division. The analysis of the religious beliefs presented here is meant to cast some light on the ideal and ideological in all its realms and forms—religious, political, and scientific.

A series of case studies makes up the substance of this book. Needless to say, the individuals studied have been disguised and pseudonyms invented. Nevertheless, I feel a certain awkwardness in presenting the case studies as justifiable representations of the real persons who provided the data on which they are based. This anxiety must stand. It is the recognition of my shortcomings as a psychologist; it is the mark of the limitations of depth psychology as a study of man; it is the representation of the discrepancies between their faiths and mine; and finally, it is the sign of the fact that psychic life cannot be comprehended within the terms of any one symbol system. It is perhaps the recognition of this last that did allow the understanding to grow between myself and each of these men that, while never pretending we shared the same premises about man and the universe, in pursuing our personal paths we were both similarly mistaken and similarly doubtful in a quest which had some common overriding human meanings. I too have certainly sought such meanings.

The tension and difference between psychological investigation and religious faith remains, however, and regardless of any commonalities, this tension will be perceived as in some way a sign of evil by those in need of an absolute system for comprehending the world. To others, even in our time, the psychological study of man itself remains inimical. To those who feel this way I ask that in reading these studies they remind themselves that the feeling in question is their own, not mine. To the theological students who worked with me, I believe I conveyed in the course of our work together my own belief that whatever we learn of man through psychological observation and thinking can ultimately contribute to his glorification—if we are only willing to so use it.

Philip M. Helfaer
*Somerville, Massachusetts, July 1971*

*Splits and gaps are in every soul . . .*
—PAUL TILLICH

# PART ONE

# Backgrounds–Psychological and Theological

# I

# Introduction: Religious Doubt as a Phenomenon for Psychological Study

Doubt SelfJealous, Wat'ry folly,
Struggling thro' Earth's Melancholy.
Naked in Air, in Shame and Fear,
Blind in Fire with shield and spear,
Two Horn'd Reasoning, Cloven Fiction,
In Doubt, which is Self contradiction,
A dark Hermaphrodite We stood,
Rational Truth, Root of Evil and Good.

WILLIAM BLAKE, FOR THE SEXES: THE GATES OF
PARADISE. OF THE GATES

Religious beliefs hold a place in psychic life similar to dreams and artistic productions. They express in symbols, images, and rituals man's most basic perception of himself and his world and the deepest, most ambiguous, and most conflictful side of human experience. The religious symbolisms are not invented arbitrarily through rational thought and decision. They lie along the raw edge where the certainties and regularities of daily life and science are met by the awesome ambiguities of deeper joyful and fearful experience, and the more primitive, creative

1

edge of the mind, wrung by such overwhelming disparities, takes dramatic images and loads them with the most powerful forces of good and evil within the realm of imagination.

Faith of any sort has associated with it a number of devoutly desired attributes. While the man of faith may have doubts, he is considered to have an essential certitude and stability of belief, a central stance, a rallying point to which he can gravitate in the face of doubt or crisis. Emotional qualities of the most important order are thought to arise from such a structure of belief: hope, trust, a sense of meaning and wholeness. Even more, it seems, faith offers antidotes to the painful existential conditions of life: an endless source of nurturance, a compensation for evil, a sense of transcendence to counteract an invidious corrosive quality of daily life, and finally an object to alleviate the painful foresight of ultimate nothingness. Belief offers a guide to living, a pathway for identity formation, and a vehicle for entering deeply into life.

And yet, for the individual, the luring promise inherent in belief, the realization of the most cherished and sought-after qualities of life, may, paradoxically, be difficult to realize. He may end up living not by his beliefs, but with them, as with a treasured possession. At the same time, the individual may find his belief system cramping, inhibiting, and he may find it limits his growth by fostering a kind of dependence. Even more disturbing to the seeker or believer is the kind of doubt that somehow finds an inevitable conjunction with faith, as if the very objects of worship that promise to be the source of meaning and hope, stir also, by their promise, a sense of meaninglessness and despair.

Nevertheless, quite apart from religious belief systems, hope, meaning, and identity are generic issues. In this sense, faith, as a deep commitment to life and a sense of the meaningfulness and hopefulness of one's own life, is a universal theme. And so too is its opposite. The lack of "faith" in this sense assumes a wide range of familiar dysphoric forms, from a deep despair to a mild but chronic, nagging sense of futility.

The "case," then, of the religious doubter—this has always seemed to me to be of peculiar interest. He does not *ask*, he *suffers*, questions about life that are not only the most general and the most impossible to answer, but the questions most in need of answering: Does God exist? What is belief? Is what I am trying to believe as ultimate about the universe true? He seeks an end to suffering, confusion, depression, emptiness, meaninglessness, lost identity, and more, through a set of beliefs whose validity he questions, but he does not know where else to look. He is not simply saying "No" to his beliefs. He tries to wring from them the nurturance he only half believes they can provide. Although his struggle may—or may not—rotate around issues of traditional belief, his experience is archetypal and universal. His condition—ambivalence and uncertainty about what in life is anyway most ambiguous—is one side of the human condition drawn to its extreme. "Splits and gaps are in every soul," as Tillich (1948) says. His pain is familiar and we dearly avoid it. He is baffled at the very heart of his life stance. Surely it is worth trying to understand. If we can understand his ambivalence, perhaps we can understand our own, and perhaps then learn something of wholeness.

The phenomena that serve as the focus and taking-off place for the investigations reported in this study are the doubts about religious faith or the polarity between faith and doubt experienced by a number of students in Protestant schools of theology. While the beliefs examined in this work are traditional Christian ones for the most part, I believe both the mode of analysis and the general conclusions have an application that goes beyond them. Ideologies of all sorts address themselves to something ultimate, to a source of hope and meaning. What can be learned about hope and wholeness, and despair and doubt, in the present context should illuminate these experiences as they occur in any context.

The broad theoretical stance toward our subject is a sociopsychological one (Levinson, 1963). This means that some of the sources of an individual's religious doubts might be seen as arising from his personal past and current emotional life, while others derive from his sociocultural milieu. In this study, however, it is the inner emotional life of the individual that receives the focused attention. At the same time, it is assumed that religious belief systems or ideologies are also features of social systems, that they have dimensions and qualities that have psychological relevance, and that these dimensions and qualities relate to aspects of individual personality.

Here the method for studying religious doubt is that of the case study. This method is "clinical" in the broader sense in which the word "case" connotes not the study of pathological conditions, but the naturalistic examination of the human condition through a series of detailed studies of the conditions of a number of individuals. The subject, in this method, becomes a collaborator in an extensive and intensive investigation into all aspects of his life and self. In addition to personal history, other kinds of data come under examination—dreams, spontaneous associations, projective test responses, even the relationship established between "subject" and "researcher"—all provide clues to the basic psychological makeup of the person. With a subject who becomes a collaborator, the researcher has the opportunity to examine in detail the actual life forms of the phenomenon he wishes to study—in our case religious doubt. The case-study method then allows the closest and most detailed examination possible of the interrelationships between the religious doubt and other aspects of the person's life, psyche, and sociocultural milieu.

Theological students seem appropriate subjects for the same reason James chose "articulate and fully self-conscious men" (James, 1902, p. 22) for his study of *The Varieties of Religious Experience*. "Interesting as the origins and early stages of a subject always are, yet when one seeks earnestly for its full significance, one must always look to its more completely evolved and perfect forms" (James, 1902, p. 22).

From the point of view of sociopsychological research, the religious belief system is an ideal avenue for the study of personality. There is no area of human living that leads more deeply into psychic life than religion. This holds both for individual psychic life and also for the evolution of collective forms of psychic life (Bellah, 1964). It is, after all, through religion that man has tried to solve the most basic problems and deep seated anxieties of life. ". . . For limited purposes only, let me define religion as a set of symbolic forms and acts which relate man to the ultimate conditions of his existence" (Bellah, 1964, p. 21). There is no tool or concept of modern depth psychology that cannot be brought to bear in the effort to gain understanding in this complex area, and conversely there is no concept of personological psychology that cannot be illumined by regarding it in the light of religious phenomena. The whole range of early experiences and identifications that go into the formation of an individual's character, his system of needs and defenses, his conception of himself and the world, and the structure of his superego (conscience and ideals) are all reflected in his religious belief system. The religious belief system, then, can be studied in terms of any of these conceptual areas, and more besides. Further, the religious belief system is an ideal vehicle for studying complex personality processes. This observation is not a new one. "James pointed out that all the psychological processes participate in religious experience and none of them is specific to religion . . ." (Pruyser, 1960).

This notion is also implied in Bellah's (1968) definition of religion upon which this study implicitly rests:

> Religion emerges in action systems with respect to two main problems. In order to function effectively it is essential that a person or group have a relatively condensed, therefore highly general, definition of its environment and itself. Such a definition of what the system is and what the world is to which it is related, in more than a transient sense, is a conception of identity. . . . In addition to the identity problem, which is concerned with the most general model the system possesses of itself and its world, there is the problem of dealing with inputs of motivation from within the system which are not under immediate control of conscious decision processes. . . . The problem of identity and of unconscious motivation are closely related. . . . It is precisely the role of religion in action systems to provide such cognitively and motivationally meaningful identity conceptions or set of identity symbols. (Bellah, 1968, pp. 11–12)

The religious belief system, then, is the individual's most general and condensed definition of himself and his environment, and it also has intimate connections with the basic psychodynamic processes which organize and direct unconscious motivational energy.

It is not our purpose to define the nature of religion in a formal way. Later discussion of specific individuals will demonstrate the aptness and applicability of Bellah's formulation, as well as the depth and complexity of the phenomena under consideration.

"Religious doubt," as used in this study, is a relatively open-ended term meant to encompass a wide variety of experiences. In simple terms, it means being uncertain or in doubt about some particular tenet of a religious belief system, or the system as a whole; or it means to be uncertain of or uncommitted to one's faith or adherence to the belief system or some aspect of it. Both faith and doubt represent a complex of thought and feeling, of basic underlying affective orientations, as well as unconscious ideas and feelings. In terms of psychic functioning, doubt can range from a cool, dispassionate, philosophical examination of the concept of God, to a person's total life being desperately caught up in the life or death question, "Does God exist?"

Some brief examples of religious doubt in conservative and liberal Protestants will illustrate the different facets of the phenomenon. A conservative, evangelical Baptist, trained in nuclear engineering, was raised in a church which taught withdrawal and isolation from worldly things and "non-Christians." He was in doubt as to whether or not to "cooperate" with more liberal Protestants in ecumenical endeavors. To cooperate may have meant only to attend meetings with such people. This problem, while it may seem minor to the observer, represented to this man an important religious doubt. It was one of a series of "little doubts" which he had always experienced, and, as he said, "If I had all those little doubts at once they would be big doubt." At the other pole is Pale (see chapter V), a Southern Baptist who was raised in a traditional, conservative culture and who came to New England where his undergraduate and seminary education exposed him to liberalism, existentialism, and psychology. This and other experiences during this period of his life made him question what had been the very core of his personality up until then: his inner relationship with Jesus Christ whom he had taken as his personal Lord and Savior at the age of eight. Such an experience is a total threat to the integrity of the personality. (See also cases of Electon and Mudge, chapters VII and VIII.)

Another type of religious doubt occurs in those committed conservative Christians who, like Pascal and Kierkegaard, see faith as a "gamble," a "risk" (Briting and Joel, chapter IX). One knowingly stakes one's life on belief that is admittedly—from the outside looking in—an irrational choice, a risk, but which, once commitment is made, has its own validation. This act of

faith is seen as an ongoing dynamic, not something gone through
once and for all, with peaceful certainty on the other side of
"the leap of faith."

> And so I say to myself: I choose; that historical fact
> (of Jesus Christ) means so much to me that I decide to
> stake my whole life upon that if. Then he lives; . . .
> He did not have a few proofs, and so believed and
> then began to live. No, the very reverse.
>     That is called risking; and without risk faith is an
> impossibility. To be related to spirit means to undergo
> a test; to believe, to wish to believe, is to change one's
> life into a trial; a daily test is the trial of faith.
> (Kierkegaard, 1959, pp. 184–185)

Doubt predominates in this context when the irrationality and
meaninglessness inherent in the risk come to outweigh the hopeful spirituality.

A different range of experiences of doubt exists within the
context of liberal Protestantism. A relatively committed liberal
may still take a characteristically open-ended view of the nature
of God, immortality, Jesus, and so on, and throughout most of a
lifetime seek an emotionally and intellectually deepened understanding of these concepts, more or less continually reviewing
and revising his conceptions (see case of Eyman, chapter XI;
also Girth and Sal, chapter XIII). In contrast to this is the
experience of some, shifting from a more conservative to a relatively liberal theology, who still desperately seek a *felt* conviction
for what they will assert intellectually—God's existence (see case
of Strindge, chapter XII; also Cliff, chapter XIII). This experience is accompanied by a disturbing awareness of their own needs
to believe in God and by intense conflicts about vocation and life
purpose in general.

The theology student who is experiencing one of the more
severe forms of religious doubt is in a psychologically poignant
condition. In the first place, he is deeply involved in doubts
about a salient ideology. Furthermore, the seminarian is beset by
the further complication that his ideological conviction is necessarily related to his present social role and to vocational choice.

There are advantages for a psychological study in working
with individuals who are in conflict. "Human nature can best be

studied in the state of conflict" (Erikson, 1958, p. 16). In conflict and doubt, psychic contents otherwise repressed and integrated are more open to observation in an undisguised form. The contents and origins of the conflicts of the religious doubter should also cast some light on the conditions which allow for religious conviction and faith.

Doubt as a general phenomenon has been discussed in psychoanalytic theory and placed in the context of obsessive-compulsive thinking, in which it is related to the primitive stage of omnipotence of thought. In the obsessional neurosis, the individual withdraws from feeling and action, attempting to replace these with thought which seems thereby to acquire an unusual power and significance. The experience of doubt represents the displacement into the intellectual field of conflicting demands upon the ego from an instinctive impulse on the one hand and the prohibitions of the superego on the other.

> The unconscious content of obsessive doubts may be manifold; yet the manifold conflicts are but special editions of a few general questions. They are conflicts of masculinity versus femininity (bisexuality), of love versus hate (ambivalence), and especially of id (instinctual demands) versus superego (demands of conscience).
>
> The last formula is the decisive one. Bisexuality and ambivalence do not form conflicts in themselves; they do so only if they represent a structural conflict between an instinctual demand and an opposing force as well. (Fenichel, p. 297)

Angyal (1965, p. 164) related doubt to pervasive uncertainty, based on confusing and contradictory early experience, as to whether the world is basically good or bad, "friendly or inimical" (p. 157). This kind of pervasive doubting may also be considered as derivative, in different forms, perhaps, from any of the first three stages of ego development as Erikson (1959) has outlined them. Basic mistrust, shame and doubt, and guilt can all be given symbolic expression in the terms of religious belief.

In this study, religious doubt will be examined primarily in the light of current psychoanalytic ego psychology. The foundations for this theory were laid in a series of Freud's papers.[1]

It is the task of the ego to deal with intrapsychic conflict from various sources and to resolve conflict between the demands of the id and of reality. To "deal with" means to find some equilibratory compromise between the forces generating the conflict. What psychoanalytic theory indicates, in part, is that doubt, in its various forms, is a manifestation of the ego's effort to resolve conflict, to integrate and balance diverse inner and outer demands. Hartmann (1939), Rapaport (1959), Erikson (1959), and others have shown that the integrative and synthesizing efforts of the ego go far beyond the conflicts involving more or less primitive demands from id, superego, and reality. It is the task of the ego to form a coherent, whole system out of the diverse, conflictful experiences of the first years of life. In doing so, it uses constitutional givens, culturally shared symbol systems, available role models, and a variety of other inner resources, to derive a sense of the self and the self's place in relationship to society and other individuals such that a social way of life and a life of one's own become possible.

> Man, to take his place in society, must acquire conflict free, habitual use of a dominant faculty, to be elaborated in an *occupation*; a limitless *resource*, of feedback, as it were, from the immediate *exercise* of this occupation, from the *companionship* it provides, and from its tradition; and finally, an intelligible *theory* of the processes of life . . . (Erikson, 1959, p. 110; his italics)

> From a genetic point of view . . . the process of identity formation emerges as an *evolving configuration* —a configuration which is gradually established by successive ego syntheses and resyntheses throughout childhood; it is a configuration gradually integrating *constitutional givens, idiosyncratic libidinal needs, favored capacities, significant identifications, effective defenses, successful sublimations, and consistent roles.* (Erikson, 1959, p. 116; his italics)

Identity formation is a function of the integrative and synthetic functions of the ego, a complex of conscious and unconscious processes. As Erikson indicates, one of the important features of identity formation is "an intelligible theory of the processes of life," or what he prefers to call an "ideology."

> . . . *ideology* will mean an unconscious tendency
> underlying religious and scientific as well as political
> thought: the tendency at a given time to make facts
> amenable to ideas, and ideas to facts, in order to create
> a world image convincing enough to support the collective
> and the individual sense of identity. (Erikson, 1958, p. 22)

Beliefs or ideologies are, of course, related to the issue of doubt. Religious doubt is in fact an example of the lack—temporary or otherwise, and from whatever sources—of an integrated wholeness within the ego. It may be seen, then, more broadly in relation to the process of ego synthesis, and may be considered the conscious, symbolic experience of some form either of the disruption of ego synthesis or of the effort to form a new integration. The impediment to the integrative functions might at the same time be an id-superego conflict or another kind of conflict, one of those "conflicts between the various identifications into which the ego comes apart, conflicts which cannot after all be described as entirely pathological" (Freud, 1923, p. 31).

The term "belief system" will be used to refer to the individual's unique form of a shared cultural (religious, theological and church) tradition. The belief system serves as a vehicle for the (attempted) coherent integration of the individual's needs, defenses, capacities, and the identifications of his childhood, as well as the roles, occupations, relationships, and life stances of his adulthood. In this sense a belief system includes articulative (conscious) values as well as underlying (unconscious) affective orientations. Faith, as the deep sense of commitment to God or an ideal which ultimately cannot be justified by rational considerations, will also be considered a feature of the belief system.

Everyday observation indicates that religious doubts are a common occurrence. Indeed, it would seem that doubt, confusion, and uncertainty are the common fate of all—at least temporarily—who make the effort to arrive at some conviction about the meaning of life. A major theme in Western literature, philosophy, and theology is the quest for certitude. In spite of the notion of faith as transcending logical argument, Western man is burdened with the quest for certain knowledge which will give a sense of meaning and provide the guidelines for a way of life. This contrasts with the quest of Eastern man for an ideal state of being without regard for propositional beliefs.

Doubt and the seeds of doubt—despair, skepticism, and angry questioning of God's justice—are central themes in the Judeo-Christian tradition. Classical examples are Job's despairing sense of abandonment, emptiness, and loss of meaning, and the Preacher's dry skepticism in Ecclesiastes. In the Gospels of the New Testament, despair and a sense of abandonment occur with a dreadful succinctness at the very climax of the narrative, the crucifixion, as Jesus "cried with a loud voice . . . 'My God, my God, why hast thou forsaken me?'" (Matthew 27:46)

Can any person involved in the Christian faith not ask what this portends, and can he theologize away Jesus's words? Bellah (1965) has commented on this feature of Western culture, contrasting it with the East.

> It is a generally admitted fact that in East Asia
> there is no literary genre which we might call tragic.
> There are conquering heroes and there are suffering
> heroes but there are not tragic heroes in the Western
> sense, men whose agony calls into question the justice
> of the cosmos itself; in a word there is no Chinese Job. . . .
> Christianity, it is claimed, overcomes the tragic. Perhaps
> so, but as long as it carries near the heart of its critical
> narrative the words "My God, my God, why hast thou
> forsaken me?" it does not destroy the tragic. However
> much exegetical effort one makes to explain this away,
> the fact remains that it is a question. Even when the
> question is in a sense answered it is not blotted out.
> The capacity to ask questions of the ultimate is perhaps a
> consequence of shifting the locus of ultimacy from the
> natural social order to a transcendent reference point.
> From the point of view of the transcendent everything
> natural has only relative value and can be questioned.
> But the questioning leads to the question of the ultimate
> itself. (Bellah, 1965, pp. 95–96)

Protestant theologians, at least in recent years, have found it necessary to treat the problem of religious doubt systematically.

A presentation of the theological treatment of the problem will help us in our subsequent psychological analysis.

It is probably Kierkegaard who is best known for first describing the place of doubt in the life of faith. His sense of *angst* in the presence of the existential gamble of faith was evident in the utterance quoted earlier (p. 7): ". . . to believe . . . is to change one's life into a trial; a daily test is the trial of faith" (*Journals*, pp. 184–185). Elsewhere he says with simplicity, "My doubt is terrible. Nothing can withstand it—it is a cursed hunger and I can swallow up every argument, every consolation and sedative . . ." (*Journals*, p. 68). Kierkegaard has described what it is like to live on a fine edge, to live a life of faith while daily confronting the most agonizing doubts and anxieties which question faith.

Karl Barth and Paul Tillich, perhaps the two greatest contemporary systematic Protestant theologians, have both recognized doubt as a problem intrinsic to faith and theology. Their *attitudes toward* doubt, however, are very different. For present purposes I shall refer to Barth's theology as "conservative" and to Tillich's theology as "liberal," recognizing that these terms can only do an injustice to their profound thinking. Barth describes doubt magnificently:

> Be it noted that in this sense as well, doubt does not mean denial or negation. Doubt only means swaying and staggering between Yes and No. It is only an uncertainty, although such uncertainty can be much worse than negation itself.
>     In [this] form, doubt means basic uncertainty with respect to the problems of theology as such. . . . This doubt produces at the outset of theological work an embarrassment with respect to the very necessity and meaning of theological questioning itself. This embarrassment puts into question God's Word itself. . . . Swaying and staggering, being uncertain and embarrassed, saying at the very beginning "perhaps, but perhaps not"—what else can all this be but a serious and threatening danger to theology? (Barth, 1963, pp. 123–124)

These words must have been written by one who himself has "swayed and staggered" under a terrible burden of anxiety and guilt-laden doubt, and who stood (or swayed) in embarrassment before his ideals. His commitment was apparently brought deeply into question:

> Swaying and staggering, life in uncertainty and
> embarrassment about our very relationship to God's work
> and word—this corresponds all too closely to the
> ambivalence in which we here and now totally exist.
> (Ibid., p. 125)

Barth recognizes that doubt "occurs within the work of theology itself, remaining to a certain extent immanent within it":

> No theologian, whether young or old, pious or less
> pious, tested or untested, should have any doubt that
> for some reason or other and in some way or other
> he is *also* a doubter. . . . In the present period no one,
> not even the theologian, can escape doubt. (1963, p. 131)

From Barth's point of view, doubt has its origins in evil and that part of man which is evil:

> . . . his doubt . . . is altogether a pernicious companion
> which has its origins not in the good creation of God
> but in the *Nihil*—the power of destruction—where not
> only the foxes and rabbits but also the most varied kind
> of demons bid one another "good night.". . . No
> one should flirt with his unbelief or with his doubt. The
> theologian should only be sincerely *ashamed* of it. (Ibid.,
> p. 131)

Tillich expresses a greater acceptance of both doubt and human nature. In his view there is no truth without doubt, and even no doubt without truth (Leibrecht, p. 4). Doubt is seen as an intrinsic element in both faith and human nature. Further, since it is part of the created world, it is good:

> All these forms of insecurity and uncertainty belong
> to man's essential finitude, to the goodness of the creative
> in so far as it is created.

. . . doubt is not the opposite of faith; it is an
element of faith. (Tillich, 1957, pp. 73, 116)

Tillich also says that Jesus had "doubt about his own work—
a doubt which breaks through most intensively on the Cross . . ."
(1957, p. 134).

The dialectical opposition between these two attitudes concerning doubt is clear. This theological difference has important
implications for a psychological analysis of religious doubt.
Doubt has a very different meaning within the context of a conservative theology from its meaning within the context of a
liberal theology. Similarly, the meanings, effects, and ways of
dealing with doubt will differ amongst individuals depending
upon whether their orientation is more liberal or more conservative.

# II

# On the Social Psychology
of the Protestant
Theological Student

What has to be accepted, the given, is—so
one could say—*forms of life.*
LUDWIG WITTGENSTEIN, PHILOSOPHICAL INVESTIGATIONS, IIxi

The case studies reported in subsequent chapters are all (with
one exception) of men who, at the time of their work with me,
were students in Protestant schools of theology. To understand
their individual psychology, it is useful to know what might be
considered their common psychology—the world of the theological student. This task is taken up in two ways in this chapter.
Previous discussion has given clear enough indications that the
nature of theology—the differences between conservative and
liberal theology, for example—has implications for understanding
the psychology of the individual experiencing religious doubt.
Further analysis of theology, then, is taken up in sections 1 and 2.
What it means to be a student in a theological school is taken
up in section 3.

A questionnaire[1] distributed in classes at a number of theological schools was the first contact with the individuals who later
collaborated with me in the case studies. The questionnaire allowed a rough assessment as to whether the individual tended to

15

be more liberal or conservative and also gave a good indication of how much and what kind of doubt about his beliefs he was experiencing. It also gave other preliminary information.

## 1. *SOCIOPSYCHOLOGICAL DIMENSIONS OF THEOLOGY*

A theology represents the most fully developed *cognitive* feature of a belief system. As such, it is a logically systematic set of propositions pertaining to the nature of and relationship between the relevant theological categories. Protestant theology is immersed in a long and complex cultural history, reaching back into the history of Israel and beyond. It participates in a rich and varied tradition, and is perpetuated and taught in a multiplicity of institutions in an explicit and formal way. The *theologian* is a specialist in this tradition and in the modes of thinking and analysis that constitute its technical features.

A theology participates in the realm of individual psychic life and also the realm of collective psychic life, the sociocultural milieu. Within the individual realm it serves to define and structure the individual's belief system, which is a complex of cognitive and affective, conscious and unconscious trends. But a theology is also a cultural *product*—it has an existence independent of any one individual's belief system. It is a feature of culture and has an impact on the social system in which the culture participates. Given the sociopsychological character of theologies, we may expect to find dimensions within theology which are pertinent both to the psychology of the individual and to the description of the sociocultural milieu. Two such dimensions are relevant to our analysis.

(1) *Absoluteness* (versus *relativity*) refers to the degree to which the theology makes *absolute dichotomies*,

    (a) between the power, greatness, and infinitude of God and the weakness, smallness, and finitude of man; and

    (b) between the goodness and purity of God and Jesus and the evilness and sinfulness of man; and

    (c) between this world and the supernatural one.

(2) *Externalization* (versus *internalization*) refers to the degree to which the theology locates religious relevance *outside* of man or *within* man himself.

Absoluteness and externalization tend to be associated with one another within theologies, as do relativity and internalization. Traditional American conservative theology is characterized by absoluteness and externalization. The contrast between man and God is absolute and unbridgeable, and religious salience exists totally outside of man. Liberalism is generally characterized by relativity and internalization. God is to be found, for example, in some sense within human nature.

Absoluteness is closely related to Erikson's (1964) concept of "totalism," discussed later (chapter III). Internalization is closely related to Murray's conception of "intraception" (Murray, 1938; Sharaf, 1962). "Intraception" refers to the tendency of an individual to value, differentiate, and make centrally salient to his life emotions and emotional nuances as well as the sense of the inner life generally. The dimension of externalization-internalization is also paralleled by the theological polarity between the "transcendence" of God as compared to the "immanence" of God. A transcendent God is located outside of this world; an immanent God is located within man, in some sense, and within society and the natural world.

Liberalism has progressively internalized God and other relevant religious phenomena. The contrast between liberal and conservative Protestant theology in this respect is again particularly clear-cut and striking in the theologies of Barth and Tillich. Just how far God is beyond and outside of man in Barth's theology is clear in the following:

> The word "God" in the symbol [of the Apostolic Creed], therefore, must not mislead us into first giving consideration to the nature and the attributes of a being which, on the basis of our most comprehensive experiences and deepest reflection, we think we have discovered as that which this name may and must fit, in order thereupon, under the guidance of the historical statements of the symbol, to ascribe to the subject so conceived this and that definite predicate, behaviour and act. On the contrary, we have to begin with the admission that of ourselves we do *not* know what we say when we say "God", i.e. that all that we think we know when we say "God" does not reach and comprehend Him who is called "God" in the symbol, but always one

of our self-conceived and self-made idols, whether
it is "spirit" or "nature," "fate" or "idea" that we really
have in view. But even this admission, of course, cannot
carry the meaning that in it we are proclaiming a
discovery of our own. . . . Only God's revelation, not
our reason despairing of itself, can carry us over from
God's incomprehensibility. (Barth, 1962, p. 12)

According to Barth, man's experience, knowledge, and thought
do not yield or contain knowledge of God. "Articles of faith"
come into existence when "God's reality, as it affects man, is
recognized by the Church in the form of definite cognitions won
from God's revelation" (Barth, 1962, p. 3). The absoluteness
with which God is externalized is also apparent in the following
remark, which is particularly interesting for other reasons as well:

But what gives faith its seriousness and power is not
that man makes a decision, nor even the way in which he
makes it, his feelings, the movement of his will, the
existential emotion generated. On the contrary, faith lives
by its *object*. (Ibid., p. 2)

In these last remarks, Barth gives expression to an anti-intracep-
tive attitude, not simply an extraceptive one. He is arguing
against an existential interpretation of faith of the sort put forth
by Kierkegaard.

There is a world of difference between this orientation and
the one expressed in Tillich's meditation on "The Depth of Existence" (1948, pp. 52ff.):

The name of this infinite and inexhaustible depth and
ground of all being is God. That depth is what the word
God means. And if that word has not much meaning
for you, translate it, and speak of the depths of your life,
of the source of your being, of your ultimate concern, of
what you take seriously without any reservation. Perhaps,
in order to do so, you must forget everything traditional
that you have learned about God, perhaps even that
word itself. For if you know that God means depth, you
know much about Him. You cannot then call yourself

an atheist or unbeliever. For you cannot think or say:
Life has no depth! Life itself is shallow. Being itself is
surface only. If you could say this in complete seriousness
you would be an atheist; but otherwise you are not.
He who knows about depth knows about God. (p. 57)

Even those unfamiliar with theological arguments can experience
the great difference between these two discussions of the concept
of "God." To read Tillich is to enter another world—a more
familiar and more human world. Here the deepest human experiences, in some sense, contain God. God has been internalized
into human experience.

The famous aphoristic summation of Barth's doctrine of
God—"God can be considered only as 'wholly other'" (Allen,
pp. 17, 18)[2]—aptly captures the absolute quality of the distinction between man and God and also expresses the external quality of this conception of God. In contrast is an utterance of
Buber who greatly influenced Tillich: "When he too, who abhors
the name, and believes himself to be godless, gives his whole being to addressing the *Thou* of his life, as a *Thou* that cannot be
limited by another, then he addresses God" (Buber, 1923,
p. 76). Tillich's conception of God expresses something very
similar to this one of Buber's. Both conceptions express a thoroughly internalized notion of God, and neither implies an
absolute distinction between man and God. A contemporary
Protestant theologian takes this trend further: "Belief in God
does not, indeed cannot mean being persuaded of the existence
of some entity, even a supreme entity" (Robinson, p. 17). This
thought attacks the externalizing, absolute conception of God
and prepares the way for a more internalized, less absolute conception.

## 2. DOUBT AND OTHER THEOLOGICAL
   CATEGORIES

There are a number of categories with which any Protestant
theology must deal. These include the nature of God, the nature
of Jesus of Nazareth, and the relationship between man and God
including some notion as to how man has knowledge of God. It

must also deal with problems of eschatology and of the meaning of the Resurrection (immortality), and also the nature of man, the church, and the secular world; and with the nature of faith and doubt and evil. Some of these categories will be discussed for the purpose of further elucidating the distinction between conservative and liberal theologies and to demonstrate how the dimensions of absoluteness-relativity and externalization-internalization run through all the theological categories. At the same time this discussion of theology will help prepare an understanding of the belief systems of the individuals discussed in following chapters.

A liberal orientation toward Jesus expressed by Tillich,

> Historical doubt concerning the existence and the life of someone with the name Jesus of Nazareth cannot be overruled. (Tillich, 1957, p. 114)

contrasts with a characteristically conservative one:

> Jesus Christ is the "moment", the point of crisis at which eternity impinges upon time; he is actually God breaking into our world of time and space. (Allen, p. 118)

The conservative proposition emphasizes the (absolute) distinction between this world and a supernatural one, and implies a supernatural interpretation of Jesus. The liberal proposition speaks of Jesus simply as an historical personage. This de-emphasizes the distinction between man and God (relativity) and brings the religious category into the human one (internalization). It implies that Jesus's "divinity" may not be supernatural, but another aspect of what is human.

Among possible liberal positions is one which would interpret Jesus simply as an historical figure. He might be considered as a model, prophet, leader, and teacher of new truths, or a revolutionary, but not as a human with supernatural attributes. Further, "God" and "the divine" in such a theology may be understood as qualities of the natural world and of human life. "God's activity" in the world, for example, then becomes nothing more nor less than a way of looking at things and of speaking about the most highly valued social processes and personal experiences. In this position, the religious functions are clearly internalized, being located in a particular quality of perception, feeling, and thinking, within the everyday processes of living.

The conservative view of human nature and man's evil is powerfully expressed in these utterances:

> The fact that man *does* evil indicates that he *is* evil—evil is lodged in the very center of his will. (Emil Brunner, quoted in Heath, p. 20)

> We must begin, each of us, by seeing ourselves as a man who has sinned, is sinning and will sin and who can recognize himself as nothing else than lost. (Barth, quoted in Heath, p. 18)

These expressions emphasize the absolute quality of man's evilness as it contrasts with God and with the goodness of Jesus. They also imply an important aspect of externalization. Man's sinfulness before God is seen as so great and absolute that it can only have the effect of making insignificant the idea of a man having an internal standard for self-judgment. In this way, the possibility of a developed inner sense of responsibility—a trend in the service of internalization—is at least partially obscured.

Certain features of traditional American conservatism are implicit in these propositions. These are the stern, penitential, and rather legalistic moral codes and certain features of evangelism. The evangelist traditionally tries to drive the individual to confession and belief by playing on his guilt. The emphasis in a religious culture of this sort is on finding salvation by "taking Jesus Christ as one's personal Lord and Savior," and "becoming a follower of Jesus." One must then strive for holiness and purity by subscribing to a particular stringent moral code and churchly participation. Barth's early theology was referred to as a "theology of crisis" (Heath, p. 20). By driving home man's sinfulness, smallness, and lostness, Barth meant to drive men, in anxiety, to a conservative faith.

This astringent, almost depersonalized, view of man contrasts with the easier acceptance of human nature on the part of the liberal.

> To be a Christian does not mean to be religious in a particular way, to cultivate some particular form of

asceticism (as a sinner, a penitent or a saint), but to be
a man. (Bonhoeffer, pp. 222–223, also quoted in
Robinson, p. 83)

Actual human activity and responsibility in this sort of position
are not obfuscated by an overwhelming cosmic sinfulness. The
way is clear to arrive at an understanding of what individual responsibility and "sin" actually represent in the course of daily
life. To put it another way, the individual has the opportunity to
experience personal, reality-oriented anxiety and guilt instead of
an overriding, nonspecific, cosmically oriented anxiety and guilt.
This is part of what is meant by internalization in the liberal
theological view of man.

The conservative view of the "secular world" and how the
Christian is to comport himself within it is congruent with the
view of human nature.

Those men who have been claimed by God's mercy are
called upon to bear witness on the one hand against the
form of this world, and on the other in favor of the
form of the coming world. (Barth, quoted in Heath, p. 42)

Again, the contrast between the natural and the supernatural is
emphasized (absoluteness), with the externalizing force being
implicit in the directive away from human forms of consciousness, "the form of this world." These notions also suggest two
other features of traditional American evangelical conservatism,
the practice of "witnessing" and a feature that shall be named
"exclusiveness." To "witness" is to share one's convincing religious experiences with another so as to reaffirm one another's
faith, or perhaps to lead the other to faith. The practice is as old
as Christianity, and has its parallels whenever one man "wit-
nesses" to another as to the benefits of a particular belief or
practice. "Exclusiveness" refers to the practice of minimal participation in the world and keeping company only with fellow
Christians. In these features of a theology are seen intimations
of the violence sometimes perpetrated in the name of faith—
aggressive evangelizing and missionary work, even atrocities.
Various trends in current liberal theologizing prepare the

way for the internalization of functions once externalized in traditional conceptions of God, sin, and so on.

> Christian belief and practice requires a new mold and we
> have to be prepared for everything to go into the melting—
> even our most cherished religious categories and moral
> absolutes; and the first thing we must be ready to let go is
> our image of God himself. (After Robinson, p. 124)

The trends toward making relative the distinction between man and God and toward internalization are also expressed in some current liberal views on the relationship between man and God: "A right relationship to God depends on nothing religious; in fact religion could be the greatest barrier to it" (Robinson, p. 61). This position brings the religious focus back to man and into man. It highlights ordinary human activity, thus dignifying man rather than subordinating him to a theological conception of sin. In this position there is nothing distinctive about a "religious" activity or role as contrasted with a "secular" one. The arena of religion is all of human life, and this position is ready to do away with the notion of religion if it interferes with this perception.

In the theology of conservatism, "Faith cannot bridge the gulf between man and God for faith renders necessary and unavoidable the perception of the contradiction between God and the world of time and things and man" (Allen, p. 15). The absolute dichotomy between man and God is powerfully summarized in this view of the relationship between man and God. Man's weakness, dependence, and sin, and his sense of estrangement, abandonment, and alienation are emphasized. Further, knowledge of God is from revelation, and knowledge and knowing of this sort are beyond and outside of man. "In the long run, it will be found that to deny the Virgin Birth is to call in question the divinity of Christ: what God has joined in his revelation, let no man therefore put asunder" (Allen, p. 35). The literalistic interpretation of the Bible implied in this utterance is tied to the conception of an absolute contrast between the world of man and the supernatural world of God that is totally external to man's world.

In the liberal position knowledge and the mechanisms of

gaining it are internalized and made continuous with other usual processes of gaining knowledge (relativity).

> The New Testament presentation of the incarnation, the redemption in Christ does not, properly speaking, describe a supernatural transaction of any kind, but it is an attempt to express the real depth, dimension and significance of the *historical* event of Jesus Christ. (Robinson, p. 34)

Mythological language, including that of the Bible, in this view, is a way of expressing what is deepest and most significant to and in man. The internalizing tendency is clear. "Redemption," "the Son of Man," and so on, are expressions of deep-lying features of the human condition—not miraculous occurrences from a realm totally outside of, and external to, man. Here, as in earlier examples, the liberal position undermines the metaphysical assumptions about a supernatural realm, and tends to reinterpret the Biblical descriptions of that realm in naturalistic terms.

The externalizing tendency of traditional American conservatism finds an important expression in the practice of seeking to "follow God's will."[3] The enormous psychological significance of this practice will be seen later (chapters V and VI). In seeking God's will, the individual looks to a source external to himself for cues and guidance. In this process, there is a sense in which certain features of the individual's decision processes, as well as experiences related to morality, the sense of responsibility, and the sense of self, are externalized. The conservative form of this practice is distinctively related to an absolute, externalized conception of God and to a number of other features of conservative theology previously discussed—the gulf between man and God, man's sinfulness, the discrepancy between human knowing and revelation, and man's weakness, dependence, and estrangement in relation to God.

The difference between the attitudes concerning doubt in conservative and liberal theology was discussed earlier. The conservative orientation rejects doubt about God's existence or nature as an indication of man's evilness and utter estrangement from God. The liberal orientation accepts doubt as an inevitable and therefore good part of human nature, and sees doubt as intrinsic to man's quest for faith and meaning.

"Doubt about the existence of God should, at some point, be seen through and despised as the act of an *insipiens*, the 'fool' of Psalm 53" (Barth, 1963, p. 123). The ideology implied in this item also rationalizes the turning against the self or others of hate and anger—"doubt . . . should . . . be . . . despised." Turning anger against the self or others in this way is appropriate to the conservative view of man as evil and sinful. In turn, the dichotomy between God and man is heightened, ultimately making that dichotomy absolute—all goodness is located in God, all evil in man. In contrast is the following expression of a liberal orientation to doubt: "If doubt appears, it should not be considered as the negation of faith, but as an intrinsic element which was always and will always be present in the act of faith" (Tillich, 1957b, p. 22). This is a characteristic liberal expression of the acceptance of doubt. Doubt is a part of faith. A much greater acceptance of human nature is implied. Man is not seen as absolutely evil. A greater range of human experience is given a positive religious meaning—in the service of internalization.

The following utterances show how the conservative orientation operates to externalize certain aspects of human experience:

> In doubt, human thought is unnatural—diseased by man's original estrangement, and consistently exposed to the corruption and error which arise and follow from a primal error, that is, the presumption to ask, "Did God say . . . ", or to boldly affirm, "There is no God," or, "I am God." (Barth, 1963, p. 125)

> No one should flirt with his unbelief or with his doubt— the theologian should only be sincerely *ashamed* of it. (Barth, 1963, p. 131)

These thoughts include directives to take certain attitudes to doubt—be ashamed of it, regard it as unnatural and "diseased," and so on. The effect on the individual of such attitudes is to make the experience of doubt or allied experiences dystonic— not a part of the self. A feeling that is regarded with shame is removed psychologically from oneself. The feeling is externalized, and social and institutional processes which support the externalization are invoked and reinforced. On the other hand the feeling still has its source from within—externalization cannot remove feeling entirely from the person—and therefore guilt is generated. Furthermore, these items clearly convey that man is evaluated by a judgment external to himself. The external source of judgment furthers the process of externalization set in motion by disowning the inevitable feelings of doubt and uncertainty. This whole cycle can only heighten in the individual a sense of helplessness, guilt, and evil for which there is no internal remedy. Guilt and hopelessness generated in this way can only be relieved by looking to a source of goodness and salvation totally outside of the self and human society—by looking to a God conceived as "wholly other." It is not coincidental, then, that Barth relates the "unnaturalness" of doubt to "man's original estrangement." Regarding doubt as unnatural leads to a sense of estrangement from the sources of goodness and meaning, and only a God conceived in an absolute dichotomy from man can heal that state of evilness and hopelessness.

The liberal position accepts doubt and uncertainty and finds positive meanings within them:

> Uncertainty and doubt belong to man's essential finitude, to the goodness of the creative in so far as it is created. (After Tillich, 1957, p. 73)

> Doubt is essentially connected with the quest for truth; there is no truth without doubt, and no doubt without truth. (Leibrecht, p. 4; after Tillich)

By taking an accepting attitude to doubt, the experience is given a meaningful place within the self. This in turn allows the individual to look within himself and the human community for meaning, goodness, and salvation. A greater range of experience is acceptable and can be internalized and recognized, making the distinction between the human and divine more relative.

The great psychological advantages that accrue from the internalizing tendency are perhaps apparent at this point. They lie above all in the greater possibility of an enrichment in the sense of self and identity and the potentially greater range of psychic contents open to being experienced as acceptable aspects of the self. In addition, along with the relativity of religious conceptions, it tends to ameliorate man's vulnerability to the sense of alienation, estrangement, abandonment, and so on, vulnerabilities which are exacerbated and to some degree manipulated by the tendency of conservative theology to dramatize them as facets of man's sinfulness and estrangement from God. At the same time, it should not be thought that there are no psychological advantages to the conservative position. It might be said, for example, that the conservative position on evil is far more realistic than that of liberalism in which the tendency to ameliorate evil with a blanket of acceptance and a readiness to see goodness becomes notoriously indiscriminate and overly passive. More important, however, for individual psychology is the fact that, by a paradoxical process, externalization itself may actually bring into decision-making processes and other experiences psychic contents not otherwise accessible to consciousness. This occurs when, in seeking God's will, the individual allows himself to be open to and becomes aware of decisive cues and feelings which the very struggle to take responsibility for might obscure. (This point is discussed in greater detail in chapter VI, section 6.)

## 3. THE WORLD OF THE THEOLOGY STUDENT

The typical divinity school offers a three-year program leading to a professional degree (Bachelor of Divinity, B.D., or Bachelor of Sacred Theology, S.T.B.). Divinity students have already completed some four-year undergraduate program, often at a denominational school or at least one which is consciously Christian in its orientation and atmosphere. Although some graduates from the theology school pursue a scholarly and teaching career and may become candidates for a graduate degree, the largest number participate in the professional clergy as ministers in a church.

Like any other professional school, the theological school teaches its students the tools of a trade: theology, Biblical studies, history of the Christian church, homiletics, and so on. Although it is not uncommon among divinity students to perceive psychology as an ideology competing with and inimical to theology, courses in psychodynamic personality theory and group psychology are now taught in most schools. Many students also have an intensive clinical experience in a mental health setting. Field training in some more traditionally pastoral setting is another feature of the training. The student may be an assistant minister at a local church, or direct the youth group associated with a church, make calls on members of the congregation, and so on. Currently students are likely to become involved with one of the social reform movements in which church and clergy are now active. For example, a student may work in an inner city area, and many students become intensively involved in the civil rights and the peace movements.

The theological student is first of all in the role of student. The student role is commonly used in our culture as an institutionalized psychosocial moratorium which permits the learning of a distinctive work identity (Erikson, 1959, p. 145). In describing this period as a moratorium, Erikson indicates that this time is set aside by the individual and his society for the purpose of engaging in a complex set of emotional and intellectual tasks—trying out and experimenting with new work roles, self-conceptions, and ideologies, as well as acquiring the technical skills of a trade or profession. Levinson (1963) speaks of this as acquiring a "professional stance," and also recognizes it as a distinctive period of adult personality development.

Erikson's, as well as Levinson's, conception addresses itself, in part, to the acquisition of a particular work role—one adapted to the person's inner needs and also adaptationally congruent with social demands and opportunities, including those of the vocational realm of which the work role is a part. Another aspect of the acquisition of a professional stance has more to do with the inner emotional work involved—reviewing, revising, and reintegrating ideology and self-conception. Our own study focuses more on this latter—inner, emotional—aspect of the acquisition of a professional stance. That is, our focus is on the student's work in reappraising his religious ideology and its meaning to him. Another focus, of course, would be possible—one which studied the ministerial student in his capacity as someone acquiring a particular professional work role. This would be an interesting social-psychological study because the role has extraordinary stresses in it, equal in psychological poignancy probably to none (cf. Wagoner, 1963; Gustafson, 1963).

Certainly the most distinctive feature of the role of the theological student lies in his capacity as a theologian—a religious ideologist, so to speak. At the time the student arrives at the divinity school, where is he in the development of his religious ideology? He has already spent four years in a college setting. This means, first, that it is likely that he has made some degree of separation from his home, especially if he lived away from home during the college years. Second, unless he attended an extremely conservative school, his education will have brought him into contact with scientific, historical, and philosophical ideas as well as a range of religious ideologies which will make it at least difficult for him to accept his home religious culture in any simple, absolute way. Both these factors make it likely that the divinity student will have gone through a period of serious reappraisal and doubt of his religious belief system before he gets to the divinity school. Whatever the beliefs are and whether they are held in faith or doubt, by the time the student comes to divinity school, they have been lived through and reworked in some measure and are experienced as a part of him. Further, the beliefs will have become associated with a vocational concern. What he believes and what he wants to become—questions which can remain separate for some years—become linked in the professional school. At this stage of their development, then, students will experience doubt, disbelief, and questions about the self and vocation as characterological. This means that rather than feeling that he may have questions about his parents' tradition, if the student has doubts and is uncertain about vocation, he will be more likely to see his uncertainties as a problematic side of himself. Part of the motivation for studying at the divinity school may then be to arrive at important answers about the self and to defer vocational plans. Other students may be ready for vocational preparation and experience themselves as apprentice ministers or scholars. In either case, the theological school will necessitate a further reworking of the religious belief system on the part of its students.

Let us draw out further the implications of what it means to be deeply involved in trying to understand for oneself the meaning of one's religious belief system. Earlier discussion referred to religion as the most general definition of the self and the world. A religious belief system does deal with the most general questions that can be asked about human life, and it deals with the most basic experiences of life. What is the meaning of life? Who and what am I? What is the ultimate nature of the universe? And how do I stand in relation to it? Within the context of Christianity, of course, these questions are asked in terms of the traditional Christian myths and symbols: Who is Jesus? What is the nature of the (trinitarian or unitarian) God, and how do I stand in relation to Him? And so on.

The religious belief system also deals with the most confounding experiences of life: basic problems of the self—the need for a sense of meaning, wholeness, and hopefulness, and for a sense of relatedness; ultimate problems of good and evil, justice and injustice; helplessness and death—the helpless fear of man before the forces of nature and, ultimately, death. The religious belief system cuts across all forms of social institutions; it is the most general ideological position a person may hold. It deals with all of life, and this is in contrast with other ideological forms which may deal specifically with some partial aspect of human living. To put it in other terms, the religious belief system contains a complex set of mythic symbols capable of being "applied" to any life situation, and it will define, within limits, the meanings of that situation. Theology is applied mythology.

It should also be borne in mind that at the heart of the religious belief system for most divinity students, although not all, is a more or less personalized God. Where this is the case the relationship with God and the nature of that relationship will occupy a good deal of theological time.

The theological student is involved, then, in a life activity of the greatest psychological interest. He is spending full time, as it were, interpreting himself and the most general problems of life, in terms of a global, complex, and highly ambiguous but highly general symbol system. The traditions, scholarly, folkloric, and mythic, of Christianity are, for him, vehicles for interpretation of the self and the world. This is a process that absorbs the total person. It means interpreting complex inner data from all levels of experience and also data from external sources in terms of the mythic symbolism. Similarly, it means reinterpreting the mythic symbolism in terms of these personal experiences. This is what it means to live by a mythology. In Christian terms, this is what it means, in part, to be a "follower of Christ." The Christian symbols serve as "extended metaphors"[4] expressed in thinking that would take such forms as the following: "This situation is like the one in the New Testament where . . . And if I am to be like Jesus, or do as he taught in this situation, I must . . ." Or this process may occur at more sophisticated levels.

> Most students quickly learn, however, that theology is not studied like ancient history or chemistry. The student cannot be content to master a set of objective principles and data which he can then objectively apply to the various pastoral situations in which he finds himself. The ultimate data of theological study are fundamental personal and social beliefs about the nature of reality, divine, human and physical, on which the life of the student rests. What he must in part objectify, evaluate and make decisions about are . . . the fundamental assumptions of his personal existence and those of the historical community in which he professes loyalty. . . . Theological education involves the total man. (Niebuhr, Williams, and Gustafson, pp. 159–160)

The depth and personal meaning of this activity are perhaps best brought home when we think of those instances in which a relationship with the Divinity, whether God or Jesus, is central. For many theological students the relationship with God, or the thought and feeling that go into trying to develop that relationship, is the most important in their life—indeed, is the affective and cognitive center of their life. This is true for the man of deep faith and a sense of constant communion with God. It may also be true for the man who is desperately seeking after a relationship with God or who is trying to come to peace with the conclusion that God is not such that one has a personal relationship with Him.

A myth leads one deeply (or it can) into one interpretation of life. It is a *lived* truth, and believers speak of a "living truth." The disadvantage of the myth is that it limits the interpretation of life to one tradition. Even though global, vague, and ambiguous, it structures and pre-structures thinking, perceiving, and experiencing. This has advantages and disadvantages. Whereas it limits and pre-structures, it also clearly can be a vehicle for individuation. Thus there is a great disadvantage in not having a myth. By virtue of its "tradition saturated imagery" (Hartmann, 1939), the myth puts the individual into context and contact with his cultural milieu and tradition. It tells a person what to *be* and *how* to be. In contrast, a *theory*, at best, leaves a man an *observer*. It does not tell him how to participate in life, or else it has the danger of becoming a shallow myth. Part of the depth of myth comes from the very ambiguity and globalness of its symbols. The symbols, images, and so on, are endlessly interpretable. Perhaps this is similar to what Tillich had in mind when he said that "the depth and ground of all being" is "inexhaustible" (Tillich, 1948, p. 57). Now it is certainly true that this depth through myth is achieved only when a person puts himself totally into the sorts of processes we have been describing. Erikson makes this clear in his portrait of Luther: it is only when those most personal and deepest inner conflicts are interpreted in terms of the myth, and similarly, when the myth is interpreted in terms of the deepest and most personal within the individual, that a meaningful approach to life through a myth is achieved. Exegesis is not living the religion.

> A theologian is born by living, nay dying, and being damned, not by thinking, reading, or speculating.
> (Luther, quoted by Erikson, 1958, p. 251)

There are, of course, individual variations on this pattern. First, how this process is carried out varies according to whether the individual has a conservative or a liberal belief system. Second, not every divinity student is a Luther who goes to the heights and depths and comes out of it with a new vision for the world. People vary according to how deeply involved they are able to become in this integration and synthesis *via* theology.

> . . . the depth of the psychic roots of ideology—the degree to which an ideology expresses, and has functions for, other aspects of personality—undoubtedly varies from individual to individual and from one ideological domain to another within a given individual. (Levinson, 1964)

What we have been describing in the case of the theological student is not only an individual for whom "the psychic roots" of the religious belief system go very deep indeed, but also a person for whom the ideology, especially at this point in his life, is the most salient feature of his personality to himself and others, and to work means to work on himself in terms of his beliefs.

Certain qualities of the divinity school itself tend to heighten the salience of the reworking of the religious ideology. The theological school, because of the nature of its enterprise, tends to recruit people who wish to come to grips with life's basic issues at an ideological level and who tend to be on the quest for identity in general. The prevalence of the identity quest is particularly apparent in the more liberal schools where it is rare nowadays to find someone who has received a "call" to be a minister. In any case there tends to be pressure from peers and from teachers to assess introspectively the integrity and nature of one's beliefs.

The theological student, then, is in the process of developing himself as a religious believer. As a clergyman, his fundamental professional equipment will be his own belief system as it is integrated within his self—its integrity, depth, and richness. In this respect the profession of the clergy falls in that category of professions in which the self or some aspect of the self is the primary professional instrument. (The profession of psychotherapy is another.)

The process of self-development in which the theology student is involved offers particular gratifications and also makes particular kinds of demands and carries certain sorts of pain. The sense of being involved in something uniquely meaningful —both in terms of self-development and as preparation for a potentially meaningful social role—is inevitably deeply gratifying. At the same time the process of self-examination and the examination of basic beliefs can be uniquely painful, arousing the deepest kinds of doubts and self-doubts.

In addition to the deep personal conflicts that may be aroused in the course of examining basic beliefs, the current ferment in Protestant theology (cf. Robinson, 1963; Harris, 1965; Wagoner, 1963, pp. 12–13) will also raise problematic questions about the form of belief, religious action, and the ministerial role. Some of these questions come together in one problem that is common among divinity students and should be mentioned specifically. For many students there is a distinct dichotomy within their belief systems between Christianity and their traditional denominational church (cf. Niebuhr, Williams, and Gustafson, 1957, p. 162). Whereas they may feel a deep loyalty to Christianity, there still may be a deep ambivalence or outright hostility in regard to the institutional aspects of organized Portestantism. The student may be looking for a way to reform the church or at least to separate what he considers his fundamental beliefs from an institutional taint.

A final psychological feature of the life of the theological student is his more or less total involvement in and commitment to a symbol system that provides *ultimate values* and *meanings*. It is generally recognized that, for the believer, God and a relationship to God represent the highest possible human values. Belief in God also bestows an unequivocal source of meaning to life. The nonbeliever must at times envy the unquestionable, incontrovertible, and final source of meaning and value that lies within a stabilized relationship to God. The divinity student, then, is looking for or expressing a *lived* truth. This contrasts with the truth of science which is relative and not an expression of life. Science does not say how to live life, religion does. Science does not give meaning or value in itself. *Doing* science provides a way of life, "a technique for the conduct of life" (Freud, 1930, p. 80, footnote 1), but its claims in this respect are by no means as majestic as those of religion.

We might say that the involvement with ultimate values and the effort to live according to them is a partial psychological translation of the first great commandment—to love God. This is to suggest that the commandment—a very general directive on how to live life—may also be considered as a highly condensed but highly effective symbolization expressing a deeplying potentiality in human life. The symbolization can be spelled out only by describing in detail many interlocking aspects of an individual's life in a particular sociocultural matrix. The second great commandment—to love one's neighbor as oneself—may also be considered as such a symbolization. As such, there is also a strand in the life of the divinity student, which we may describe in psychological terms which correspond to it. Commonly, divinity students do give expression to the wish to love and serve their fellow men. This also is a great area of values in which the divinity student is deeply involved in various ways and to which he is striving to be deeply committed. Being good and trying to be better, being kind and gentle, and serving others are orienting values for many students.

Orientation to these particular values—commitment to the source of ultimate value, living according to it, and participating in society with an ethic of love based on the source of ultimate value—can be taken as the general description of one specific value orientation which is modal in our society. As such it contrasts with other characteristic value orientations such as the achievement orientation or the emphasis on knowledge and truth in scientific terms. Perhaps through it as much might be "achieved" as through other value orientations. Which is to suggest, of course, that achievement in itself is not a separate or separable motive—it remains to be directed by overriding values; just as it is possible for a vocal commitment to the great commandments to lead to no action or evil action. It is also to suggest that science too, as scientists' participation in war has shown, needs a value context. Man is at his best only when he is responding to the totality of his self, and no one symbol system has yet been able to contain and condense with wisdom all of that.

# III

# The Religious Belief System
# as an Aspect of Personality

The woods of Arcady are dead,
And over is their antique joy;
Of old the world on dreaming fed;
Grey Truth is now her painted toy;
Yet still she turns her restless head . . .

W. B. YEATS, "THE SONG OF THE HAPPY SHEPHERD"

## 1. *EGO SYNTHESIS*

The purpose of this chapter is to review the theory that guided the initial approach in this study and is the underlying rationale for the particular approach taken in the case studies. The major concepts used to think about personality dynamics have been taken from psychoanalytic ego psychology, and some of these concepts are reviewed here. The theoretical format of the case studies, however, is not meant to be understood as conforming with a model provided by ego psychology. While the issue is not taken up in an explicit technical way, it is possible that consideration of the materials presented in the case studies will suggest extension or modification of ego psychological concepts. Possible candidates for the direction of such modification include the discussion in the concluding chapter of the holistic principle and the irreducibility of symbols of identity, and the approach to characterology taken in the case studies.

The sociopsychological point of view is also an extension of the framework of ego psychology. Within this point of view, a religious belief system is viewed as an expression of personality and also as derived from the sociocultural and familial milieu in which the individual was raised. The belief system lies between the two conceptual spheres of individual personality and the historical-cultural matrix of the society. Through the belief system, we may "discover the psyche in the socious and the socious in the psyche" (Levinson, 1963).

To say that the belief system is an aspect of personality is to say not only that a person's beliefs are *him*, or an aspect of him, but it is to say also that the belief system is related to and an expression of other aspects of personality. In seeking the connections with those other aspects, we look particularly for those connections to the deeper underlying personality processes, the emotional currents that establish broader repetitive meanings within the individual's life, processes not entirely within conscious awareness. The context of these processes within the family milieu will receive careful attention in the case studies, while the extension into the broader social-historical context remains largely unexplored.

The specific theoretical focus may be stated as follows: the religious belief system is a vehicle for, an expression of, and an outcome of the synthesizing functions of the ego.

> The continued influence on the human mind and the
> synthetic achievement of religions rest on their integrative
> imagery and on their being tradition-saturated, socially
> unifying wholes which are fed by the contributions
> of all the three mental institutions, and provide a pattern,
> accessible to many people, for satisfying the demands of
> all these three institutions. (Hartmann, 1939, p. 79)

The ego itself, one of the three mental "institutions" referred to (the "id" and the "superego" are the other two), is considered to be that set of psychic functions which integrates complex inner psychic reality in such a way that an internal harmony tends to be maintained or striven for as well as the tendency to an adaptive equilibrium with complex outer social reality. As that part of the mind which contains consciousness and controls motility, the ego is also that part of the personality which contains the phenomenological center of self-awareness.

There are two features of psychic life with which ego synthesis must deal. The first, the "structural" feature, has to do with the fact that at any one time inner reality (id, superego, ego) and outer reality contain a diversity of contradictory demands. The second, the "developmental" feature, has to do with longitudinal temporality—the fact that reality changes as the organism matures and past syntheses must constantly be modified. The "epigenetic principle" suggests that any one stage of ego synthesis contains past integrations and prepares the way for new ones, "an ontogenetic beginning and a reintegration on ever higher levels of development" (Erikson, 1965).

> . . . the epigenetic principle [asserts] that development consists of a successive and cumulative series of critical encounters between emergent maturational and convergent environmental forces, each of which in normal development is both preadaptive in respect to succeeding encounters and re-adaptive in respect to preceding encounters . . . (Jones, 1962, p. 55)

To the extent that the religious belief system is an outcome of ego synthesis, it will derive some of its meanings from and will in part represent the contents of the fantasies, wishes, ambivalences, and conflicts of the psychosexual stages of development. There is every reason to expect, for example, that the religious belief systems in the following case studies will bear the marks of the resolution of the oedipal conflict and will also be an expression of "the fulfillment of the oldest, strongest and most urgent wishes of mankind . . . protection through love" (Freud, 1927, p. 30). By virtue of its being a function of ego synthesis, the religious belief system will similarly have specific dynamic relationships with other ego processes, particularly object identification, and other ego structures, namely, the ego-ideal, superego, and ego-identity. These are the major technical terms employed in studying the belief systems of individuals in the following chapters, and they will be discussed further in what follows.

## 2. EGO PROCESSES RELATING TO THE RELIGIOUS BELIEF SYSTEM: IDENTIFICATION

The process of identification is central in the establishment of the character of the individual. Through it and related processes, various aspects of character can be understood in terms of the individual's earliest important familial relationships. Some of the deeper meanings of the religious belief system, for example, derive from these early relationships. At the same time identification is directly involved in the establishment of the other ego structures—the superego, ego-ideal, and ego-identity.

The process of identification was first described by Freud in "Mourning and Melancholia" (1917). In the instance he described in this paper, an object identification is established in the ego when an ambivalently cathected, narcissistically based object-choice is undermined in one way or another or the loved person is actually lost. The cathexes previously attached to the abandoned object are used to establish an identification of the ego with it. The word "object" generally means "person"; "cathexis" is a form of libidinous energy expressed in, say, the child's attachment to his mother. An ambivalently cathected object is one which is both loved and hated. The relationship has a narcissistic basis when the individual's self-esteem and, even more generally, his sense of self and needs for love are dependent upon the relationship, again, as in the mother-child relationship. The idea here is that the energy that is withdrawn from the relationship is taken into the ego and becomes a permanent internal structure within the ego. It will inevitably bear the impression of the relationship from which the original energy was withdrawn.

In "The Ego and the Id" (1923), Freud stated that this process was much more common and of greater significance than he had realized:

. . . we did not appreciate the full significance of this process and did not know how common and typical it is.

Since then we have come to understand that this kind
of substitution has a great share in determining the
form taken by the ego and that it makes an essential
contribution towards building up what is called its
"character." (1923, p. 28)

. . . the process . . . is a very frequent one, and it
makes it possible to suppose that the character of the
ego is a precipitate of abandoned object-cathexes and
that it contains the history of those object choices.
(Ibid., p. 19)

Freud also stated here that he felt "the effects of the first
identifications made in earliest childhood will be general and
lasting" (1923, p. 31). In particular, the complex of identifications with the parents through which the resolution of the oedipal complex is achieved have a powerful lasting influence. The
early identifications occur at a time when the ego is weak and
when instinctual life is intense and more or less primitive, and
these conditions account for the lasting effect of early identifications.

The culminating identifications of the oedipal period rest
upon and integrate earlier identifications with the parents. The
quality and character of an identification are determined by the
maturational level of the individual when it occurs and the
quality of the relationship with the person identified with.
Earlier identifications (prior to the oedipal period) are usually
referred to as "introjects," based upon the process of "introjection," which supposedly follows the model of oral incorporation.
The lasting effects of early characteristic affective states which
arise in the context of the mothering relationship are based
upon such precursors of the process of identification and have
a similar though more diffuse and primitive effect. The establishment of such general life orientations as basic trust or basic
mistrust is related to the process of introjection.

Identifications occur under various conditions. Those conditions which result in the pathology of depression or "melancholia" are one particular set of conditions. The oedipal complex
in a typical family situation provides another common set
of conditions in which a set of identifications with the parents

is bound to occur. In this case, the child's wishes, in confrontation with reality, put him in an impossible situation. Exclusive claims to love and sexual privileges with one or another parent (or both at different times) must be relinquished, and the reality of the claims and power of the other parent and family members must be recognized and accepted. At the same time, the child must recognize that the parent who arouses his hostility as a competitor and limit to potentially boundless entitlements is the same parent who is loved and loves and protects. Some more or less sophisticated resolution of this ambivalence is therefore also necessary. The intolerable conflictful aspects of these crosscurrents of feelings can be resolved through a complex of identifications with the parents. These identifications involve relinquishing infantile claims on both parents and internalizing the controlling, guiding, limiting aspects of the parental imagoes (superego). While some features of the child's early relationships to his parents are thereby given up, the real relationships are preserved at a higher level of development and the way is paved for future maturation.

The formation of the superego—the controlling, limiting, guiding functions of the internalized parental imagoes—is one outcome of the identifications which resolve the oedipal complex. The ego-ideal may be differentiated as a psychic institution from the superego. Its characteristics and contents are only in part established during the oedipal period. The functions of the ego-ideal are expressed in those ideals, goals, and ultimate values which explicitly and implicitly define the good for the individual and which—if one lives by them—hold the promise and expectation of future happiness and self-realization.

In general, an identification with an object occurs when, for one reason or another, an intense real relationship is intruded upon, and the object or some feature of the relationship with the object must be relinquished. The process is heightened and intensified when the real relationship meets a multiplicity of the person's most important needs. In particular, this is the case where there is both strong love, or especially strong love and hate (ambivalence), and also dependency upon the object for a sense of the self, self-esteem, and also actual resources for survival (narcissistic and self-preservative needs). These conditions occur most commonly, of course, in childhood, but they may persist, in pathological and other conditions in adult life. Certain kinds of situations may be contrived in adult life that also reestablish these conditions—brainwashing and revival services are examples.

> When the ego assumes the features of the object, it is forcing itself, so to speak, upon the id as a love-object and is trying to make good the id's loss by saying: "Look, you can love me too—I am so like the object." (Freud, 1923, p. 30)

Another implication of this process that is extremely important has to do with the developments of "secondary narcissism" (Freud, 1923, p. 30, footnote 1). Secondary narcissism refers to rather special kinds of feelings that a person has about himself. Although they lay claims to specialness, such feelings are nevertheless closely related to a sense of injury or loss and to some form of feeling a lack of self-worth, perhaps of a very profound order. Such feelings may not be entirely conscious. They receive further discussion below and also detailed illustration in the case studies.

Out of the earliest familial relationships, then, arise identifications which in fact are defining structural properties of the ego or character. Identifications established in early life may be expressed in the character of the adult through the family culture and ideologies and their subsequent transformations. In the families of the individuals described in later chapters, for example, it will be seen that religious language and symbolism had a central role. In such families, the religious symbolism is a vehicle for expressing and preserving any number of features of various relationships. The family's underlying basic feelings, values, and world orientations find expression in the religious language and symbols. Prohibitions, ideals, and covert hostilities also are particularly amenable to communication in religious language. The symbolisms of religion are in themselves powerful ones, and they acquire further power since it is very easy for a child to attach his own most powerful conscious and unconscious fantasies, feelings, and wishes to the religious imagery. In this way the child early on can come to express the deepest and most significant of his experiences in religious symbolisms and the moral symbolisms attached thereto.

## 3. SUPEREGO, EGO-IDEAL, AND EGO-IDENTITY

The conceptualization of the functions attributed to the ego-ideal, superego, and ego-identity are useful in an examination of religious belief systems, and so the discussion of the preceding section will continue with a further delineation and contrasting of these concepts.

Briefly, the ego-ideal is that set of psychic functions which projects ideal goals for the self which if followed or strived for promise the fulfillment of hopes and expectations and an overall sense of satisfaction. The superego, on the other hand, is a mainly prohibitive function, deriving its energy from internalized aggression and limiting, more or less severely, instinctual expression. Features of the description of the social psychology of the divinity student are pertinent in a general way to these two mental institutions. The involvement in ideologies, theologizing, various aspects of the general value orientation characteristic of the divinity student, and in general the close pursuit of identity formation through religious ideals, are all actions which may be considered in relation to the functions of the ego-ideal. Similarly, the lack of aggressive and competitive actions and the emphasis on the desexualized aspects of love bespeak the prevalence of a particularly severe superego formation.

In a major paper, "On Narcissism," Freud related the development and functions of the ego-ideal to transformations of narcissism. The superego, in "The Ego and the Id" and elsewhere, is related to the cluster of identifications through which the oedipal complex is resolved. This differentiation and its attendant implications seem to have considerable clinical and theoretical usefulness, and it will be followed here.

To begin contrasting the ego-ideal and superego, some central features of Freud's discussion in "On Narcissism" will be summarized. One of the initial hypotheses for this discussion is that every person originally has two sexual objects: his self (body) and the mothering one (Freud, 1914, p. 88). Thus there is in every person a primary narcissism. Associated with this stage of life, before there is clear separation between self and world, is also the "belief" in the omnipotence of thought; that is, because of lack of separation between self and world, a thought or feeling is "assumed" to have an effect on the world. The ego-ideal is the development that results when some life experience forces a departure from the state of primary narcissism. The ego-ideal is the effort to restore the state of primary narcissism. It is based upon external and internal criticisms of the self, and comparison with and identifications with idealized parents or aspects of parents. The original narcissism is now displaced onto the ideal, and it is felt to have all the perfections which the child once felt himself to possess.

Repression proceeds on the basis of comparison of the self with the ideal. Where the ideal is not instituted in one or another aspect, a perversion may result or the individual will retain one or another pregenital form of gratification. John Murray (1964) has chosen the apt word "entitlement" to express the sense of "having the right" to infantile gratifications. As in the case of the development of secondary narcissism described earlier, feelings of self-esteem and the sense of self in general are closely dependent upon the quality and contents of the ego ideal.[1] Freud summarizes these developments as follows:

> The development of the ego consists in a departure from primary narcissism and gives rise to a vigorous attempt to recover that state. This departure is brought about by means of the displacement of libido on to an ego-ideal imposed from without; and satisfaction is brought about from fulfilling this ideal. (1914, p. 100)

The superego arises out of the oedipal complex, and its "executive agent" (J. Murray, 1964) is castration anxiety. The child resolves the complex of conflicting feelings by identifying with the same-sex parent, relinquishing sexual claims on the cross-sex parent and maintaining a desexualized affectionate relationship with that parent. The identification with the same-sex parent is inevitably ambivalent. In the simplest case, the sexual claims on the cross-sex parent are given up by intensifying the identification with the same-sex parent. However, this latter achievement may also occur through identifying with the cross-sex parent as well. Freud (1923) said that the simplest case rarely occurs, and in general, because of the inherent bisexuality of the child, one must assume a negative and positive oedipal complex:

> For one gets the impression that the simple Oedipus complex is by no means its commonest form, but rather represents a simplification or schematization which, to be sure, is often enough justified for practical purposes. Closer study usually discloses the more complete Oedipus complex, which is twofold, positive and negative, and is due to the bisexuality originally present in children: that is to say, a boy has not merely an ambivalent attitude towards his father and an affectionate object-choice towards his mother, but at the same time he also behaves like a girl and displays an affectionate feminine attitude to his father and a corresponding jealousy and hostility towards his mother. It is this complicating element introduced by bisexuality that makes it so difficult to obtain a clear view of the facts in connection with the earliest object-choices and identifications, and still more difficult to describe them intelligibly. . . .
>
> In my opinion it is advisable in general, and quite especially where neurotics are concerned, to assume the existence of the complete Oedipus complex. (Freud, 1923, p. 33)

Character development, then, in the case of the male, may be expected to be influenced by both masculine and feminine identifications and superego functions that may have arisen in connection with one or another or both. In particular, these observations prepare the way for seeing in the religious belief system the major influence of a feminine identification, that is, an identification with the mother.

The superego derives its energy from aggression, once directed in jealousy at one or the other or both parents, and then turned against the self in the form of castration anxiety. The more intense the oedipal complex and the more quickly repression is instituted, the "stricter will be the domination of the superego over the ego later on—in the form of conscience or perhaps in an unconscious sense of guilt" (Freud, 1923, p. 35). The superego plays the role of Simon Legree (J. Murray, 1964). This suggests the typical pathological developments. The ego-ideal, on the other hand, "is born as an effort to restore the lost Shangri-La of the relations with the all-giving primary mother" (J. Murray, p. 478). The anxiety associated with it is the fear of the loss of the mother—fears of abandonment or "starving to death" and associated feelings of helplessness. Murray uses the following imagery to convey the quality of the ego-ideal and to imply some psychopathological possibilities:

> The ego ideal . . . can effect its purpose with promises
> and the seductive, alluring smile of the Mona Lisa.
> The future and even the present holds so much of hope
> and expectation if it is followed. When life is not
> lived in harmony with the ideal, however, or when the
> ideal is so narcissistically based that it is infantile and
> socially unrealistic, anxiety inevitably ensues and further
> regressive tendencies are prone to follow. (Murray, 1964,
> p. 478)

The idea that the ego-ideal "is born as an effort to restore the lost Shangri-La of the relations with the all-giving primary mother" and the observations of the phenomena upon which this idea is based are seminal in all that follows. This idea prepares the way for seeing the religious belief system as a part of that effort to make restitution for the relationship with the primary mother relinquished in the course of development. In later chapters, the idea is presented that the psychological meaning of the concept of God derives from the primary maternal relationship and represents, in part, the wish for fusion with the maternal imago and the restoration and never-ending reestablishment of the sense of wholeness, meaning, and nurturance felt to lie therein. Religious doubt, in part, is then the dread of fusion, the fear of loss of self, annihilation. A rather formal caveat should suffice at this point as the qualification to these generalizations: the emphasis throughout on these factors should not be taken as an indication that they are considered to be the only ones.

Erikson (1959) sees the superego as it contrasts with the

ego-ideal as a more "archaic and thoroughly internalized representative of . . . man's congenital proclivity toward the development of a primitive, categorical conscience" (p. 148). It is more closely related to early introjects which can be harshly punitive and "remains a rigidly vindictive and punitive inner agency of 'blind' morality" (ibid.). In contrast, the ego-ideal is more flexible, more closely related to the ego's function of reality-testing and more a representative of the ideals of a particular historical period.

Ego-identity, as it contrasts with the ego-ideal, is even closer to social reality.

> . . . as a subsystem of the ego it would test, select, and
> integrate the self-representations derived from the
> psycho-social crises of childhood. It could be said to be
> characterized by the more or less *actually attained but
> forever-to-be-revised* sense of the reality of the self
> within social reality; while the imagery of the ego ideal
> could be said to represent a set of *to-be-strived-for
> but forever-not-quite-attainable ideal* goals for the self.
> (Erikson, 1959, p. 149)

The notion of ego-identity also may be directly related to the earlier discussion of the social psychology of the divinity student. We noted the theological student's deep involvement in "theologizing"—the process of interpreting himself and the world in terms of his religious beliefs, and conversely reinterpreting and filling in the meaning of religious symbols and myths in terms of his most personal experiences. His evaluation and integration of basic life assumptions proceed at conscious and unconscious levels of the personality and also at affective and cognitive levels. This process itself—the development of an ideology—is a central feature of identity formation. ". . . Identity and ideology are two aspects of the same process" (Erikson, 1959, p. 157). The theological student is thus intensely engaged in one central feature of identity formation in a uniquely pure way: he is working out for himself the traditional ideology that binds him to the historic Christian community. For many students the feeling of being a Christian in the sense of being a member, in one way or another, of this historical community assumes a central role in identity. It should be evident also that, for the doubter especially, the working out of an ideology may be an expression of the quest for identity.

## 4. PSYCHIC ROOTS OF THE RELIGIOUS BELIEF SYSTEM

The psychological sources and meanings of the religious belief system lie in the history of the individual's earliest object relationships as they occur in the family context. Ego synthesis, making use of the salient religious imagery, finds in the religious belief system a ready medium to express and preserve the contents and qualities of the early object relationships. Religious symbolism will be readily used in ego synthesis particularly in those families where religious language and activity is a primary vehicle for communicating important overt and covert feelings, values and underlying world views. Even when religious imagery has little place in a family, it is easy for the child to pick up and use available religious imagery. Religious symbolisms are common in society, and they are easily put to use in childhood and adolescent mental life as well as later (see the case of Eyman, chapter XI).

It is the usual case, for the theological student, that the religious belief system is the ideological manifestation and culmination of identity, as well as the vehicle for seeking identity. It is the object of his current study and development and the primary tool of his future professional work. The religious belief system is the primary representation of *himself*—to the world and to himself. The religious symbols, imagery, and literature are "tradition-saturated," and thus are powerful ties with the historic and contemporary Christian community. They form a common language in which the most diverse aspects of life may be discussed and experienced.

The religious belief system is a manifestation of and gives expression to basic underlying attitudes and feelings toward the self and the world. Any sort of religious doubt which is at all pervasive or deep will represent a profound lack of closure, conflict, or confusion in the coherence of the ego. There will be difficulties in establishing a sense of self-esteem and a sense of the self generally, and there will be concomitant adaptational difficulties and subjective discomfort.

While the above considerations relate in particular to the process of identity formation, other considerations we have mentioned relate quite specifically to the development and functions of the ego-ideal. What should be reemphasized is the profound effect on self-esteem and self-concept deriving from a belief in God. Of all cultural symbols, "God" is the most powerful in its capacity to bestow a sense of meaning and esteem. In the face of a profound sense of an underlying division within the self and chronic diffuse feelings of shame and guilt, it is often enough that only a relationship with God can restore a sense of wholeness, meaning, and self-esteem and the ability to accept the self and life. We must, in fact, infer a greatness of need equal to the power of the remedy. Belief in God must in many instances function above all as an effort to make restitution for a profound narcissistic wound that occurs when, in the context of the early relationship with the mother, there is a "departure from the primary narcissism" (Freud, 1914, p. 100) of the sort that gives rise to the ego-ideal. The religious belief system, then, and the relationship with God in particular may be seen as a restitution for the relationship with the primary mother, a defense against the loss of that relationship and the effort to restore its good effects. In the effort to make restitution for the departure from primary narcissism, the ego-ideal may come to contain more or less grandiose and socially unrealistic claims which may then find expression in the religious belief system. A development of this sort is particularly likely to occur and have central salience in the personality where, in addition to the inevitable departure from primary narcissism, the mother-child relationship is prolonged and, in one way or another, keeps alive issues of secondary narcissism. Secondary narcissism will find expression in the adult personality in such feelings as being special, holy, having "great expectations" (J. Murray, 1964) for an extraordinary future, or a dream of a golden future. The feeling of being special, which in one form or another is apparently very common in the divinity student,[2] can become expressed in the religious belief system in a variety of ways. It varies with the way in which the student conceives of his ministry, his conception of God, and what type of internalized relationship he has established with God and with Jesus. To be a follower of Jesus, for example, in any of a number of possible ways, may imply an identification with Jesus, and thereby some sense of the self not only as holy, pure, good, or whatever, but also as unique among men by virtue of a special relationship with God. The traditional experience, rare now in the more liberal schools, of having been called to the ministry by God, is a good example of one religious form these feelings take. It should be borne in mind that the feelings of being special, of having a great entitlement to a glorious future, and so on, are feelings that are by no means unique to the theological student, nor do they necessarily fall within the realm of the pathological. They are a very general type of human affective experience that finds expression in the context of religious belief systems among others. Their vicissitudes in other realms would make an interesting and complex study. Suffice it to note further that they may also take the form of an unconscious conviction of immortality or even of being God.

The descriptions given here are very general and have any number of possible variations, some of which are described in the case studies. It is not assumed that they hold universally.

It is tempting to speculate that, in the case of the theological student with his overriding preoccupations with ideologies and values, the ego-identity is peculiarly under the domination of the ego-ideal. This would imply that his actions and general life course have a tone and color unusually or especially influenced by ideological, belief, and value considerations. This, however, is a comparative judgment for which I have no empirical basis. But it does suggest a more general psychological observation for which there is some basis. The ego-ideal in contrast with the ego-identity has somewhat more distance from social reality and the ego's function of reality-testing (see above, p. 46). Actions then, in the life of the individual or group, taken under the aegis of ideals or beliefs may well override other considerations of reality, even human well-being. For example, in the more extreme instance, a considerable degree of pathology and generally tenuous reality relations may be "masked" by the religious belief system. Considering its development, the ego-ideal may contain relatively primitive, archaic, and grandiose ideals, and be related to similarly primitive and archaic impulses and fantasies. Because of the communal quality of the symbols of the religious belief system, however, the most primitive feelings and fantasies may achieve more or less direct symbolic expression. In a relatively closed community of believers, psychic life may remain quite undifferentiated and primitive and still be socially adaptive. This sort of instance may be expected to occur with particular frequency in homogeneous subcultures whose child-rearing practices involve early severe inhibition of instinctual expression.

Further, where the ego-ideal is dominated by ideological contents that have become attached to very early experiences and primitive fantasies, the direction of identity formation by such an ideal would seem to preclude the development of strong ties to and understanding of external realities. The attaching of highly valued, communal symbol systems to early psychic structures tends to fixate the psychic structures at an early age, making further individuation difficult, if not impossible. (An instance of this sort is discussed in chapter IV.)

## 5. DOUBT AND LIBERAL AND CONSERVATIVE THEOLOGIES AS FUNCTIONS OF EGO SYNTHESIS

In chapter II, two aspects of the world of the theological student were described, the domain of theology and some of its sociopsychological dimensions, and the social psychology of the immediate life of the student. It is in regard to the latter that, to this point in this chapter, concepts have been elucidated pertinent to understanding psychological processes underlying a general value orientation, the quest for identity, and some aspects of theologizing. It is time now to draw more closely together the domain of theology and that of personality. Doing so will prepare the way for being able to observe and understand the personality processes related to and underlying the individual belief system, for being able to "discover the psyche in the socious and the socious in the psyche" (Levinson).

That there are dimensions of theology that have psychological significance and relate to aspects of personality has already been indicated. At this point there remains the elucidation of the more specific psychologically relevant qualities of liberal and conservative theology and the aspects of personality with which they are congruent. We are saying, in simple terms, that the person who holds to a liberal theology will have particular characteristics which distinguish him from a person who holds to a conservative theology, and that the latter will have his own distinctive characteristics.

Erikson (1953) has used the terms "wholeness" and "totality" to describe the kinds of personality structures congruent with those types of ideologies which have important elements in common with, respectively, the liberal and conservative theologies. In the totalistic personality organization, a low tolerance of anxiety (and other dysphoric psychic tensions) is dealt with by the relatively primitive mechanisms involved in establishing absolute boundaries and psychic demarcations which provide absolute internal and external definitions once and for all. The earliest model for this process is dealing with the ambivalence toward primary objects by "splitting" the object and establishing the love and hate in two distinct and separate images. This is an effort to reduce the psychic strain introduced by ambivalence into the real relationship. With healthy ego development, the individual can bear the tension involved in establishing a unified image, containing his positive and negative feelings, of the parents. An immediate inference from this is that the person who tends toward liberal theologies would be more likely to have a more unified view of the parents as having both good and bad qualities, and he would be able to express mixed feelings about them, and about people he loves in general. The conservative would tend to idealize parents and manifest the need to express and consciously have only positive feelings about parents and loved ones.

Erikson (1953) points out sources of anxiety in three major psychosocial crises that may demand a totalistic personality organization. The earliest period of life may leave a deep sense of division, malevolence, or emptiness which may demand the personification of the sense of evil and institutionalizing and projecting nostalgically felt sources of good and never-ending supply of meaning. We may look here and in the primitive splitting of objects for the source in conservative theology of absoluteness, the profound dichotomy between man and God: the deep sense of sin, man's puniness and helplessness, the unbridgeable estrangement from God, and the underlying sense of omnipresent evil. The pervasive sense of estrangement, isolation, and evil would tend to pervade all aspects of living in the case of the individual who maintains a conservative theology. To bridge the gap between himself and other people, for example, he may fall back on stereotyped forms of religious inter-change (see case of Pale, chapter V).

The tensions aroused in the oedipal period may demand that the child determine once and for all whether he is good or bad, and he may set out to be absolutely good (see the case of Mudge, chapter VIII). Similarly the tensions aroused in adolescence by tendencies to identity diffusion and attendant falls in self-esteem, may be responded to by some form of absolute self-delineation (see the case of Electon, chapter VII).

The term "wholeness" refers to a quality of psychic or-ganization in which a greater tolerance of tension allows for the integration of a greater range and diversity of psychic materials at a higher level. Such a personality organization allows for more flexibility, openness, and relativity, and would find the liberal theologies more compatible.

The totalistically organized personality is generally domi-nated by a primitive superego. Baranger (1958) has discussed these same distinctions by distinguishing between superego and ego-ideal ideologies. The former type of ideology is highly idealized, puts forth apocalyptic utopian promises, and contains a persecutory quality in one way or another. The ego-ideal type of ideology is more relative, nearer to reality, and better synthe-sized with the experiences of the ego.

Certain aspects of the description of the authoritarian per-sonality (Adorno et al., 1950; Levinson, 1964) also aptly cap-ture some of the qualities of totalism. While I am freely drawing on these descriptions to enlarge the picture of totality and wholeness, I wish to make it absolutely explicit that conservative theology is *not* being equated with an authoritarian ideology, and there is in fact no basis for so doing. The personality struc-ture underlying authoritarian ideologies has also been presented as being superego-dominated. What occurs in this instance is that a relatively weak, ineffective ego is caught between a polar-ized, severe, primitive superego and an id whose contents have remained primitive and unintegrated. The result is a rigid, energy-consuming defensive structure, which relies on the more primitive mechanisms of defense such as projection, denial, and distortion, and a severe narrowing of consciousness and its contents. The individual experiences a relatively narrow range of thought and feeling, and there is a tendency therefore to fall back on stereotyped thinking and conventionalism. Some sort of authority hierarchy is relied upon and rigidly defined, and unacceptable impulses and feelings are externalized onto an outgroup, or perhaps, in the case of the religionist, personified partly or wholly as evil.

The contrasting case is the one in which identity formation and development in general can proceed by integrating a wider range of feeling, thought, and impulse into the ego organization. The id is not sealed off and thereby allowed to retain a primitive impact on the personality. There is a relatively greater range of consciousness, and more energy and fantasy are available for creative work and relationship.

Under the term "totalistic" will be subsumed those absolute organizations of personality arising out of the psychosocial crises as described by Erikson, and also the mechanisms determined by the splitting of objects as a method to deal with ambivalence, as well as the personality features resulting from the type of superego dominance just described. The term "wholeness" will be used in a parallel, contrasting way. The hypothesis is, then, that conservative theology is more congruent with the totalistic personality structure. Similarly the more liberal theologies are congruent with the personality organization characterized by wholeness.

The importance of the implications of this formulation finds one illustration in the process of theologizing described as central in the social psychology of the theology student. The style in which theologizing is carried out by the conservative as it contrasts with that of the liberal may be seen to follow extremely closely the contrasts between personality structures characterized by totality and wholeness respectively. Conservative theologizing is geared to reduce the ambiguity of the symbols of the religious belief system, and the doctrines tend to be applied as absolutes to the personality. Liberal theologizing allows for more idiosyncratic and personal interpretation of the symbols of the belief system. In conservative theologizing, the doctrines are applied to the person, and if he has experiences which do not fit the doctrines, he is wrong. In the liberal position, the individual's experience is more a key to interpreting the religious symbols. This corresponds to the internalized dimension of liberal theology. And this in turn corresponds to the greater flexibility and internal richness of the "whole" personality. In contrast, the abnegation of the personality before the doctrines in conservative theology corresponds to the subjugation of inner life in the totalistic personality, and is the basis for externalization. The rejection of doubt in conservative theology corresponds to the severe repression of large areas of psychic life in the totalistic personality structure. The greater acceptance of doubt in liberalism corresponds to the greater tolerance of anxiety and tension and the broader range of consciousness in the "whole" personality. The liberal theological student is also more likely to have investment in other ideologies or forms of finding truth and to be integrating these into his theology. For the conservative there may be no truth outside of the religious belief system. Depth psychology nowadays is one common test case for the flexibility and tolerance of the theological student— a challenge to integrate an "ideology" that initially, at least, may set up a tension with religious belief.

Conservative theology can be seen to be congruent with a totalistic personality, and similarly, liberal theology may be seen as being more congruent with the personality structure characterized by wholeness. In this case, as in all others, the generalization sounds absolute, when in fact subtle tendencies with many possible variations are under consideration. In any case, this general observation may now be related to our theoretical focus—the process of ego synthesis—and our empirical focus— religious doubt as it occurs in either the conservative or liberal context. Now wholeness and totality may be seen as outcomes, or perhaps more accurately, as *styles* of ego synthesis. Totality is one *form* of accommodating inner and outer stress and conflict, while wholeness is another. They represent different ways of achieving personality integration, and different ways of dealing with anxiety and conflict.

> . . . the ego . . . has the task of mastering experience
> and . . . guiding action in such a way that a certain
> wholesome synthesis is, ever again, created between the
> diverse and conflicting stages and aspects of life. . . .
> To do its job, the ego develops modes of synthesis as
> well as screening methods and mechanisms of defense.
> As it matures through the constant interaction of
> maturational forces and environmental influences, a

> certain duality develops between higher levels of
> integration (which permit a greater tolerance of tension
> and of diversity) and lower levels of integration where
> totalities and conformities must help to preserve a
> sense of security. (Erikson, 1953, p. 162)

In the case of the individual belief system, too, the tendency to
a conservative theology may be seen as the outcome of a particular mode of ego synthesis, just as is the tendency to a totalistic
personality structure. The tendency to a liberal belief system
will then represent a different style of ego synthesis.

Religious doubt has already been discussed as the conscious
symbolic manifestation of ego synthesis at work. It would seem
then that two sets of phenomena—doubt and the choice between either a liberal or a conservative theology—which appear
on the surface to be psychologically unrelated are in fact expressions of the same psychological processes. One implication
that may be mentioned, although this will be much clearer in
the chapters that follow, is that the individual may seek to resolve religious doubt by becoming more liberal (at the same
time, say, he becomes more naturalistic or psychological), *or* by
becoming more conservative (at the same time he rejects liberal
or naturalistic ideologies).

## 6. A NOTE ON METHOD

The case studies themselves will have to stand as the basic description of method, and whatever illumination may be derived
from them will be the justification for the case-study method.
In several of the main chapters, the effort is made to give a
fairly complete account of the individual—his belief system, his
personal and family past, and his current personality functioning as these latter relate to the belief system. In other instances,
the account of an individual is quite brief and is used only to
illustrate a particular point. While in the more complete accounts of individuals, the style is determined by the aim of
drawing a psychologically apt picture, rather than by previously
determined categories, some of the data (not all) of the life
histories do, for our purposes, nevertheless fall into certain
categories:

*Family constellation.* Important aspects of the subject's relationships with his mother and father are examined, including changes, if discernible, at different developmental periods. More than this, however, the subject's position in the overall family structure is taken into account. That is, any one familial relationship is understood as one relationship existing in an interlocking complex of relationships. For example, the subject's meaning to or impact on the relationship between the parents may be of significance.

*Role of religion within the family.* As with any social structure, a particular family may be seen as having its own culture and ideology. Religion, in the families of the subjects, may be seen to play a specific role in that culture and ideology. Even in a relatively homogeneous subculture, the structure and function of religion may be expected to vary among families. Similarly, the way the religion is communicated to the child, and the use of religious language in particular familial relationships (e.g., mother–child) may be expected to vary. These sorts of variations have important consequences for the eventual function of religious symbolism in the personality of the adult.

*Fate of the infantile neurosis.* Even an effectively functioning adult may retain memory fragments of a period of infantile or adolescent conflict. Such memories are precious clues to the conflicts around which development took place, as well as to covert emotional trends in important familial relationships and the overall family structure. Also, the manner in which such conflicts are resolved gives the adult character its lasting form. Resolution may be accomplished through harsh, rigid defenses which tend to give the personality a totalistic cast. Or it may be accomplished through more flexible defenses and the development of adult coping mechanisms learned from a valued parent. And so on.

*Narcissism and self-esteem.* The fate of infantile narcissism is of particular interest because of its association with the development of the ego-ideal and important feelings about the self. The earlier theoretical discussion leads us to pay particular attention to the maternal relationship as a possible source for the development of significant trends in secondary narcissism. It is also important to look for the main sources of healthy self-esteem and for the individual's real capacities for relating to the world and others.

*Sexuality and masculinity-femininity.* The profound connections between religious symbolism and sexuality and sexual identity are pursued only very partially. The important identifications with the parents, of course, have implications for the development of sexual identity and for closely associated capacities for adaptation. Where the maternal identification plays a central role in the man's character development, the sense of masculinity and phallic aggressiveness are deeply effected. These character developments can only be of great importance for understanding the belief system as an aspect of personality.

The data for the life studies were gathered by several hours of interviewing (between six and twelve, over three or four sessions) and by the administration of the Rorschach cards and Thematic Apperception Test. The interviewing was all done by the author as was the test administration. That there may be bias in both interviewing and test administration and interpretation goes without saying. The style of the interviews was associative. That is, while I had in mind the important areas I wished to cover, I always followed as closely as I could during any one session the subject's own flow of thought and feeling. A mutual task was agreed upon at the start of interviewing, the exploration, as broadly and deeply as possible, of the subject's belief system, his past, and his current experience. This task was an agreeable one, or at least an interesting one, by and large, for those who participated in it. While I myself did not try to remain professionally aloof, my participation in the relationship was primarily determined by the agreed-upon task. I certainly also felt free at times to relate my own experiences, express interest, offer sympathy, and so on.

The Rorschach procedure and Thematic Apperception Test (TAT) will need little explanation for this study. With the exception of one very brief discussion of a Rorschach protocol, the use made of the test materials is not technical and will be self-explanatory for most readers. The word "test" in both instances is, of course, inapplicable. Both procedures are devices used to allow the individual the opportunity to express himself in characteristic ways. Each procedure is effective in displaying prevailing fantasies, repetitive emotional meanings, cognitive style, modes of defense, ways of dealing with feeling, interpersonal themes, and so on. The Rorschach procedure is the famous "inkblot" test. It does in fact consist of a standard series of ten cards with inkblots on them, some colored. The subject is instructed to tell whatever he "sees" in the card. The TAT procedure consists of a series of pictures (the ones used are described in Appendix B). The subject is instructed to make up a story on the basis of the picture. As mentioned, the interpretive use of the resulting materials will, I believe, be quite clear in the context of the case studies.

## PART TWO

# Faith and Doubt in the Precocious Identity Formation

# IV

## Chelly: A Texas Idyll

. . . there can be no depth without the way to the depth.
Truth without the way to truth is dead; if it still be
used, it contributes only to the surface of things.

PAUL TILLICH, "THE DEPTH OF EXISTENCE," IN THE
SHAKING OF THE FOUNDATIONS

Our series of studies of religious doubt in the Protestant divinity
student opens with one in which there is very little intrusive
doubt. This belief system, then, will provide us with a comparative anchor for those belief systems in which doubt exists.
Chelly, an intelligent man, holds to a conservative form of
Protestantism. Chelly's life pattern illustrates another concept
to be introduced, namely the "precocious identity formation."
Precocious identity formation, we will hypothesize, is a modal
pattern in the conservative subculture in our society. The concept is defined below and through the description of Chelly in
this chapter. Chapter VI is a brief theoretical sketch of the pattern of precocious identity formation.

### 1. BACKGROUND, EARLY BAPTISM, AND PRECOCIOUS IDENTITY FORMATION

Chelly is twenty-five, married, and a student in a liberal divinity
school. He grew up in Texas cities and went to a very large high
school. But his paternal grandparents had a ranch where he

spent his summers, so he is immersed in the folklore of the Texas farm and ranch. In four years at a conservative Christian college, attended mostly by members of his denomination, he finished his A.B. and M.A. He was active and sociable throughout his schooling, dramatics being a favorite activity.

Among the brethren of his church he is considered a liberal, sometimes with suspicion. His theology is, in our terms, relatively conservative. He holds traditional Christian beliefs in the Virgin Birth, and believes that he will participate, when the day comes, in Christ's Resurrection and triumph over death. He summarized his belief in this way:

> I believe He created something new in Mary's womb
> and that on Easter morning He created something else,
> and that someday, when all this business is over,
> He will create again something, and that something will
> be a new Heaven and a new Earth, and I'll have a place
> in it, and so will everyone who lives according to the
> light he has received from God. It's very mythological
> —I'm embarrassed to have to confess it, but I don't
> see anything from my [liberal] friends at —— who no
> longer accept that view of things, that really is that
> satisfactory, that useful, that pleasant, that systematic,
> that rewarding, either intellectually or, as you say, in
> your guts. . . . It is only this recent heresy of disbelief
> that has led us to question these things.

What, in the eyes of his brethren, is his liberalism, consists in his knowledge of liberal Protestantism, which, like his theological scholarship in general, is extensive. It is, however, an intellectual acquaintanceship, not having encroached upon his belief and faith in the least.

Chelly's baptism at the age of ten signals the establishment of a precocious identity formation. As Erikson (1959) presents the concept of ego-identity, it is a process that takes its initial forms in late adolescence or perhaps some years later, in the event of a psychosocial moratorium. The precocious ego-identity, as it will be described in the case of Chelly and others, is established before adolescence, and before puberty. In these cases, it *is* an identity that is established, not simply a finalization of the identifications and defenses which resolve the oedipal period, although that is also involved. The precocious identity formation, we will assume, is a characteristic of a very conservative and homogeneous culture. In the case of the conservative Protestant subculture, the social identity around which the ego-identity is formed is that of the "Christian," or "follower of Christ." The identity is a relatively simple one, and it represents an internalization of the mutually recognized values and symbols of the community. The precocious identity may be established at the height of a period of infantile conflict and represents its characterological resolution. A social ritual, baptism, heightens the social meaning of the individual development and provides the consensual symbols around which identity can coalesce. Major characterological lines are laid down at the time—patterns of defense, self-concepts, instinctual and motivational patterns, and the system for maintaining self-esteem. Adolescence is not a time for major reorganization of the personality. Conflicts precipitated at this time by sexuality are construed in terms of already established categories, and may precipitate a new religious commitment which reaffirms the earlier form of identity. The emotional core of the personality, then, remains essentially the same from childhood, relatively unaffected by subsequent possibilities for development or later intellectual sophistication. If the individual leaves his homogeneous subculture, he may have difficulty establishing a more complex identity adaptively required in the society at large (cf. Pale, chapter V).

Precocious identity formation will be studied in Chelly first by examining the manifold intertwining strands of his early life which lead up to and culminate in his baptism.

Chelly was launched on the career ecclesiastical early indeed. The maternal grandmother decided, when he was three years old, that he was to be a preacher and she started his preparation at that age. She had him administer the sacraments to her with sunshine crackers and water, and she stood him on her ottoman footstool as a little pulpit and had him sermonize. Grandmother was the first of a series of women who encouraged him in his religious vocation.

My life apparently has been studded by spiritual women.
I never realized that I could periodize it so in terms
of the Christian women I've known, but apparently I can.

Outstanding, of course, among these influences, was his mother. "She's been my intellectual, spiritual guide . . ." It is in this context that he comments, "Really, we've had just an idyllic life," adding separately and subsequently that he and his wife have too. Chelly was the only child, and the father's job took him away from home for most of the week, "which put him there only over the weekends, and Mother and me together all week long." The atmosphere of those early years, as he fondly retains it at the conscious level, is summarized in these remarks:

> Mother, you know, Mother and I were just companions. Daddy would leave and say, "Now you're the man in the house while I'm gone. So you take care of Mother." I accepted that as full responsibility. . . . They always treated me as, you know, a small-sized grown-up, really. . . . My opinions were worth something, and my says were listened to, and whenever there was a decision to be made, if I had an opinion on it, I was welcomed to express it.

Mother, as Chelly presents her, seems to have manifested a certain degree of neurotic hysteria, although this picture is compounded by physical illness. She married when she was seventeen and Father was twenty-two. Chelly comments, "She didn't know anything," indicating both Mother's prolonged naïveté and some degree of sharing of her sexual life with her son. He describes Mother as a very nervous person who had been ill all her life.

> She's just a very tense, nervous person. You know, being sick so much . . . her heart beats too fast, and she gets all fluttered . . . [PH: Is that how she expresses it?] Well, she just gets going so fast sometimes that she just can't keep up with herself.

Other symptoms were apparently genuinely somatic, and perhaps congenital. Chelly adds, "And, she's a tall, and dark and very gracious person . . . Very, very good-looking. And very sweet, gentle, nice, good in every way."

During the Korean War, for a period of some years, when Chelly was between five and ten, Mother and son were thrown even closer together. They lived in a boardinghouse in a city on the northwest coast and Chelly sometimes shared Mother's bed. We will return to a consideration of this period after sketching the family constellation further and the masculine influences in Chelly's life.

Part of the idyll was the paternal grandparents' ranch where Chelly spent his boyhood summers. What boy wouldn't love a Texas ranch, a horse of his own, dogs, and loving grandparents? Both grandfathers were church elders, and theology was a family pastime. Certainly it was between the paternal grandfather and grandson.

> I always thought he was a beautiful old man. He always had gray hair. Such a wonderful old gentleman, and an elder . . . The summer evenings were times of just sitting out on the porch at night and talking about things, everything theological . . . where you wrangle, and argue, discuss, agree, disagree, look for points where you disagree so you'll have a real good go-at-it.
>
> It makes Grandma mad, she says, "Why are you always out there arguing?" Grandpa grins. Whenever she gets mad she goes in and rattles her pots and pans around on the stove.

This was "one of the givens" in Chelly's early life.

It was this grandfather who arranged for him to give his first sermon when he was twelve. Chelly preached regularly from the summer before his senior high-school year. On one occasion he preached to a largely teen-age audience, telling them they should try to convert their dates.

Chelly's feelings about his father have a distinctive ambivalence. While, on the one hand Chelly presents his father as a firm, solid, masculine figure, clearly the authority in the household, on the other hand Chelly himself, it is implied, is a better Christian, that is, holier. A shared religiosity between mother and son, from which the father is partially excluded or contrasted, is a powerful medium which heightens the son's sense of being special and holy—indeed, the chosen son. This would be a particularly strong developmental influence when other influences also incline the child to be precociously good and spiritual anyway, as in Chelly's case.

Other family circumstances further heighten the quality of special meaningfulness and influence of the mother-son relationship. Chelly was the *only* child, and, as he says, "I was the only one." Circumstances surrounding Chelly's birth also augmented this quality of the mother-son relationship. His mother had two, perhaps three, miscarriages in the effort to have more children. It is part of the family mythology that it was very hard on the mother to bear Chelly, and he says, "I nearly killed her." The specificity of the following bit of his theology reflects his identification of his own experience with that of Jesus:

> God can speak Christ into existence into the womb of
> Mary. He can then be born, and come to an increasing
> awareness of the fact (of his divinity) by listening to
> what she tells him about the miraculous event of his birth.

That is, the son, Chelly, comes to feel special by being told of his miraculous, painful birth, and he identifies with Jesus in this respect.

Chelly's later feelings about sex and marriage were certainly affected by these experiences. In his adolescence, he seriously considered that perhaps he should not marry. Marriage, as Paul said, could interfere with his Christian mission, the most important thing in his life. This semi-resolve quickly wavered when he met his wife-to-be during his first year of college, but he keeps alive a curious fantasy.

> There are all kinds of horrible circumstances that I
> suppose a person could dream up. . . . These poor people
> in the Congo now, and these savages that are killing
> them, and if I were, you know, a Christian missionary
> with my wife there and they were torturing her before my
> eyes and asking me to renounce my faith,  I would find it
> very difficult not to.

When the low likelihood of this situation ever actually occurring in the light of his present plans was presented to Chelly, he said that one never knows where one will be in a number of years, and he added, "Certainly it's a possibility that I ought to entertain in quieter moments so that I'll have my thinking on it worked out when the time comes, if it ever does."

Father was a hard-working go-getter, a successful man in a highly competitive business setting. Final decisions always waited on his word. Mother, while knowing how to get what she wanted in an appropriately feminine, submissive way, always deferred to him. Chelly often had to hear, "We had better wait until Daddy gets home to decide . . ." In getting ahead, Father was not always as Christianly passive as he should have been, and he was sorry about this. Like every other moral and religious question, it was discussed in the family. It was not just this, however, that tarnished the paternal image. Father was in the tobacco business, and tobacco was considered sinful by many in the family's pietistic community. Father would say, "I just don't know if I ought to be in this business or not," and he would discuss the issue with his son, who had early on become the family theological expert. It was decided that tobacco, like alcohol, which was sometimes consumed in the home, was acceptable in moderation. Chelly also describes Father as something of a philistine, in comparison with himself and Mother. Chelly also presents him as naïve. Father has never had doubts about the ultimate questions, "because these things just don't occur to you when you're on the theological level that he's on."

Nevertheless, Chelly regarded him as a "perfect father." Only in recent years has he been able to see and appreciate Father as another man who could also make mistakes. He had felt a good deal of protection from his father, and felt the pangs of relinquishing an idealized image and becoming someone who could manage situations on his own, rather than the boy who could always turn to Father. He feels that Father taught him to be confident in his own area—theology.

Many strands of his early years, then, could find full expression in his baptism and in his wholeheartedly assuming the role of the little theologian and preacher that Grandmother had first selected for him. He was following, in the close-knit pietistic community, the tradition of his grandfathers, and their fathers before them. And above all the ecclesiastical life with its rich symbolisms and moral righteousness, the love for and of Jesus, and finally the expectations of heaven—all gave expression to, and replaced what had to be given up in, the relationship with

Mother. We will return shortly to the later specific forms of what Chelly would call the "outworking" of these qualities of being special, what we call the vicissitudes of narcissism and the processes of idealization.

## 2. CHILDHOOD INTRAPSYCHIC CONFLICTS AND BAPTISM

Evidence Chelly provides indicates that his baptism occurred at the height of an intensely conflictful developmental period, and that the inner conflicts tapered off sharply after the baptism. This suggests that the baptism, as a symbol of commitment as a Christian, as a believer in Christ, instituted or finalized defensive and other processes that helped control the conflicts and allay the anxiety. Other evidence indicates that his current personality functioning rests essentially on the same dynamic core as it did when he was ten. That is, a precocious identity formation occurred at ten and has carried over essentially unchanged into adult life.

The developmental conflict remained, within the otherwise open family, largely covert. Perhaps the only overt expression of an inner disturbance was the fact that he sleepwalked a good deal at this time, that is between five and ten. Another overt expression of an inner anxiety was a concern with death which was one of the motivations for his baptism. This fear was interpreted in religious terms within the family. The minimal external disturbance in his daily and family life indicates that for the little theologian most of the life developments we have described so far were ego-syntonic, and this would include the close identification with his mother and the other feminine influences in his life.

The primary clues to Chelly's childhood developmental conflicts lie in his memory of three frightening, "terrible" dreams, each of which he had repetitively between the ages of five and ten. They declined before junior high school, that is after the baptism, and he recalls enjoying his dream life after age eleven.

The dreams seem to reflect a conflict between a trend to establish the person as a separate male individual and the wish to yield passively to an active, all too present and overpowering closeness with the mother. The outcome of the conflict, as it is represented in his current personality, seems to be the relinquishment of some aspects of a sense of maleness, including phallic impulses and a sense of masculine heterosexuality in general. It is notable that in early adolescence masturbation and sexual play with a male cousin, although conflictful activities, were subject to less repression than phallic and heterosexual impulses.

The activities with the cousin provided the material for one of his anxiety dreams. He and K were in the habit, at one point, of playing with each other's rectums. They did this at times when they were supposedly napping. On one occasion, Mother came in and found them lying side by side doing this. She slapped their hands in rebuke, but she said nothing.

> But this dream involved me in—it seemed like the basement of a house, and there with K and Aunt M, Mother's sister, K's mother, and I think Mother was there too, and Aunt M and Mother would talk. But Mother was not predominant, nor was she the active one. K and I were there together and we were paired up, and I think we had our, we were either without clothes, or scantily dressed or something. And the point of the dream was that Aunt M had a square of white paper with red blood on it. And if she wiped you across your rectum with this red blood, you know, then you died. And it was a process of, there was some conversation about it, you know— should this be done or not. And it was all very hazy and very misty, but it was a frightening dream.

Activity, judgment, and punishment are displaced from Mother to another less important, but still female, figure. Chelly was familiar with the menstrual cycle at the time, an idea that seems reflected in the blood on the aunt's square of paper. He had also seen his mother nude, as it was customary in the family to be casual in this respect, although mother was more modest than he or father. One magical, or primary process meaning, of "being touched by" (wiped) is "to be turned into." The dream seems to express the fear of (wishes related to) being turned into a menstruating woman, a passive, "dead" person. More generally, it expresses the wishes for and fears of fusing with and being overwhelmed by Mother, wiping out his efforts to achieve a masculine integrity and interpretation of his own body.

A second dream repeats the "red blood" theme in a different manner. Every night for a time, Chelly dreamed he was being chased by a horde of Indians led by "Red Shirt." The character was from a movie. This was the most frightening of the dreams.

For his third dream, he also used a scene from a movie: A woman comes into a dark room and sees, with horror, her husband who has hanged himself. The spectator and the dreamer see the spooky shadow of the hanging man, although not the man himself. And they see the horror registered on the woman's face.

This dream repeats the theme of the active female and the totally threatened, passive, in this case, dead, male.

The dreams seem clearly enough to be related to each other. The central theme of our interpretation of these materials is the conflictful wish for and fear of fusion with the mother during a period in which the boy was trying to differentiate himself from her as a phallic male. The threat is one in which the ego is in danger of being inundated by too much closeness and lack of differentiation from the mother.[1]

To the extent that this interpretation is relevant, it offers an insight into religious symbolism. God is understood, in the Judeo-Christian tradition, as God the Father. Psychoanalytic writers on religion have accepted this symbolism at face value—interpreting God as a projection of the father or aspects of him.[2] It is curious, however, that a discipline that is so used to seeking the latent meaning beneath manifest ones should accept the manifest symbolism in this instance without question. What I wish to suggest is that, in an important number of cases at least, the symbolism of God the Father is a defense against maternal engulfment, and the actual affective content and meaning of the symbol "God" is derived from various aspects of the maternal relationship. Specifically, the salience within the personality of the symbol "God" and the God relationship may, in part, represent the wish for fusion with the primary maternal imago. Such a fusion seems to promise the restoration of a sense of wholeness and completeness, of a time of being totally loved and secure, of being smiled upon by the gods. Secondarily, the sense of self is enhanced, its existence, continuity, value, and specialness. In this sense, God may represent a restitution for the early mother relationship. At the same time, a dread may accompany the wish for fusion, because fusion also means a loss of ego boundaries, a loss of the self, death. Fusion is thus feared as well. The symbolization of God as male, Father, and as ultimate value protects the individual from the sense of a dreaded fusion. Where such protective measures are ineffective, for one or another reason, the dread of fusion throws the individual into the deepest conflicts about his religious commitment. It is the dread of fusion which I hypothesize as the deepest underlying source of religious doubt.

This interpretation parallels an aspect of the normal oedipal phase. The identification of the son with the father and the relinquishment of the feelings of exclusive entitlement to the mother serve not only reality and the incest taboo. These developments preserve the young child's ego from being engulfed in the maternal matrix in such a way as to preclude its development and individuation. Circumstances that prolong and heighten the son's sense of entitlement in the relationship with the mother, as in Chelly's case, inevitably have as one of their consequences an intertwining of the child's ego with the mother's. A variety of interferences in ego development and formation of masculine identity may result.

In his dreams Chelly experienced the dread of death—loss of the self, destruction of the body. At the time of his baptism he was also very much afraid of death in his waking hours.

> The week or so just before I was baptized when all the theological implications of the things began to fit into place, you know, the little ten-year-old systematic theology, then it [death] became a fearsome aspect because in my belief at that time, if you hadn't been baptized and knew that you *ought* to be in response to the Gospel of Jesus Christ, that as he was dead and buried and was resurrected from the tomb, so we must be. We must die to our sins and be buried in baptism, and then be raised up from baptism so that at the end of the world it all comes about and then we will be resurrected from our tombs—then fear of death was a very salient factor . . .

So he describes it and its implications in retrospect. It may be assumed that the waking and the dreaming dread had the same source.

As it also turns out, "We had a ripsnorter of a preacher, who preached hellfire and brimstone." He recalls that at the time he wanted to be baptized because Jesus loved him and wanted him to be, "and that if I did I'd go to heaven and if I didn't I'd go to hell." So one Sunday, after his credal knowledge had been tested by parents and teachers, he went forward to the pulpit when the time during the services came, and said that he wanted to be baptized. His confession that Jesus Christ is the son of God was made public, and he was immersed in the baptistry before the large congregation. The preacher commented to his father that if he had any sins, they certainly weren't very big ones. He was congratulated, and he believed that the angels, of whom he had tried to steal glimpses during dull sermons, were rejoicing.

### 3. CURRENT PERSONALITY FUNCTIONING: RETENTION OF EARLY CONFLICT

It remains for us now to consider Chelly's current personality functioning, particularly as it pertains to the notion of precocious identity formation and the vicissitudes of narcissism. Chelly's Rorschach imagery, particularly, suggests the retention within his ego of a too powerful and too close Mother-imago. Three of the four well-developed M responses (human figures in motion) are of vigorously active females.

> Two old ladies . . . talking over the back-yard fence shaking their fists at one another. (R*II*)[3]

> African tom-tom beaters . . . women because they have breasts. (R*III*)

> Two high-school girls . . . excited and animated conversation—maybe they're mad . . . (R*VII*)

These images reflect women as savage and angry. This is congruent with the judgmental and punitive function of women in the dream discussed earlier. Both these apparently unconscious qualities of Chelly's perception of women contrast sharply with his assessment of his mother as "sweet, gentle, nice, good in every way." Another "grand-dame" appears: "This is a grand-dame of the opera." (The image is highly elaborated, and she has all sorts of decorations.) ". . . The glory that follows her" (RX).

The male figures, in contrast, are "straining . . . trying to lift something" (R*III*), or small and comical "court jesters" (RV). Some sturdy male symbolism appears but remains very undeveloped: "This central thing is some sort of column but I don't know what kind of a column or I don't know what it's doing and I don't know why it's there . . ." (R*IV*).

From an apparently deeper psychic level come frightening, engulfing images: "The fellow on Bald Mountain . . . the Devil really . . . Here's his gaping maw." Chelly describes his memory of the image from a Walt Disney movie: "This black person . . . fierce-looking . . . a frightful thing, but just delightful" (R*III*). Also on R*II* and R*IX* are frightening masks which have a nightmarish quality, and in fact they reminded Chelly that he had been having dreams lately.

Chelly's comments on the Bald Mountain image suggest the quality of defense against the affect and unconscious imagery informing these percepts. The fearful aspects are put out of consciousness and the idea is converted into a harmless, entertaining one. Below we will note that this parallels the way Chelly handles certain theological problems.

Too much physical closeness to the mother of the kind Chelly reports, and sometimes, specifically, a boy's new knowledge of menstruation can result in feelings of repulsion for women. Such feelings are reflected in the TAT:

> This one is about sex. She's lying in bed and she doesn't have any clothes on. She's either his wife or perhaps a seductress of some kind or perhaps a girlfriend, and he's not married to her. Yet, for some reason, he's not willing to go to bed with her. Because he still has his clothes on, number one. And because he's repulsed, number two. He's changed his mind. . . . She's ready. Because she's in bed *sans* clothing. And yet for some reason, he changed his mind, I don't know just why. Maybe he just came in the room and he didn't plan—this wasn't a mutual agreement. And so he sees this naked woman lying there and he's embarrassed by it perhaps or repulsed by the idea of seeing this person whom he knows, naked . . . (T*13*MF)

The uncertainty about the woman's category—wife, seductress "of some kind," or girlfriend—is noteworthy. It may be taken to reflect an oedipal dilemma. That is, heterosexual impulses still retain a close association with the relationship with Mother. As a result, the sexuality portrayed here is aseptic, overly delicate and lacking in vigorous spontaneity.

## 4. CHARACTER AND THEOLOGY

Chelly's contemporary religious beliefs are, at core, exactly the same as those he held when he was ten, despite a great deal of sophistication in terms of historical knowledge and theological scholarship. The later sophistication simply surrounds, enclothes, and buffers, as it were, the core beliefs. This seems to be typical of the character development following the precocious identity formation. Later characterological developments function to protect the core identity, crystallized around the basic religious beliefs.

The precocious identity formation proceeds, in part, by a relatively severe repression of infantile conflicts, and that repression leaves a heavy mark on adult character. In Chelly's case, this mark takes the form of what we may call a *characterological barrier against experience*. In some way, feelings and events arising from an inner or an outer source are not strongly experienced and are not allowed to really impinge upon the personality core which contains the basic religious belief system. As with any characterological development, this has many ramifications in Chelly's life, and his protocols are replete with rich and uniquely interesting examples. We can go into only a few.

Chelly talked a good deal about the "necessity" of God's existence, and he was queried about what this meant. Here, as elsewhere in theological discussions, Chelly nearly drowned the interviewer in a sea of fluent scholarship and theological sophistication. He spoke of the extremities man would be in without God, that everything would be meaningless, and that suicide would be the logical out. He even applied all this to himself.

It just seems to me that if God is not to underwrite the whole thing, that the whole thing then is just not worth it all. And that's what I really mean by necessity. God's

*got* to be there. It's kind of a frantic necessity for me.
God's *got* to be there. Or all this is just not worth it.

Now, on the one hand, there is every reason to take Chelly seriously here, and it would be a mistake not to. He is deeply committed to what he says, and he means it. However, the fact is
Chelly does not *sound* frantic in the least, and the listener is
always left wondering what his locutions about liberal positions,
uncertainty, doubt, and existential *angst* really mean to him.
What are the burdens for him that would be unbearable without God? One way to find data relevant to a question like this
is to ask:

> PH: Do you really feel that? I mean, how much do you
> feel that in your guts, as opposed to how much is it
> intellectual?

> Chelly: Yeah. Well, I don't know, you see, 'cause I've
> always been a Christian. We believe and I believe that a
> person has to be converted to become a Christian, which
> implies a previous state as a non-Christian. But after
> all, if you've been raised as a Christian all your life and
> you come to Christ when you're ten years old, you hardly
> know the extremities of life, at the tender age of ten.
> So I've never known what it's like to be without God . . .
> So, *primarily* I would say, this is intellectual argument
> against people who are at the moment in ambiguity, with
> regard to their faith . . .

What Chelly indicates is that he has preserved the tender ex-
periential innocence of the ten-year-old. We also see that he
handles ideas that are essentially nihilistic with regard to his
faith in the same way he handled the devilish figure with the
gaping maw on card III of the Rorschach. The fearful, anxiety-
laden meanings are successfully repressed and isolated, and the
ideational contents are turned into harmless intellectual toys.
   At another point when discussing doubt and alternative possibilities in his life, he commented:

> Well now that's hard to do [think what he would be if he
> were not a faithful believer] because I've rarely entertained

the thought along, you know. As I told you, ever since I was three—it was decided what I was to do.

At the core of Chelly's belief system is the idea of the Resurrection in Jesus Christ and the eternal life. What occurs is the presentation of all sorts of liberal theological considerations, intimations of doubts and uncertainties, and locutions about meaninglessness and existential *angst*. On closer inquiry, however, it is clear that these do not come from the center of a more or less deeply and genuinely, personally experiencing self. Sometimes the flood of ideas seems to be an effort to baffle the listener. The approach to the Rorschach is exactly parallel:

> Oh this is a wonderful thing! . . . [PH: Look at that please—] Great! [PH: And tell me what it might appear to be.] Oh about three things, four things. Does it matter which one comes first? [PH: No. Go ahead.] It looks like a bobcat's hide hanging on a smokehouse wall; it looks like a butterfly; it looks something like a beetle; it looks something like a skeleton to some sort of an animal. Uh, it looks like something with wings that has pinchers. And then it looks like a—some sort of crab, I suppose, sea beast—these things always look alike. I'm glad you paint them different colors. I never know whether to look at the outside or the inside to decide. . . . And it's hard to decide which thing to say. (RI)

His initial exclamations of delight establish the procedure as a kind of refined entertainment, tending to remove it from the realm of an opportunity for a serious, personal, and deep expression of the self. He follows this with the statement that it looks like several things, and this also serves to indicate that no one thing is to be taken as a representation of a meaning to which he is personally committed. There then follows a little flood of percepts, one upon the other. The listener is somewhat overwhelmed, and he cannot really focus on any one. None are highly developed, and in fact the quality of the percepts distinctly trails off toward the end ("something with wings that has pinchers"), indicating that the pressure to put forth a quantity is displacing the task of finding personal meaning in the blot. In his final comments he indicates that he himself experiences a lack of focus, but he tends to project its source to something external: "These things always look alike. . . . It's hard to decide which thing to say." He gives expression to this latter feeling a number of other times during the projective tests. He says that there are innumerable possibilities, and no one more than another should take on the implications for personal meaning that accrue from articulation as the response. What is indicated is the lack of a centered focus, and the handling of anxiety by this defensive strategy.

The trait we are considering then is characterological. It is not simply a peripheral quality that appears in his discussions of theology.

It is as if the fluency and flood of ideas serve as a buffer or smoke screen. While this quality appears on the Rorschach, we also see a sense of vulnerability and a need for protection:

> . . . fur coat—wrapped around a pole of some kind . . . some sort of a fur coat—hanging around a billy club . . . (RVI)

> At first I thought a corset, but that then reminded me of . . . the breastplates . . . the Greeks used to wear in their battles . . . the top part of the breast . . . the lower parts and the part that goes between your legs and over your front things . . . (RVIII)

There also is "a big, black billow of smoke coming off of an oil fire—the flames of South Texas" (RV). Also, there is an angelfish:

> You know that if you scare an angelfish they can lose their color. Sometimes if you do so much as tap on the glass that it frightens them so it's a traumatic experience and they'll lose their color. And if it frightens them enough they die. [PH: Is there a moral in that?] I don't know. Angels are delicate creatures [*chuckling*]. Angelfish are. (RVIII)

One can hardly not be reminded of the ten-year-old boy who peeked out the church window, trying to catch a glimpse of the angels, and who was told, after all, that he was nearly as pure. Angels *are* delicate.

The apparent lack of central personal focus and the quality of deeply *meaning it* appear also in the heart of the belief system. The following interchange illustrates this.

> PH: Well, let me ask you a different kind of question, then. Suppose someone asked you to describe your relationship with God, how would you do that? I mean your own, I mean, sort of experientially as opposed to theoretically . . .

> Chelly: That's a highly interesting question, of course, 'cause that's what everyone's interested in these days, since James and everyone. Well, let's see. Philosophically I have an existential association with God, relationship to God. And theologically I have kind of an academic, intellectual relationship to God. Emotionally, I have a kind—of a well—what? [*laughs*] Uh, come back to that. As far as living my life day to day is concerned, I have a churchly relationship, a relationship to God that's mediated by the church and the sacraments, that's mediated by my profession, my vocation as a minister, an official Christian. And then emotionally, my relationship to God is something I suppose that's derived from these other three. It's not the kind of relationship you know, where I saw a blinding light once, nor is it a relationship where I hear God speaking to me. I'm no Joan of Arc. Nor is it a relationship where I watch each succeeding session uh second, to see the hand of God acting in my life.

Now God for Chelly, as for many conservatives, is more distant than Jesus Christ. However, the same quality of description appears when he is asked about his relationship with Jesus: "Hm, well, it's all very theological . . ."

It is clear that Chelly does not experience an internalized, personal relationship with the deity. The question arises as to what, more specifically, is the part played by the concept of God in his personality and belief system. The following discussion bears directly on this question.

## 5. THE DREAD OF DEATH

Chelley's discussions often center around some idea that could be best termed a "conceit." An archaic meaning of the word is "Conception or concept; a thought." And currently, "A quaint, artificial, or affected notion, or a witty thought or turn of expression."[4] Technically the term may be used to refer to literary forms such as the quaint, drawn-out metaphors used by the metaphysical poets of the seventeenth century. Essentially, in the quotation above, Chelly has used the notion of "relationship to God" as a conceit. Now he is conscious of using particular imagery or ideas as literary forms and says as much. He is not conscious of it as a characterological manifestation. He commented, for example, that his word "necessity" has "worked" in our conversations.

Another of his conceits arises in the context of discussions about death. When man dies, if he be without God, or there is no God, then he is "dead like Rover, dead all over, *or*, it's the door to a higher existence and a new life." "Dead like Rover, dead all over" had appeared on his questionnaire. The doggerel turned out to be one of those idiosyncratic fragments of imagery that condenses a central feature of identity. In a curious way, it is through this phrase that intimations of the real, persisting anxiety about death make themselves known, to Chelly and to the observer. It is in thinking about the death of dogs that the reality of death makes itself felt, because, "dogs don't go to heaven." "The dog that dies is just dead, but a man that dies is not just dead." The phrase and its personal origins take him back to his boyhood, and he comments, "That's a terrible piece of theology to tell a little boy" (that dogs don't go to heaven). It is terrible, of course, because it speaks to the reality of death.

Inquiry about the phrase was pursued, while trying not to attach any immediate interpretation thereby. Two of Chelly's spontaneous comments indicate its poignancy to him.

I fully expect to see [in heaven] those who have lived in accordance with the Son of God, who himself was raised

by God's power. Except my dogs. I don't know why I
keep thinking of dogs tonight for some reason. I've never
thought about my dogs to such an extent before.
But I've always loved my dogs . . .

It's kind of not fair to one statement to make a whole
life revolve around it actually, a whole system of thought,
but I suppose you could say that.

"Dead like Rover" had intruded itself into the interviewer's
awareness by its repeated sporadic appearance. By following out
its meanings Chelly revealed that he occasionally has intimations
of the dread of death experienced in childhood and that therefore that dread is still dynamically active and powerful. We thus
learn the real, continued "necessity" of God to Chelly, a necessity that in some ways he no longer experiences, nor would he
wish to. His belief in the Son of God reassures him that his
dread is unnecessary. Paradoxically, however, his very dread is
kept alive by his belief. The dread of death, according to our
earlier analysis, is an expression of the dread of the loss of ego
boundaries which accompanies an active wish for fusion with
the primary mother. But it is the positive aspects of this same
wish—the promise of wholeness and so on—which are given
expression to in the relationship to God.

## 6. THE "OUTWORKINGS" OF NARCISSISM

It was suggested earlier that the quality of Chelly's closeness
with his mother, particularly in the context of a partial exclusion of the father, along with other conditions of the relationship such as his being "the only one," would give rise in Chelly
to a kind of feeling that might take such a form as "the chosen
one." This category of feeling about the self, establishing the
self as in some way special, exceptional, chosen, and so on, will
be referred to as "narcissistic." Such feelings derive, in part,
from the maternal relationship, and I believe they may be considered as not simply compensation for injury to self-esteem,
although they also function in this capacity. Chelly gives expression in a number of ways to such feelings, a few of which need
to be mentioned.
In his feelings about his own person he betrays a slight

grandiosity that is expressed by a tendency to associate himself with the great. This occurs on the Rorschach and in interviews. His denials of being great or holy incline one to think that the fantasies being denied are present:

> Of course there are still [*sic*] very few people who take my categories to the extremes to which I take them. Not to say that I'm the great one with all the new and wonderful categories, and that sooner or later everybody will come to my way of thinking . . .

> The Holy Spirit came to me when I received Jesus Christ . . . the thing that makes the difference between me and, say, somebody else who doesn't depend on Jesus Christ. Now that's not going to say that I'm holier than anybody else, but it does say that I ought to be—perhaps . . .

On the Thematic Apperception Test (TAT), a little boy pictured is "one of two things . . . a budding genius or [he] wishes he didn't have to [practice]" (T1BM). The boy is a genius or "mother is making him practice."

The last alternative—mother is making him—introduces a theme that is even stronger in other subjects (Mudge, Electon). I shall call this theme *the fear of determinism.* This anxiety is one facet of the inevitable negative converse of feeling special—that is, feeling worthless, like nothing. With Chelly this fear came up in the first minutes of our first meeting. He was concerned that the interviewer not interpret everything that he *is* as mechanically determined by his past—specifically, the influence of mother and grandmother. His concern reflects his own doubt. That he had no choice in his belief and vocation, that they were forced upon him by his circumstances, especially by the "spiritual women" in his life, is his most profound doubt. This doubt ties in with the earlier discussion of the maternal relationship, and the fear of being engulfed thereby.[5] Because of his doubt, Chelly has a deep reluctance to consider those aspects of life and the self that in fact are perfectly clearly determined. In all of this is the persistent retention of the more infantile forms of narcissism supported by the denial. In Chelly's case, the denial would support the "budding genius" perception of the self.

Chelly considers himself a systematic theologian. He rarely speaks of an idea or a belief, and even his beliefs as a ten-year-old are referred to as theology, so that one soon gets the idea that it is a majestic edifice that is in question. As a theologian, he does not hesitate to spell out in detail the mechanisms of supernatural mysteries, as if the workings of the Deity, Himself, were his special domain, and he were only settling a family discussion. Indeed, he sometimes puts it in this context. He refers to the metaphysical problems of how Jesus could be both man and God, as, "This is my Daddy's question. This is my father's problem more than it is mine. I'm working on it for him." In resolving this problem he does not hesitate to go into how Jesus and God both experience the problem, how Jesus grew in his awareness of his divinity, how God was not sure of what Jesus might do, and so on:

> My father would say, "Yes, but what about God?
> Didn't God after all see the whole thing? Didn't he know
> that Christ will make it, where is the sacrifice on God's
> part?" Well, in two places. First of all, we believe that
> man chooses right or wrong according to his own free will
> and not according to what God gives him, or tells him to
> do, and consequently at any of these points, Christ, divine
> person that he was, *still* could have chosen not to go
> through with it. And he himself even admits to this.
> "Why I could call down legions of angels, if I wanted to,
> but I'm going to go through this." Anyway, his faith is that
> he can call the angels, but he knows that if he does, it's
> going to mess up the system that he's got going of
> redemptive suffering, of the suffering servant that he draws
> on from the Old Testament. Jesus had to choose for
> himself, and consequently, since the creativity of the
> choice came from within the depths of the human person
> Jesus himself, God didn't *know* which way he would
> choose, because we limit the knowledge of God there, or at
> least, we limit it effectively, not actually, because God
> can look ahead. . . . But more important even than this
> would be the fact that God, as it were emanating, if I
> may use gnostic terminology, heretical though it be—by
> emanating into the person of Jesus and separating from
> his eternal self a portion of himself that becomes a *relative*

being. He thereby divides himself and suffers a loss of
his own plenitude, *which because* Christ was also Jesus,
that is to say, because the human and the divine were
united, God can never have back, because he cannot
subsume Christ into himself ultimately . . .

The tendency to force a somewhat arbitrary, only partially
justifiable, closure on ambiguous, inherently disconnected or
inexplicable data by means of a theory appears also in the
Rorschach:

I don't really see anything in it but I'm kind of interested
in the central part here because whereas all these are
different—and although this section is one color and this
section is a color, and this section and this section, the,
they don't bear any relevance to one another or any—
internal connection but here whatever this is running
through here does the same thing although it—no matter
what color it is so it is the unifying principle in the whole
—it could be a gunshot fired from over here, going through
all of this—and out the other side—or it could be uh—the
number of stages in a rocket . . . (RVIII)

In this example and others, the insistent, closed, and relatively
arbitrary quality of the construction reveal a kind of entitlement
to impose one's own view or beliefs on the world. The pervasiveness of the tendency indicates also that it is in the service of
controlling a continuous underlying anxiety.

Chelly's image of himself as a churchman and "official
Christian" also has a narcissistic tinge. He seems to be aiming
toward becoming *the* leading theologian of his church, an outcome that may not be unlikely. His educational plans are
extensive.

No end in sight . . . I've got to hear it all from the
horse's mouth, on all sides. . . . Heard what the best
Protestant school has to offer, so now why shouldn't I go
to the best Catholic school . . . this side of the Atlantic?

Ultimately, he wants to establish a divinity school of his own.
There is an enormous sense of self-esteem that can accrue

from seeing oneself as an upholder of righteousness. Chelly sees this as part of his mission in his church, feeling that morality is a large part of Christianity. He was called in to arbitrate a dispute within a congregation, and he commented, "I'm excited about one thing, that they're doing something wrong and I'm going over there and tell them not to."

It is, of course, the idea of heaven that most clearly and grandly preserves and expresses the ego's greatest expectations and entitlements of all sorts. Heaven confirms the ultimate value and goodness of the self (in contrast with hell which confirms the evilness of the self). Heaven and immortality promise recompense for all the outrages suffered in this life, as Freud (1927) said. Certainly the greatest protection heaven offers is protection against loss—of loved ones and ultimately of the self. The latter is the profoundest real anxiety involved in the idea of death—the necessity of the ego to give itself up.[6] To face *this* idea and this form of anxiety does in fact demand the relinquishment of the less developed, more childish, form of narcissism expressed in the expectation of heaven. This latter is closely related to the component of infantile narcissism that is confirmed, in a biography such as Chelly's, by the prolonged relationship with the mother.

We may now understand further Chelly's dictum that for him, God is necessary. The conception of God does in fact "underwrite" the tapestry that we have been drawing out of his self-image, feelings about the self, self-evaluations, expectations and entitlements for the self, and his professional identity. Relinquishing the notion of God would require major reorganization of all this, the temporary loss of important sources of self-esteem, and the need for the very difficult effort of finding new sources.


## 7. ON CHELLY'S CERTAINTY

For Chelly, the belief system provided and was developed into an effective vehicle for fostering the integration of multiple facets of the personality, from the deepest intrapsychic conflicts to aspects of the self-image and an adaptive ego-identity and social role. It is, in part, the synthesizing effectiveness of the belief system that accounts for, or perhaps simply represents, his stability of faith and belief. There are, however, another set of considerations which provide a basis for stability.

Before we consider these, it must be admitted that the very way in which Chelly's certainty has been presented raises a question about it. Can we speak of "certainty of faith" in the case of a belief system whose characterological context is the exclusion of important and relevant experience and knowledge, the buffering of belief from any perceptions potentially inimical to it? This raises the question of what criteria should be used to assess "certainty," apart from or in addition to professed certainty or doubt. These problems are discussed in the concluding chapter.

Quite apart from his belief system, Chelly presents a reasonably well integrated personality. The defensive system functions effectively. The ego is not threatened with primitive affects, imagery, or unacceptable impulses. Although he has otherworldly expectations, Chelly has stable, dependable sources for self-esteem and gratification in his work and churchly activities. He has found his life comfortable so far, and he has not been torn by inner conflicts since his early years. His precociously formulated identity led him into a life pattern which was successful and highly valued in his community. His relationship with his wife, although we did not discuss it in detail, seems to be stabilizing and improving after some initial storms, mostly before marriage.

The family constellation out of which his character developed is of particular importance in understanding the certainty and stability of his faith. Much of the content of his religious belief system and the narcissistic components and gratifications of his religious career derive from the maternal relationship. However, he derived a sufficiently strong masculine identification from the father to push through effectively on the practical necessities of his career, at least so far. While the father was the secular "philistine" in the family, he was nevertheless respected by the mother, and, whatever else may have gone on, his position as the masculine head of the household was accepted in at least some basic measure. His business success and effectiveness in this realm clearly constitute a part of Chelly's image of him. Chelly retains memories of incidents from childhood which clearly indicate Father as a firm, efficient, limit-setting father—someone who believed in getting the job done efficiently.

Chelly's ego-ideal is firm, and although it may contain the grandiose expectations of eternal heaven, it still has sufficiently reality-oriented aspects for him to deal with the part of social reality that makes up his world. One measure or indicator of the stability and flexibility of personality functioning is the type and quality of feeling, imagery, and fantasy that a person reveals to be associated with the idea of loss of the current form of the ego-ideal.

> I would retire to my ranch in central Texas, become
> a game warden with the Texas game and fish commission
> for profession, lead a life of quiet Epicureanism—
> indulging in good books, good wines, and, on occasion,
> women other than my wife whom I love. I would breed
> fine cattle, have an enormous flower and vegetable
> garden, and construct an aviary in which to keep colorful
> and interesting birds. I would expect that when I die,
> like Rover, I'd be dead all over. There would be a note
> of slight melancholy, but nothing overpowering. I would
> fish and hunt and walk in my woods. I would relax.
> (Actually this sounds to me like what I expect in
> Heaven!)

Chelly gave this as the answer to an item of the questionnaire asking for response to the idea of being led to relinquish current beliefs as the result of experience, study, and thinking. His answer here reflects similar indications that occurred during interviews. This mode of life is a viable option for Chelly. His answer here indicates a healthy narcissistic cathexis of the ego and its functions. It indicates that if the ego-ideal were partially lost, or its contents changed, the sense of self and self-worth would not be completely destroyed (as Pale indicates it would be for him, see chapter V). The reality for Chelly of these fantasies and of this form of pleasurable existence was brought home when he brought in a recent dream for our examination. The dream had to do with his pleasure in acting, in walking in the country with friends and family, and the whole way of life —"quiet Epicureanism"—that is represented by such activities. It reflected very closely the above quotation from his question-naire. Perhaps we should take seriously his quip that this reflects what he expects of heaven.

The flexibility of the ego-ideal reflected in the above questionnaire response indicates that although the religious belief system may be carrying a heavy dynamic burden in terms of meeting needs and maintaining self-esteem, it is not carrying an intolerable burden. Chelly's whole sense of self does not rest on it. Where this occurs, doubts are sure to encroach, because a belief system can carry only so much weight in terms of fulfilling basic personality functions. It is sometimes easier to have faith, when faith is not a life-and-death matter. When a person is trying to use the religious belief system to meet basic needs, and these needs are not being met, doubts will arise. The inner tensions and anxieties arising from unmet or conflictful needs will inevitably lead the individual to question the belief system. Chelly is relatively free of such anxieties, and so does not have this inner source of doubt.

# V

## Pervasive Doubt and the Precocious Identity: The Case of Pale

My God, my God, why hast thou forsaken me?
Why art thou so far from helping me, from
the words of my groaning?
O my God, I cry by day, but thou dost not answer;
and by night, but find no rest.  —PSALM 22

Among conservatives, the type of global, all-pervasive doubt experienced by Pale is rare. The general tendency of conservative theology to reject doubt would lead us to expect that strong doubt of any kind would be less frequent in a group of conservative believers than in the liberal groups. We are fortunate, then, to have an unusual case which gives some suggestive insights into the genesis and effects of religious doubt in a theologically conservative individual whose life and character also illustrate the pattern of precocious identity formation.

Pale's roots, also, are in Texas. He and his family—parents and their parents—have always been members of the conservative evangelical Southern Baptist church. The church was an important arena for Pale's development. Although the warm fellowship and the audience of the congregation have always been important to Pale, the sense of a community of brethren is not as developed as in Chelly's case. The family moved a great deal in his early years, but remained for the most part in Texas and for the most part in small rural towns. In any case, the church community provided a homogeneous culture, relatively the same, from town to town.

Pale is twenty-three; he has been married for a little over a year, and he has a baby son. He is the oldest of four siblings, a sister being two and a brother four years younger. The parents had a fourth child after these three had grown up and left the home. From Pale's description of the home situation, it is clear that having this child forestalled the separation which Father had claimed for many years was in the offing when the children were all grown.

### 1. CONVERSION AND BELIEF SYSTEM

Pale experienced a conversion when he was eight. It was a moment of high feeling, after a sermon in which "probably the preacher had said if you don't accept Jesus Christ yourself, personally, that your sins are not forgiven, and perhaps he elaborated what the consequences of one's sins not being forgiven are." He conveyed a feeling of confusion and upset to his parents.

> So my father led me to accept Jesus Christ as my Savior, and I think with the extent that I understood at this time, I prayed there on the floorboard of the car in tears. "Father, thank you for saving me, for forgiving my sins and for giving me eternal life." And it seems to me an integral part of this was that I accepted Christ as my personal Savior. Now I was a child of God, and I *knew* it personally.

It would seem that a moment such as this is of the greatest importance for understanding not only character development and life patterns, but it also contains implications for the function of religious symbolism in ego synthesis. Two features of the situation may be singled out which bear on the problem of ego synthesis. One aspect of this event is that diffuse, vague anxiety, guilt, and other feelings which Pale experienced were given definite religious labels. He says:

> I told my father and mother that something was
> wrong. I kind of tried to express myself. But I wasn't sure,
> and I remember saying that I had a lump in my throat
> and I was choked up. So they began to talk to me. During
> this ride home, then, I expressed the emotional upheaval
> —suppose through my actions and some words. By
> the time we got home, we stopped the car and they
> turned around and were talking to me. And I think my
> father talked to me . . .

Pale expressed vague, inarticulate feelings, tensions, and so on, and the parents gave these feelings the appropriate religious labels. No doubt Pale had been prepared for this to some extent by previous religious instruction. However, his upset at this particular moment was very real and immediate for him. He was told what the upset *meant* by his parents, and then he *knew* what the religious language *meant*—he had been converted. In such a way, religious symbolism may become inextricably a part of, an expression of, and a vehicle for the early infantile conflicts.[1]

The second feature of the situation relevant to the problem of ego synthesis is that it was the parents, the arbiters of reality themselves, who proffered to Pale the explanation of his feelings. The nature of reality, to a child, is determined in one important way by what the parents *say* it is. *Meanings* of all sorts are arbitrated first and foremost within the family by the parents.

From the time of his conversion, the social front of Pale's life was lived as a Christian. He was a good boy in school and Sunday school. "I was the cute little sixth-grader—grade boy in the group whose father was the principal of the high school and all the girls, including the seventh-grade girls, sort of ran around after me in the playground." His intelligence and religiosity were recognized in school and church, and his years up to the second year in college were successes in these respects. He was active and a leader in several high-school organizations.

Within himself and within the family, however, there was more disruption. His upset at the time of his conversion was one incident in this side of his life. The conversion provided new modes of relief from guilt and anxiety. As with Chelly, it marked the crystallization of the pattern of defenses and character development that gave his life its form and content up to the time doubts encroached upon his faith.

The core of the religious belief system was and remains basically simple. Pale summarized, in retrospect, how it was and how he would like it still to be:

> I'm trying to think of what I felt then, I mean now—now.
> Jesus was God's son—only son—and Jesus mediates
> between God and man in the sense that Jesus died for
> us. God so loved the world—he gave his only son—and
> Jesus loved us so much that he died for us. Won't you
> trust him? As a sacrifice for your sins? That you may be
> forgiven—and God will forgive you and give you
> eternal life. That's the way I understood it: My all—for
> —Christ—that little card I have [from ninth grade]—
> I think was very central to my relationship. I mean
> it expressed very centrally . . . whatever I may do in the
> future. My all for Christ . . .

Pale, in contrast with Chelly, emphasizes the sense of *relationship* to Jesus Christ, and the concern with salvation and forgiveness for sin is more active. Also, Pale's core beliefs are not as successfully enmeshed and buffered in a web of relatively ·disciplined scholarship and theological knowledge. He began the attempt to do this his sophomore year in college when doubts and uncertainties first assailed his beliefs. Between immersion in the great voices of liberalism—Tillich· and Bultmann—and the existentialists, the effort led as much to an undoing as a reinforcement of his basic beliefs. What this indicates, of course, is a more tenuous hold on the basic propositions of his belief system to begin with. The lack of closure and development in the personality is also reflected in less systematic and disciplined efforts at developing a theology that would preserve and protect his basic early beliefs and his sense of relationship with Jesus.

The sorts of differences indicated between Pale's belief system and Chelly's raise the question of their source. We have suggested one very general such source—the differences in personality structure that hold between Chelly and Pale. Pale's character and life reflect a long-standing lack of closure. Chelly's give indication of an effective defensive system and relatively firm crystallization of identity. Assuming that the basic theologies and cultures of the Church of Christ and of the Southern Baptist church are not that different, there are still two other sources of differences between Chelly's and Pale's belief systems.

The first is the different ways in which religious beliefs and language were used in the families and by the primary figures from whom the children learned to be religious. Theology and the church were family matters in Chelly's family. He says, "Our small talk was scripture." There was less emphasis on sin and salvation from sin. Being more at home with God, they were also not as dependent upon His judgment in their every act. In Pale's household, the religiosity and piety masked a good deal of family pathology. Mother managed to maintain an air of righteousness in the face of her contribution to the severest sorts of strains in her relationship with her husband. Father's image as a Christian, on the other hand, was undermined. Pale interpreted the stresses in religious language which left Mother virtuous and Father not.

Second, the religious belief system meets different basic needs in Pale and in Chelly. This is related to what was expressed more generally above—that the difference in belief system reflects a difference in personality structure. The emphasis on sin and salvation, for Pale, helps to control and to relieve the guilt attendant upon a great deal of only partially repressed primitive impulse, affect, and imagery. Also, the religiosity actually permits in Pale the retention of sexual preoccupations and ruminations. These can be expressed in terms of concepts of sin and idealized relations such as the "I-Thou" terminology which has become very important to him. The sense of righteousness and heightened self-esteem that accrues from considering oneself a repenting sinner (who is, after all, doing a lot better than most others in retaining purity) must not be underestimated.

The sexual preoccupation, the lack of repression, and the righteous reworking of these contents into religious language all appear on the Rorschach:

It reminds me of the protruding lips of . . . a woman's sexual organs 'cause it's on the bottom—and she seems to be spread wide open. [PH: What suggested that?] The feeling that these desires came in and—made themselves

strong—occupied an idle mind like a devil's workshop
or something, not building anything in the workshop
worthwhile—or anything that would last . . . sort of
spilled something very impermanent . . . so that you've
got this one spr—the one with the spread-out legs and
of course this is sort of a central feeling in a lusty
man. . . . I sort of conclude that not only do I have the
central fact that man is a sinner—that all men are
basically I-centered . . . [He goes on at much greater
length.] (R*I*)

It is notable that this percept appears so quickly on card I. There
is a similar percept and lengthy justification on card II:

. . . the woman's organs again here in—in sort of a
similar way but cuts, I mean there seems to be blood
involved in this. [Inquiry.] Oh the symmetry—open lips—
the fact that when you use a person you don't care
how they're treated. You don't care how you treat them.
And therefore whether blood flows or not is of no
consequence. I remember reading about this guy who
went around raping all these women . . . and thinking
how—that I felt that probably all men would—could
fall under this same pattern—let much blood and using
everything around them to do anything that they'd like
but for the restraints at different times on them. (R*II*)

Religious language here seems to have become a magical weapon
to ward off unacceptable, mostly primitive impulse. The sheer
length of Pale's rambling associations, justifications, and explanations of his percepts indicate how frightening are the impulses
which have been aroused. The degree of anxiety and the sense,
conveyed in the final remarks quoted, of the possibility of imminent irruption of primitive, egocentric impulse, indicate a shaky,
fragile ego-ideal. It is an intimation through fantasy of what
might be attendant upon the loss of the ego-ideal. The ego-ideal
is in fact threatened when the ego is not strong enough to repress or suppress fantasies or behavior contrary to it. This is one
source of doubt in Pale, and will receive further comment.

The central difference of content between the religious

belief systems of Pale and Chelly is that Pale developed a sense of a personal, inner relationship to Jesus and consciously sought continually to do the Lord's will, whereas Chelly did not. This difference also reflects a difference in the needs met by the religious belief system. These features of Pale's belief system are crucial for our understanding of his doubts.

Pale reports that he started to become aware of a relationship with his Lord in about the ninth grade. We may assume that his effort to do the Lord's will became more conscious and more concerted as he himself had more central life decisions to make. These demanded of him some sense of his own identity and in turn would heighten that sense. Thus, he reports a feeling of having prayer answered in eleventh grade when he prayed for three friends, and they all made public confessions the same night. However, his first report of trying to discern the Lord's will was when he was trying to make a decision about where to go to college:

> I was praying—I still remember in the bathroom kneeling
> —playing altar there with the commode and praying.
> I knelt there and began praying that the Lord would
> definitely make known whether I—that I should go to X
> because I got an early acceptance from them, even before
> I got the scholarship.

Coming to New England to attend a great university, for Pale, was like entering the darkest unknown. It seemed to be surrounded by the mysteries of death, and this may have been one of his reasons for coming.

The effort to do the Lord's will grew in the face of greater demands from reality and greater demands for self-definition and identity. This occurred, of course, after he left home, at the university, where there was no longer so much cultural support and ease of success. It expressed, in part, the effort to be relieved of the anxiety that comes from assuming the responsibility for one's own life and the decisions which determine it. Growth in identity is inevitably accompanied by anxiety. Externalizing the source of success or failure and of decisions relieves the anxiety which comes from taking responsibility for them—as *my* successes or failures or decisions. They then become to a lesser degree *definitional of me*. In Pale's case, the ardent seeking for the Lord's will expresses the wish, not only for relief from such anxiety, but the wish for a state of absolute peace and bliss. His prayer is:

> I pray, then I take a deep breath and I relax and I trust
> and I say, "Lord, all is well—I can depend on you,
> for I have always depended on you, and I can trust in
> you, both for my past and for my future and—" a great
> feeling of relief—for the lack of having to depend
> on myself to get these things done—those things done—
> I have to accomplish this or that and a lack of having
> to feel ultimately responsible for myself. But that
> the Lord cares as much for me as I care for myself. And
> that I can trust Him wholly.

Even in his current state of uncertainty he seeks to understand the minutiae of his everyday life as being determined by the Lord:

> And I would almost, Lord, for a sign. If there could
> be a sign. I want something. Of course during all
> this time, He's also leading me to read this or that, or
> hear this or that speaker. To think these thoughts or that
> thought, make these observations. Just like this with you
> —going to be another one of these opportunities to look
> at my experience, to ask and see where the Lord
> is working in it, and to turn again to Him and have
> Him interpret it all to me.

The wish is for a passive state in which there is a "a feeling that God Himself was directing and guiding and loving me."

Love, of course, is the other feature of the dependent relationship with the Lord—loving and feeling loved. He spoke of walking home with his wife-to-be during one of their early encounters.

> I told her I just *love* Jesus Christ. I just *love* Him.
> And I'm not ashamed to say it to anyone. The simple
> matter of the fact is that I just love Him. And that the

> whole—that the relationship I've had with Him is that
> for which I live. That which makes my life—life
> worth having. That which makes the future not
> completely desolate, but that which gives me hope
> about the future . . .

It is no exaggeration that he said this with a lover's passion. He did not indicate any awareness that to her he had implicitly contrasted his love for Jesus with his love for his fiancée. He also said, "I don't feel like I've *ever* related myself in such an intimate way to anyone as I have to Jesus Christ. I look to my mother, to my father, to my good friends . . ."

### 2. *THE IRRUPTION OF DOUBT*

The sense of a relationship with Jesus Christ became the center of Pale's religious belief system. Around this center were formulated his deepest wishes and hopes. Since this was the center, and since it also had certain vulnerabilities, it was the sense of relationship with the Deity which was eroded by doubt. Pale's sophomore slump at the university culminated in an angry letter to the Lord:

> Lord, you surely have something better for me than this.
> If you don't I'd rather go home. I'd rather be taken
> from this world if I have no greater ministry. If I have no
> greater *success* in terms of doing your will here, which
> I know is schooling. I realize that—I'm not being honest
> in not realizing the amount of blame that falls on me,
> and yet I wish that I could more clearly discern
> your will, and I feel like that you have not as clearly
> revealed it to me now as you have in the past . . .

To feel in the Lord's will, it is necessary to feel with some certitude that what one is doing is *right*—that it is the right thing to do, that it is right now, and that it is right for *me*. Many are the possibilities for doubt being cast on these feelings. Conversely, a person may persevere in the face of heavy burdens if he feels that nevertheless what he is doing is in the Lord's will. Pale's sense of being in the Lord's will was probably particularly vulnerable. He had been successful earlier, in high school, and he had not known adversity in the world—he had not been tried. Further, although his interests were varied, his identity was as a Christian witness. There was no need to develop an identity as a scientist, for example, with a corresponding commitment that could push him through the rough spots in college. Lacking *focused* interests, he was also deprived of one source of cues for feeling in the Lord's will—a deep interest in something. (Later he was to pray for this very thing, so that he would have motivation to push the studies.)

In any event, Pale's feeling that he was in the Lord's will foundered when, among other things, college became too great a burden with too few successes. When Pale had first arrived at the university, he almost immediately discovered a conservative, evangelical Baptist group with whom he felt very much at home. He felt this was a confirmation from the Lord of his journey into the distant, unknown lands of New England. A year and a half later, however, he was overburdened with work, could not decide on a major, and was not as successful in his studies as his expectations demanded. He was not active outside of studies. He felt depressed, burdened, abandoned, and confused, and the Lord's will became obscured.

> Here I was with *great* pressure on me about this,
> you know, what will my major be? What am I going to
> teach after I get out. And not doing too well, and all
> this. So I was not sure about what the Lord's will was.

There was more on his mind at this time than matters academic. The summer before this sophomore year, he had had a relationship with a girl to whom he had been very attracted sexually. There had been some petting. The whole affair stirred him strangely and deeply. On the one hand he wanted her and mourned her after they parted. On the other hand he felt he had to give her up because she was not as good a Christian as he demanded. He had tried to mold her in their talks and through the mails. He had used Bible study methods on her. He felt the Lord would have it no way other than that he should marry someone as dedicated to Him as he felt himself to be. The sex with her could be justified on these grounds only. The whole affair obsessed him throughout the year, and he had endless theological discourses on it with a friend who also had been sexually involved with a girl.

The summer following, they broke up. She said to him that it appeared the devil was using her in his life, and she didn't want to be "the devil's handmaiden."

This girl, C, remains for him the person with whom lust is associated. He seems to indicate at times that if she had not appeared in his life, lust never would have entered it.

> I feel like she didn't draw the line. Now I feel like that
> she should have, and that we would not have—that I
> would not have done it. Because I was greatly trusted
> by everyone, you know. I mean, if anybody would
> guess out of the whole, you know, school or something,
> who would be not engaged in this sort of thing, I
> think they'd tend to point to me. In other words, I didn't
> cuss, and I didn't swear, drink, or smoke, and I was
> a regular attender at church, and I had good reasons
> for this. Just all of a sudden, just like a patsy here, who
> never has realized the strength of all of this stuff, and
> you know, the power of it, and everything, and
> then just all of a sudden big pushover, you know, in the
> period of three weeks or something, I'm caught up in
> this.

His sexual activities with her shook his conception of himself as pure.

> I felt like that here I've ruined my chances of
> being able to come through all this time in the Lord's will,
> spotless, without having yielded myself to a lot of lust
> and to things that I knew would not be upbuilding
> to me. [T13MF]

In contrast, he has managed, in some way, to keep lust from entering the relationship with his wife. There is no indication that she excites him sexually as C did. He indicates that intercourse is relatively infrequent, and that he has tried to keep lust out of the relationship.

The sexual play with C had not only been contrary to the

image of purity, it had stirred very deep, vague fears which he expressed on the TAT:

> She has been very yielding and he has used her.
> Now he has a vague fear and wishes now that he had *not*
> done what he felt called into doing with this woman.
> This looks like a woman older than a normal girl would
> be for him. Perhaps a prostitute, perhaps an older
> girlfriend. It reminded me of C, although she was younger
> than my wife by several years—seemed in her way to be
> older. Not necessarily older than my wife, but you would
> think of her as being an older woman and that since
> this young man is younger. (T13MF)

Notice that he associates sexual feelings with C, not with his wife. It is his wife, in fact, who is two years older than he is. He continues:

> So I see this young man as having completed some
> act with this woman; seems to be either dead afterward
> —of course you always have—when you treat someone
> else as an It in lust you—it doesn't make sort of much
> difference in fantasy at least whether or not they're—they
> die afterward. Whether you've killed them, you've
> slain them. So she could either be dead or she could
> just be asleep . . . This is something that can only lead
> to eventual dissolution, despair. So the future holds no
> hope for this type of relationship.

> Perhaps his life in all of its feeling and tonal aspects are—
> being dissolved, disintegrated and all this. Insofar as he
> yielded himself up to an undisciplined situation, an
> undisciplined life. He realizes that this very act and
> that all this feeling and what he has felt in this are all
> part of untruth. They're all part of what should not be.
> They hinder him from what is truth; from feeling whole
> and clean and fulfilled. (T13MF)

There is a fusion of incestuous sexual wishes with aggressive ones here, and the sexual imagery has become fused with that of death. The stirrings of lust, then, can lead to the disintegration of the person, the loss of the self. These fears must have been stirred by his relationship with C, and they must have made his need for the felt presence of the Lord—to heal and make whole —all the greater.

With the heightening of anxiety and stress from several sources, we may expect that about this time an old obsessive thought and fear took new meaning and salience. The fears had to do with eternity. He had learned very young that "whosoever shall trust shall not perish but have everlasting life." He developed a deep fear of eternity, the earliest remembered instance going back to the ninth grade. He will start thinking about eternity, everlasting life, endless temporality, and so on, and a strong anxiety will take him. He will have to jump up or hit the wall with his fist to shake himself out of this.

> And even during the last term, I would start thinking about this. About eternity, and on, and forever. No end. And I'd sit up all of a sudden in bed, you know, my wife would be asleep, and I'd sit up and I'd try to shake myself away from it. One time I ran out of a theater.

These comments suggest the possibility that, in the darkened theater or bedroom, the presence of his wife may be one of the conditions which precipitates his anxiety.

What happens at these moments is that an idea of "eternity" becomes so real to Pale that it seems to him that it is all suddenly about to happen—the living endlessly.

> . . . fear in the sense of suddenness. Fear in the sense that it all of a sudden oooohhh. You know. Gets going down a certain path, maybe one that's way down in my brain and well worn by now. I'll get to a certain point and it'll just scare me. I'll grab myself to go some other direction in thought. It just frightens me very strongly and I have to—I beat my fist against the wall or jump up. It just becomes so real until I realize in fact that it's going to happen! I get to the point where I say it's going to happen! And that just *scares* me to death! [PH: Something's going to happen?] Not something! The living endlessly!

Further inquiry did not yield more details about the content of the fear. The way Pale expresses it, one thinks that he is saying he might suddenly die. However, when this was suggested to him, he was receptive to the idea, but had not made the connection himself. He pointed out that if he were going to live eternally, he would already be in the process of doing so, death or no death. The realities of death have been lost for Pale in the confusion of a more nameless fear.

A specific image that does seem to be associated with this anxiety is one of disintegration of the person:

> Or if my soul doesn't live on, well then I will live
> on endlessly if there is endless time, and since I
> can't conceive of anything else, then what will happen
> is all the molecules will go all over creation, but at some
> other point in eternity I'll come again together [in
> this] configuration. So in a way I can conceive I'm not
> living endlessly.

One of the fantasies about death expressed on the TAT is that it is a kind of discontinuity—one suddenly wakes up and has neither past, present, nor future, only the immediate confusion:

> I would try to figure out what time of history I was in.
> If I had been slung back there by a time machine or
> something like that, or if I died and woke up again to
> find myself in this unknown situation, or if I happened to
> have had amnesia or something and I'm awakened in
> this new and strange environment . . . I'd be looking
> around. I'd be trying to seek security—safety. Having
> something solid against my back which I knew wasn't
> going to fall on top of me . . . (T11)

We noted another image of dissolution earlier, in his associations to the sexual imagery stirred up by card 13MF of the TAT. It was also associated with a woman.

The anxiety Pale describes probably derives from an early oral period. Erikson places it in the "second part of the first year" and describes it in terms very reminiscent of Pale's:

> What it means *not* to be able to behold a face in mutual
> affirmation can be learned from young patients, who,

> unable to love, see, in their more regressed states, the face
> of the therapist disintegrate before their horrified eyes,
> and feel themselves fall apart into fragments of oblivion.
> (1962, p. 115)

Pale is trying to save himself from this kind of disintegration of
the sense of self. His fear is that this *might* happen, or that it is
*suddenly about* to happen. This intimation of the loss of self has
become interwoven with the ideas of eternity and death.

The sense of self that develops during this period is part of
the development of basic trust. Erikson says that part of the
process is based upon the mutual recognition between mother
and child that is centered perceptually in the recognition of the
familiar face (ibid.; also cf. 1968, 713–15). In periods of frustration, tension, and fear, the familiar maternal face appears horrible and strange. Pale's projective protocols are, in fact, replete
with strange, malevolent faces, faces whose owners have inscrut-
able and questionable intentions.

> Well, this man through the way he's looking at his son is
> . . . well he's got a curve—his facial expression is a
> calculating one toward his son. And both has a sadness in
> it and yet has . . . he's calculating in some way. Just
> sort of gazing upon him . . . he's looking at his son.
> He's got sort of this sadness, but he's got this . . .
> closedness as he looks. . . . He's looking . . . calculating,
> because the eyes . . . have a calculating kind of look.
> His eyes are closely placed. He's looking—he's almost
> cross-eyed in a way . . . (T7BM)

Pale assesses and reassesses the father's expression as he gazes
upon his son. Is the expression one of sadness at the loss of the
son, or is it malevolence? Pale cannot decide.

> A man . . . looking down at something with a contempt,
> with his lip turned over. And with his eyes looking very
> diabolical. . . . I can almost see a wo—a wo—a head of
> a woman . . . so that you could see a woman—woman's
> long flowing hair . . . almost as if it's so warped and
> misshapen and everything that you could probably see—
> I suspect you could see several figures here. . . . Sort of

reminds me of one of the guys . . . whose face is very
difficult to read . . . (TIV)[2]

The face seems to change before his eyes, becoming more malevolent as it turns into a woman. There is analogous imagery on the
Rorschach:

> . . . two dancing partners—with a very mysterious look—
> on each of their faces and on their eyes. (RIII)

> . . . a weird-looking dolphin . . . weird because its
> —look in its eye. (RVIII)

> . . . a man with a beard—odd look on his face. (RVIII)

> Two pig's faces with women's hair flowing back. (RIX)

As with previous imagery, the image becomes more grotesque
as it becomes more specifically associated with women. We may
assume that this imagery extends into "a witch" (RI) and "a
large, black frog-like monster" (RIII). That is, these last two
images express the monster-like turn taken by the maternal image
grown strange and destructive.

When Pale went to college, he felt as if he were venturing into a
distant land, dark, mysterious, beckoning at the same time that
it repelled. He had received a sign, a confirmation, that he was
in the Lord's will almost immediately upon arrival—his discovery
of a group of warm, accepting, fellow evangelical conservatives.
By the time a year had passed with one summer home and then
back to New England, life had smitten him with stresses of
which he had not dreamed and for which he felt himself unpre-
pared. The sexual encounter with C had stirred lusts and strange
fears that seemed never to have been a part of him. The burdens
and above all the lack of success in studies stunned and frustrated him. He felt the Lord had let him down. If the Lord had
wanted him here, He should have given him the interest and the
drive to do well.

> I could not understand—it was beyond my comprehension
> to understand why I was in this situation and was not

making any success. Why I was seemingly no good to
anyone or to any task that I was engaged in during this
term. . . . So that I—I was praying—I was knowing that
God wanted me to be doing these things.

Or perhaps he should not be here at all, in which case the Lord
should show him how to get out of it and where to go. On the
other hand, he knew he could not blame only the Lord. He felt
"hard things" in himself which kept him from turning back to
the Lord. He felt perhaps "He doesn't love me" and, after all,
"not feeling I can retreat to the Lord because He has an awful
lot to do with the fact that these tasks are here." In other words,
Pale felt unrepentant. He felt unwilling and unable to do what
he had to do to improve himself and his studies and to return to
the Lord. He no longer felt like God's child.

All of this could only obscure and finally lose for Pale the
sense of being in the Lord's will. It is a short step from losing
track of the Lord's will to losing the sense of relationship with
Him, of being loved by Him. This is what happened to Pale.
With the loss of the inner relationship with Jesus Christ, Pale
lost the positive effects of those restitutive derivatives of the early
maternal relationship which alone could make him feel whole
and well. Relinquishing the relationship with his Lord unleashed
a sense of evil malevolence which he projected into the external
world, and from which he then felt an overwhelming threat. The
feelings of potential disintegration and loss of self also colored
the ideas of death and eternity.

The unknown for me is not simply an unknown like X.
It is also tinged with fear. With uncertainty. With some
despair. I'm not the Christian always looking forward
to a glorious hope and rapture in the Second Coming.
And I've asked myself the question in view of what
I'm thinking after death. Not thinking, but my feelings
about this. How can I be joyous now? If I turn my eyes
away from death? . . . But—how can I have great joy
when I—death is so uncertain? It's all a question mark.

Pale suffered the extremes of doubt because the restitutions
of the early maternal matrix did not protect him from and in
life. Promising and beckoning, the ego-ideals had led him on to

high aspirations, great expectations and hopes. They were not flexible enough to yield to reality—either the reality of his sexual feelings for C or the stiff academic competition at the university. With greater ego strengths he might have put in a performance at college that would have satisfied him. He might have had a stronger defensive system to protect the ego from its own impulses and regressive tendencies. If the ego-ideal had been more reality-oriented, he would have felt less stress. Any or all of these might have allowed him to keep the inner sense of being in relationship with the Lord. When this was lost, he lost the effects of those derivatives from the early maternal matrix that had protected him in life and had protected him from the inner evils that Erikson calls basic mistrust. With this loss, he was thrust into the middle of the conflict as to whether the world is basically good or basically evil. His alternating positions and often mutually self-contradictory statements reflect this basic ambivalence toward the world.

This basic ambivalence toward the world and God expressed itself in less central areas of the belief system as well. Ironically, it attacked and turned upside down the meaning of a favorite scriptural passage: "Whosoever shall trust shall not perish but have everlasting life." Perhaps because he no longer trusted, Pale, that same sophomore term, worked out his "perish" theory of judgment. Since life had come to seem, at least at times, meaningless, he came to ask: Is there anything that could go on for endless time that would be worth it? He questioned whether an everlasting life of praising the Lord were such. He decided that it is only just that man be given a choice of "to be or not to be" on the Day of Judgment. That is, man should be allowed to choose death, if he wishes. He had ceased to feel with much certainty that God "is forever wooing me into life, forever wooing me into giving of myself, as Christ gave himself." Perhaps it is better to perish.

Pale's repetitious return to the puzzlement about the contents of eternity suggests that he has more or less specific unconscious fantasies about what does occur "there." He repeatedly returns to the question, with such comments as, "I can't imagine what's going to happen here [*sic*]." Later we will offer a speculation about this.

To return, briefly, to his college career, Pale pulled himself together that sophomore year. He involved himself—flung himself—into more activities, especially with his church, and he did much better scholastically the second term. Curiously, he is reluctant now to consider this an answer to prayer:

> I felt like this was an answer to prayer. I haven't pushed
> that real hard because I usually think of answers to prayer
> —or I most often think of answers to prayer as being a
> more—immediate answer. Whereas this took place over the
> whole—the semester. Now that I reflect on it I realize
> that I'd urgently prayed at Christmas time and then—then
> see what happened—now, was that an answer to prayer
> or not?

It is an example of his reluctance to trust again, having once been badly burned. Neither is he willing to relinquish the search for trust in the Lord, and say, like the existentialists he soon started to study: Man is on his own—I did it myself.

He plugged through the next two years, never really taking a decisive major. His religious and philosophical preoccupations naturally led him into taking courses in these areas even though he felt a science degree would be more respectable. He read Freud and rejected him because he felt his own experience clearly showed Freud to be wrong. During his senior year, he was in the midst of Sartre, Bultmann, and Tillich, none of whom he could as easily dismiss; he was also planning his marriage. The stresses precipitated another crisis of doubt. He sought but again could not find the Lord's will.

> I've often remembered looking up at the stars as I would
> cross over the bridge there coming home from my fianceé's
> apartment last year before we were married and looking
> down the river. Made me wonder and speak—speak to the
> Lord. And ask him to show me a sign that I might feel
> at home in the universe. That I might feel that everything
> is warm toward me, and that I might feel that I was in
> His will. That I might know that—I have security in
> trusting Him.

Since he received no sign indicating one path or another, the marriage, after graduation, proceeded, but not before Pale had had a good case of cold feet.

We will return to a brief consideration of Pale's present life after further examination of his early years.

### 3. FAMILY CONSTELLATION AND THE TRANSFORMATIONS OF NARCISSISM

As Pale reports it, a long storm raged between the parents, at quite an infantile level, off and on up to his twelfth or thirteenth year. Family pietistic and religious practices within the home were sporadic and short-lived, and the family religiosity only veneered the tension between the parents. It provided rationalizations and recriminations but was not a source for mediation, although no doubt, without it, things could have been worse. Pale feels that the first development in the parental difficulties was that Mother became jealous of Father. From his reports the jealousy was pathological and intense. Father was an elementary-school teacher in the early days. He loved teaching and the children. He coached athletic teams, sometimes was principal of his school, and generally put in a great expenditure of time and energy on his work. Mother would single out one attractive female teacher as the focus for her suspicions. Father would come home at night to a barrage of accusations. There were apparently no grounds to her accusations, but they resulted in the family having to move a great many times before Pale left home for college. Father would have to leave his job and find a new one, because of Mother's fantasies that he was carrying on with one of the women teachers. Pale says that they moved forty times.

Pale was born during the first year of the parents' marriage. When he was about four or five, Father went into the Army. Mother was in charge of the family for the first time. Father accuses her of taking over then and never letting go, never again allowing him to be the head of the household. Pale feels that he was broken by then. Father in his turn became querulous, starting fights, jealous of his position in the family and deeply insecure about it. He came to feel that the mother was alienating the children from him, that no one in the family loved him or respected him.

The specific details of these painful struggles are less important than the poignancy and intensity of Pale's continued involvement in them. The way in which Pale was and continues to be involved in his parents' conflicts is also significant. In all of it, he identifies almost completely with his mother's side. He puts himself in her shoes, sees her as virtuous, Father as inadequate. He has no perspective on Mother's jealousy, which in all likelihood is a pathological symptom. The mother remains over-idealized. Complementing this is the fact that Pale has not integrated into his image of his father the father's effectiveness as a teacher, the fact that he was respected in the community, held responsible positions for a government agency, that he knew how to deal with people, and so on. Father's worldly effectiveness was not a part of his familial image, as far as Pale was concerned. Pale has, nonetheless, identified with his father as a Texan, a talker, and a teacher.

Pale saw the mother as open, unselfish, and loving—that is, as a good Christian. He felt Father was selfish, unloving. "I think she opened herself both to him and to us [the children], but that he knew not how to receive her."

Pale learned too much (to be good for his own development) about the parental sexual life. He had listened at the key-hole of his parents' bedroom and overheard discussions about his father's partial impotence and his lack of interest in intercourse with Mother. He felt that Mother was sexually unfulfilled, and that this was the cause of her jealousy.

> My impression is that—she was jealous without cause, and she was jealous because she was not fulfilled and it redirected itself in jealousy. She wondered why he was so dead tired when he came home and couldn't have intercourse with her, maybe. I can speculate. In fact, when I was in sixth grade, I overheard them and I knew that they were mentioning—Dad—whether or not he was potent. Dad was saying something like, "Well, there used to be something—white came out." . . . I *knew* what they were talking about.

On another occasion, when Pale listened to his parents discussing their relationship, Father said "they're probably out there listening now." However, there did not seem to be limits set on this curiosity of Pale's. Again, what is of significance here is not simply the details of Pale's report but the degree and intensity of his intrusion into the parental life and his lack of separation from its dramas and tragedies. It is this lack of separation which is the condition for his vulnerability, weakness of ego boundaries, and inner sense of imminent dissolution.

Currently Pale seems to be living out with his wife a pattern like Father's:

> . . . the fact that my wife and I haven't had intercourse
> in a week or so because I've been so dead tired from
> swimming at noon and from several activities that we've
> done this week—up till late hours . . . (From an
> association on the Rorschach)

Even with the disparagement of Father, and his identification with his mother, Pale must feel a deep yearning for his father to be or to have been a man who would stand up to the mother, who could guarantee his own, Pale's, masculinity, and who could protect him from maternal engulfment. Perhaps it is for reasons associated with this that, in spite of a characteristic initial fearful suspicion, he almost immediately developed a powerful transference to the interviewer, pouring out vast amounts of material. He commented at the end of the first interview that he had had the thought during our talk that perhaps God had led him into this experience.

Father was seen as inadequate sexually. Pale also felt that the father could not meet his mother's emotional needs. He could not communicate with her.

> See—when she said I never have been able to talk to him,
> she meant, I never have been able to deeply share myself
> and problems. Like if I know I'm not sexually fulfilled,
> I haven't really been able to talk to him about it—
> paraphrasing what she could say. He hasn't really been
> able—been open himself to know deeply where I'm hurt
> or where I have needs. But he has been only communicative
> to me—well not exclusively selfishly, but more so than
> I—than has been good for our relationship.

Pale has not *talked* with Mother about her sexual life with Father, it should be noted. The degree and detail into which he intrudes himself into her sexual and emotional life in his fantasy, however, is striking. It seems like a kind of breach of the incest barrier.

Pale's description of his relationship with his mother implies that he succeeded where Father failed, at least in terms of having an emotionally close, religiously toned relationship with her. He feels that she turned to the children:

> My mother is a person who gives herself. She didn't find fulfillment in her husband. She finds fulfillment in the children. She loves them. She gives herself to them. She —it's hard to give herself to her husband, because her husband doesn't reciprocate this love, like we did. . . . She is the most unselfish person I know.

Pale will not quite say explicitly that he, of all the children, had a special relationship to Mother, but he does intimate that there are feelings of being special to her:

> I was her firstborn—two years there before she had another child [daughter]. The fact that I was the leader among the children. I had the most attainments in every way. Although they were not sluggards themselves. And I *always tried* to not build barriers between me and her. Her own unselfishness helped to point me this way too. And the fact that I was—when I became a Christian at eight—I began to grow. And *always* going to church. And always in the fellowship of a certain number of Christians who helped me to grow. So that—just a natural strong bond that would have grown there between anyone and her who had been under that same influence and who opened themselves from the center in this way. [PH: Did the other kids?] They did—but—I suppose. I would guess that each one of us if you asked us would say that we felt that we had a special place. And I think that it's because God loves us individually.

It is no accident that he explains the "natural strong bond" with his mother by, in part, explaining that he became an ardent Christian. Religion is the medium, so to speak, which preserved and expressed the deepest yearnings, expectations, and mysteries of an intense maternal relationship. By becoming that holy, he could meet his mother on a spiritual plane which his father could not, and he could meet the high expectations of goodness which were part of his idealized image of her. It is no accident, either, that he jumps, in his associations, from being loved by Mother to loved by God. It is the sense of being loved by God that preserves and makes restitution for that early participation in the maternal relationship which confers the sense of unique self-worth, the ineluctable sense of being of value and being protected.

The maternal relationship was intense and, in certain important respects, prolonged. Pale's attachment to his mother undoubtedly remains his deepest.

> She has been the greatest—probably the greatest single
> influence in my life. In—every way. I would say in a
> religious way, but it's in every way. I wrote her a letter this
> past year and told her—I guess maybe a Mother's Day card
> or something—and told her that the greatest gift that
> she had ever given me was that she loved me. With a
> genuine love. And that I hoped I could love my child in
> this way. And give it this gift.

His identification with her is expressed in the last comments. He wants to love his child the way he feels his mother loved him—to be a mother to his son.

> Because it changes a person's life. It just—I can see—uh,
> not being proud—but I can see a difference between my
> life and people that I meet—in their ability to give of
> themselves at all. In my wife, for instance. Her parents
> are not Christian. She is less able to give to me than I am
> to her . . . there's not a great disparity here.

At another point we discussed how anger might be expressed in the family. He felt that he had kept back any anger he might have for Mother, explaining how much he loved her:

> Simply because someone that you may love more [than
> Father] or that you may love on a face-to-face level, not
> the type of love that sort of expresses itself in that squeeze
> before you leave for school [as with Father]. But the type
> of love that expresses itself through continuing and
> constant dialogue over a period of time about personal
> problems, about other members of the family. About your

> relation—Mom talking with me about my relationship
> with Dad. Or about Daddy's work or about P [sister], my
> future, and about our relationship with the Lord.

Out of such a matrix arise those developments of secondary narcissism that become expressed in terms of feeling special, holy, selected for a special calling, and so on. By becoming particularly religious, Pale preserved, into his adolescence and young adulthood, early and archetypal qualities of the maternal relationship. These are reworked into the later characterological developments and become expressed as feelings of the sort just mentioned. They become expressed as the high ideals, the great expectations, the sense of being holy, and so on. The religious career with its mysteries and promises of eternal paradise can uniquely appeal to such feelings.

We have already seen some expression of these developments. Pale wanted to remain spotless and pure, in the Lord's will. The sexual activities with C had sullied this ideal. Other comments are equally specific:

> My life . . . oriented around urgently seeking the Lord's
> will because I felt that He has things special in mind
> for me in terms of the fact that He'd given me gifts of
> this and that and the other. I think I probably made the
> response in the questionnaire—that I was God's gift to
> His people to a certain degree. I mean in the sense of all
> that He has poured out on me that a lot of my fellows and
> peers had not gotten, had not been blessed with.

It is important to Pale to feel that he is open and loving. He sees this as an ideal of the Southern culture in which he was raised as well as an expression of Christ's commandments. Typically, he raises this virtue, in his self-image, to a pitch which excludes the perception in himself of all those human fallibilities which are contradictory to it:

> Let me say [excitedly] that I feel like I'm less hard
> [in the sense of egocentric] than anyone else, or than most
> people I've ever met in my life. I must not be too modest
> about this. I must say that I feel like I'm just as loving

a creature as I've ever met except for maybe two or three
people in my life. Maybe my mother, maybe this pastor
at home. I tend to think that I may be as loving as both
of them, because I've grown over the years as a Christian.

It should be mentioned that this outburst occurred on the heels
of a description of how he finds that he sometimes has to put
his foot down and make final decisions when he and his wife
disagree. It indicates the need for absolute control over his
aggression.

More than in any specific comment, though, the grandiose
claims of his religiosity are implicitly expressed in the constant
use of the language of religion and morality. The claims to guilt,
the claims to being forgiven, the constant reformulation of interpersonal dealings in the I-Thou language, the continual refer-
ences to struggling to find the Lord's will, and so on and so forth
—all these can only add up to an expression of a Christ-like sense
of holiness. Such an unconscious self-perception is based upon
exclusion from critical awareness and integration into the self-
concept of that massive array of human experience that runs contrary to it. On the other hand, in the context of such a system
of self-esteem, the constant claim to guilt and culpability is itself
by no means a minor mechanism for asserting one's own righteousness and maintaining a heightened sense of self-worth.

Of further interest in this complex of Christ-like feelings
about the self is the role that Pale assumed within the family.
For one thing, he took into himself what he saw as his mother's
burden:

When you've got someone this close to you like this, you
know, you talk with, you just don't want to hurt them.
In fact I felt maybe that after—the ninth grade maybe
that my mother had been hurt too much. Maybe she had
enough trouble—with the fact that my father got into
these emotional tantrums and so forth. I just felt like that
she had a hard enough time, trying to both handle the
burden of being interested in all of us children as
individuals, and trying to meet our needs and our problems,
trying to bear with and the burden trying to give us
some guidance and so forth.

In recent years particularly he has made attempts to assume a mediating role between the mother and father. In his own life he wants to "right a lot of things I think my father did wrong." He does not express anger at Father for hurting Mother or being as he is. Pale is identified with the masochistic submission of the mother, and struggles for reconciliation from this position. In the family as a whole he seems to be recognized as the gifted one and the religious one. During a church service on one occasion, the minister suggested that the members of the congregation "confess our thoughts one to another" and tell each other where they have appreciated one another. As Pale stood in the choir, his sister came up and thanked him for the influence he had been in her life, in drawing her into different activities, especially music, which she had "been immensely blessed by." His father then came up,

> and said that he was thankful for the influence that I had been on him, you know, in his Christian life. And it was a very honest and sincere expression. And I was very appreciative and glad about this; shows that the relationship between my father and me are really at basis warm. That we have a great love for one another. But in terms of the working of this and the growing of this, it just hasn't come to pass as I hope it will in the future. I think my brother would say this too.

He says that his brother has expressed similar appreciation of him. Indeed, the whole family has: "I have been one who—maybe looked up to—my—I think my whole family—maybe including my mother in some ways." The father thanked the son for having been an influence in his, the father's, Christian life. Pale accepted the thanks but feels that there is growing to be done. He feels that Father is jealous of him and of his success.

In terms of the structure of his oedipus complex and its resolution, Pale has achieved a kind of triumph over the father. There is a predominating identification with the mother and a massive rejection of phallic masculinity and little capacity for genital expression of heterosexuality. He has preserved his sense of entitlement to the mother by becoming more religious than the father, a better Christian. In the economics of his system for establishing and maintaining self-esteem this outweighs the fall in self-esteem that comes from relinquishing genital masculinity.

One other feature of the family constellation must be enlarged upon. Contrasting with the family's official religious stance was the irruption of rather primitive impulses within the family. There were the outbursts between Father and Mother. Father left home for a week when Pale was about six, and he threatened to shoot himself one night when Pale was eight. Also, there was Pale's aural and possibly visual intrusion into the parental bedroom. Limits did not seem to be set on this activity, on the occasions of which he reports. We do not know how extensive this practice was. However, his apparent preoccupation with sexual imagery on the Rorschach as well as his fear of affects associated with sexuality may be related to traumatic witnessing of the primal scene. The children in the household apparently all slept together a good deal. Pale and his brother slept in the same bed during most of the latter's boyhood. He reported only one incident of sexual play with the brother, but it was notable because it had occurred as late as Pale's first or second year of college. Pale also reported a period in which he and his sister, two years younger, had slept in the same bed, and there had been a small amount of sexual play. He reports having attempted intercourse with her on at least two occasions when he was about twelve or thirteen. His efforts were unsuccessful. His comments are interesting because they do not indicate any feeling about the fact that it was incestuous:

> We were running around and got each other excited, and
> I attempted to have intercourse with my sister and very
> unsuccessfully, although I had erection. I just didn't you
> know—I asked myself later why was it unsuccessful. But
> I just did not make a successful approach someway. Even
> though she was desirous.

There is some indication, in other words, that certain fundamental limits were not firmly established between the generations and on the taboos of incest. The expression "running around and got each other excited" seems to convey the feeling of a more ordinary occurrence than an unusual one.

Religion within the family, then, seems to have a function

similar to that which it has within Pale's own personality. It neutralized, or perhaps even allowed the retention of, a certain amount of infantile, primitive affectivity and impulse expression.

### 4. CURRENT ADAPTATION AND EFFECTS OF DOUBT

Pale feels that he never returned to the Lord in the relationship that nostalgic memory tells him he once possessed. He says that both he and the Lord have withdrawn, but with characteristic assertion of a contrary feeling also says that God has planned this for him in order that he may go to his extremity and grow. He speaks of "playing the doubter." But he also makes clear that he is not studying the liberal positions in a liberal theological school simply to understand them objectively from his own standpoint. As he says, he does not have a theology. He is trying to recapture a partly remembered, partly longed-for experience. He hopes to return to orthodoxy and feel in the Lord's will once more, but he is also frightened about the path down which his intellectual pursuit of the Lord may take him. Playing the doubter is not what he wants to do. He has to do it because he really doubts. At the same time he also says that he would die now with a firm faith, believing that

> God so loved the world that he gave his only begotten son,
> that whosoever trust in Him shall not perish but have
> everlasting life. . . . This is everlasting life, that ye may
> know Him and the One whom He has sent.

He would return, in other words, to the faith of his childhood. In the meantime, though, liberalism leaves him with an openness that is intolerable: how do you interpret scripture? How does atonement and forgiveness for sins come about? There are a thousand ways to interpret everything.

Fortunately his quest and his effort at pulling things together take an intellectual bent. Being intelligent he does well in seminary. He is in a social institution where his particular combination of strengths and weaknesses is functional.

In fact the intellectual expressions of doubt only thinly disguise a deep inner rift. The sense of a relationship with Jesus was a restitution for the early maternal relationship. With it, and the sense it gave him of being loved, protected, and of value, he felt whole and could live in the world. Without it, he is left with a deep sense of emptiness, evil division, pervasive malevolence in the world, and vague fears and threats seeming to come from the outside.

> Here's the young man who should be able to trust, with the church at his back there. But from behind the tower we see a—skeleton waving, saying you haven't really figured out—you haven't got it all in your bag. It isn't all clear to you—here's something you have to fear—a question you have to ask. . . . And out behind him there's a trick being played on him. Here death is waiting for him and saying—sort of laughing at him that—he will die and —laughing that death has the final say in this gentleman's life. (TVI)

The extensive theologizing is a desperate effort to capture reality, to sort out a deep confusion, to peek into every corner from which danger might come.

> Very dangerous and the unknown is here. Very much unknown. There is much looking around to be done. If I were standing in a spot from where this picture was taken, I'd look around quickly to see that nothing was sneaking up from behind. I'd get the heck out of there as quick as I could. And I would seek safety. I would seek to make myself invulnerable to all of the dangers that lie in the situation, probably including the unknown aspect of all of it. . . . Having something solid against my back which I knew wasn't going to fall on top of me . . . would be able to look out and protect myself up front. I would take precautions to do all these and to—seek some kind of a respite from the ever-lurking dangers. . . . And what I'm afraid of in this instance, not so much that I would be hurt, but the unknown thing involved. (T11)

The TAT card arouses such real feelings that he puts himself right into the scene, and he describes the fear of the unknown, the fear of a primordial engulfment and annihilation.

With the disruption by life of those features of the personality that preserved the restitutions of the early maternal relationship, Pale is thrust into the conflict over whether the world is basically good or basically evil. Since the heart of personality functioning has been left vulnerable so are other aspects of it. The defenses are extremely fragile and permeable. The ego tends to be flooded with primitive, archaic affect and imagery. Reality relations can be relatively loose at times. Homosexual libido is poorly sublimated and becomes rather clearly expressed in mutual witnessing which is always with male friends. In witnessing, he can love his male friend (and himself) in the way he felt his mother loved him for his expressions of piety and devotion. "We had a good time in prayer together. . . . My greatest joy has been in leading several fellows to the Lord."

In the face of all this there is a strong effort to reestablish firm boundaries and limits, to reduce ambiguities, to escape the fear of the unknown. Every interpersonal event seems to be worked and reworked through a filter of religious and moral concepts in an effort magically to control and ward off primitive impulse and affect and to retain an idealized version of the situation. The fear and rejection of psychic contents and the effort to contain them and to reestablish firm boundaries became expressed dramatically during the Rorschach testing. After having let down his defenses in the course of an hour-long interview before we started the test, the imagery and feelings aroused in response to the first three cards frightened him so much, we had to stop the procedure for the time:

These ink splots are all so misshapen and grotesque-looking. There's so few straight firm lines in them that I can get a monster out of every one. I think it's uncalled for. It's because of the black, the dark, or gray that all of this has always symbolized to me—gathering doom or the gathering storm or the lurking monsters or this sort of thing; where the bright colors and the straighter firmer lines —the known and all of this sort of thing gives me— . . . I mentioned when I came to New England—*Wuthering Heights* and Nathaniel Hawthorne and some of the stuff here that all reminded me or gave—formed the impression that I had of New England. . . . So that these pictures— most of those pictures and inkblots and all that are gray and they all are warped and misshapen like the pictures

I saw on *Wuthering Heights* so that it gives me the same
kind of a feeling.

There can be little doubt, from this, that a vague mysterious
fear had been a part of his idea of New England when he first
came. And yet he came. The unknown must attract and repel.
The feelings called up here are similar to those central fears and
images associated with death and eternity. Could it be that
*Wuthering Heights* really does express his deepest unconscious
fantasy: the union in death with a loved one who in life is torn
away by fate to be married to another? Pale says that according
to the Christian notion one is united in the afterlife with loved
ones. He elaborates this in a vague yet curiously specific way in
a bit of his own theologizing:

> Since it didn't make too much sense to me just on the
> surface of things for God to just create us to exist—and
> then separate us and let one go on existing in one state of
> life and another go on existing in another state of life . . .

Pale does not say, nor does the context indicate, which "us" and
which "one" he has in mind. The comments are introduced
seemingly extraneously as a purported explanation of why he developed his "perish" theory—the theory that man should be given
the choice to perish, to die, on the Day of Judgment. Now the
first and original "us" is the bipolar mother-child relationship in
which there first occurs the sense of "one" over against the other
"one." This experience of "us" and "one" is there in the beginning, as if God created it. It is the bipolar mother-child relationship in regard to which Pale could say, without second thought,
that separation did not make sense. That is, emotionally it is
inconceivable and intolerable. However, this was the separation
he was experiencing. He therefore invented his "perish" theory:
if man has to bear the suffering of separation from the maternal
matrix, it is better to perish.

The internalized relationship with God protects the individual from experiencing this earliest and most painful separation. It is also a restitution for the loss that has occurred in
reality. I am also suggesting, in Pale's case, that there is the
archetypal fantasy that in death there will be a reunion, at the
early primordial level, with the mother. This inference is not

based upon the one bit of data just discussed. As with any clinical inference, it represents a convergence of a large number of trends and pieces of information. Other pieces of data are equally suggestive.

Recently he and Father had an argument that upset Mother very much. Charcteristically, Pale tried to mediate between Mother and Father, telling Mother not to side with him against Father. He explained, "I know that I'm not with her always. But he is with her always," and he added, "while she's alive." The implication is that things will be different after their death—when he will be with her always. In a TAT story he describes a woman as "part of the reality of this man's life, in either the distant past or the distant future." Since the man in question is very old, the "distant future" may mean the future after death.

Of particular interest in this complex of fantasies is the intertwining of the ideas of sex and death. Some examples of this have been previously noted. Pale uses one TAT card to provide a classical symbolization of this fusion: "The first thing this picture—I looked at the open door with the stairs leading up to it; immediately saw a grave or two there" (TIII).[3] There are no graves in the picture. The idea of the graves are aroused, we may assume, as a response to the classical symbolism of the sexual act as mounting stairs and entering the doorway of a building. "But then as I looked and saw the flower, 'course that would go along with the graves. Yet then I looked down at the young man" (TIII). Flowers are the symbol of death, but also of life and sexuality, as Pale himself adds a little later: "The flower of course signifies hope—there's life in a flower. I think of both death and life when I think of a flower" (TIII). Pale sees the building in the picture as a church, and he also almost immediately brings in the idea of the Resurrection. Pale does not make a coherent story from this card. The imagery of the card and his associations to it have aroused in him his vague fears and longings associated with the mysteries of death, eternity, and Resurrection. He spends several minutes trying to clarify his feelings and juggling the symbols.

> This young man is there—very pensive, thinking about what will happen when he walks through this door. What —where the doorway leads. Or what his relationships are with people in this house or through this doorway. . . . Thinking of a flower, say in relationship to the unknown

future—either he sees the future holding a tomb, holding a tomb and death, and yet also thinking that there's hope. We are before the event of death or before the event of the unknown future, or whatever it may be, and we're not after that event, and therefore we cannot say absolutely, and therefore we think thoughtfully about what shall happen afterward . . . (T*III*)

The mysteries of the unknown, death, and eternity are continuing underlying preoccupations with Pale. The imagery and feelings associated with these preoccupations are easily aroused by the ambiguous stimuli of the projective tests, both Rorschach and TAT. Occasionally the severe anxiety associated with these preoccupations breaks through along with the accompanying thought that living endlessly may suddenly happen *now*. We have tried to locate these preoccupations and this anxiety as derivative of separation anxiety experienced in the later part of the first year of life. At this time erotic needs are closely intertwined in the mothering relation with those for food and protection. We have shown other indications that sexual imagery and ideas are currently associated with those of death. It is above all the sheer power of the ruminations about the unknown and so on, with the various meanings which we have tried to assign to it, which suggest that Pale is currently under the sway of the fantasy of reunion with the mother in death.

This fantasy is not uncommon. What is distinctive in Pale's case is the degree to which his life is under its influence, as indicated by the strength and persistence of his preoccupations with death and the unknown. Archaic or archetypal fantasies have power in the personality when there are powerful regressive pulls to early periods of development and when defenses are fragile and permeable. Both these conditions hold in Pale's case. Chelly might very well have an unconscious fantasy of reunion with the mother in death. For that matter, some features of the idea are not unconscious in the least, since he too looks forward to seeing loved ones in the afterlife. Other features of the fantasy, in his case, may be unconscious. On the other hand, his current functioning is not dominated by these ideas, whereas Pale's is. In Pale's case the mechanisms of sublimation are not serving their purpose. In the TAT story quoted just above, he brings in church and Resurrection, but these concepts do not protect him from the anxiety associated with his preoccupations about death and the unknown. He tries to use religious concepts to express his fears, longings, and ideas, but they cannot be made to serve as a protecting, adaptive vehicle for them.

This reunion, fantasy, it may be added, sheds light on the major step in his life: leaving Texas for New England—leaving Mother in reality, but also living out a fantasy of reunion in the future. It explains, that is, his attraction to a place that for him, at the time, had all the qualities of the mysterious unknown.

Our discussion of Pale may close with some comment on what he is today trying to *become*. He is trying to shift his focus of attention *away* from the unknown future onto the present. His interest in Buber's I-Thou concept is an expression of the effort to establish meaning in the *present* and in the present relationship. His central quandaries reawaken when he also tries to reestablish the relationship with Jesus as a *present* relationship. That inevitably brings in questions about death and eternity, since he has not taken Jesus out of a supernatural interpretation. He remains in conflicted uncertainty about his relationship with the Lord. On the one hand, he yearns for it and the feeling of "satisfaction in being an instrument—in being one who is rightly related in going through these experiences." And he still, some of the time, insists that what is now happening is planned by the Lord and will lead him back to the Lord. On the other hand, he knows he does not experience a relationship with the Lord in the way he once may have. He knows also that he is not attending to that relationship, trying to create it anew. He has turned his mind to other things. But he is not sure where his journey into liberalism is taking him. Scientific and psychological attacks on religious belief have apparently had little effect on Pale. He cannot, however, dismiss the liberal theologians.

The uncertainty about the relationship with the Lord derives its force and persistence from the very ambivalences and conflicts that such a sense of inner relationship with God could repair. It is informed by the basic mistrust—the sense of loss and evil division springing from the early maternal matrix—as well as later ambivalences to the mother. The fact that Pale's religious conflict has a psychological basis, however, must not obscure for us the fact that his conflict still demands a religious solution. That is, for Pale to grow together again and move toward his goals in life, he must either relinquish his yearnings for a personal relationship with God or he must be able to reaffirm with new fervor his faith and sense of being "rightly related." Either move involves both theological and psychological processes. If, for example, Pale relinquished his yearnings for the religious relationship, he would have to rethink, in theological terms, the meaning of Jesus Christ, what he believed about the Resurrection, and so on. Psychologically, he would move through an emotionally painful experience of separation. He would experience depression, emptiness, and loss. He would feel the world to be meaningless. He would be faced with the difficult task of finding and committing himself to an ideology with less majestic claims and promises. (The following two chapters will illustrate in more detail the sorts of processes involved in resolving pervasive doubt of the sort suffered by Pale.)

In the meantime, Pale is making adaptive use of two roles which can accommodate both his strengths and his weaknesses, that of the student and that of the mediator. The former role gives him the time and the materials to do the intellectual and emotional work that he must do. As for the role of mediator, his wish is to return to the conservative culture of his childhood and early youth, and to be a mediating voice between the Southern conservative traditions and the Northern liberal ones. The role of mediator is one he learned in the family. It is fraught with emotional and also religious significance. If he can carry this off, he will have found an adaptive and socially valuable vehicle for channeling not only his intellectual strengths but also some of the offshoots of his psychological conflicts—his doubts and uncertainties about the culture of his early years.

## 5. SUMMARY

Doubts and uncertainties irrupted within Pale's belief system when it—that is, the restitutions of the early maternal relationship—did not protect him in and from the stresses of life. The high ego-ideals were fragile and the self-esteem system not flexible enough to withstand the confrontations with reality he met when he left the warm, less demanding culture of his early years. The high narcissistic expectations about the self—the sense of being pure, highly pious, special—were confirmed within the family and the home community. But they could not receive the same support later in his life. Part of the stress came from within in the form of vague fears and sexual impulses. The latter, acted upon, could only be a contradiction to all he had believed about himself. Their continual felt presence led him into doubts, since he felt thereby out of the Lord's will. As doubts encroached upon the inner relationship with Jesus, the Lord, the loss of that restitutive complex exposed Pale to separation anxiety and a sense of pervasive evil and danger. The defensive system was weakened further, and there was a more primitive threat to the ego from impulses, affects, and imagery which were perceived as extremely dangerous. The old faith, the earlier religious sublimations, could not possibly do the psychological work needed to contain these inner and outer threats. Since it could not provide the protection of faith, it was doubted. It is possible that the inner tension that precipitated his conversion when he was eight was the same form of anxiety that later became expressed, first in his early teens, as the fear of endless time.

His problem might have been somewhat simpler, and Pale less tried, if he had chosen to be a minister or some other purely religious vocation. To combine the religious vocation with a secular one demands, as does any marginal, complex role, greater psychological development. The ideology and identity formation are more complex. For Pale this effort put greater strains on his simple faith of childhood.

It would be easy to say that Pale doubted God because he doubted his father. I do not believe it works this way, however. If Pale, like Chelly, had identified with a stronger father, at least partially, it is true that he might have had a more stable belief system. With a firmer masculine identification with a valued father, he would have been more effective in life. The defensive structure would be more stable, and the self-image firmer and more valued without the need for as much compensatory grandiosity. He might have learned workable coping mechanisms from the father. What all this suggests is that identification with a stronger father would have protected, *within Pale's personality*, that good which he had been able to derive from the early maternal relationship. It would also have protected him from the devouring, annihilating aspects of the early maternal relationship.

A predominating and prolonged maternal influence is apparent in the lives of both Pale and Chelly. There is some indication that both mothers used their boys for their own narcissistic needs in the face of an absent or unsatisfactory mate. It seems clear enough also that neither mother supported the growing boy's phallic, aggressive drives. They fostered in their sensitive children piety, tenderness, and religiosity. It is within such a context, perhaps, that they "seduced" their boys, drawing them close and being intimate over a prolonged time through the medium of religion. Through such enticements, the religious belief system comes to contain the greatest hopes and expectations, the fulfillment of the grandest narcissistic feelings about the self and the regaining in heaven of the lost, but promised again, paradise.

# VI

# Precocious Identity Formation in Conservative Protestantism

> I have implied that the original faith which Luther tried to
> restore goes back to the basic trust of early infancy.
> In doing so I have not, I believe, diminished the wonder
> of what Luther calls God's disguise. If I assume that it is
> the smiling face and the guiding voice of infantile parent
> images which religion projects onto the benevolent sky,
> I have no apologies to render to an age which thinks of
> painting the moon red. Peace comes from the inner space.
>
> ERIK H. ERIKSON, YOUNG MAN LUTHER

## 1. INTRODUCTION

In this chapter, the precocious formation of identity will be discussed in general and theoretical terms. The hypothesis is presented that precocious formation of identity is a modal personality
pattern in the subculture of conservative Protestantism. This
hypothesis is based on clinical interpretation of limited case
material and obviously requires further substantiation. Central aspects of the personality and life pattern characterized by precocious formation of personality will be described. In addition to
describing a hypothetical modal personality type, our purpose is
to shed further light on Chelly, Pale, and Joel (chapter IX), as
well as to provide a comparative anchor for our other case
studies.

Precocious identity formation is the lasting establishment of ego-identity before adolescence. The basic features of ego-identity are formed before the age of twelve or thirteen. In conservative Protestantism, the child, in his and the community's eyes, becomes a "Christian" and a "follower of Christ." It is as such that he henceforth regards himself, and this is the core of identity. The notion of being a Christian includes the basic concepts of sin and salvation and eternal life, and that one is saved through Christ, despite one's sins. The stern morality of the community is internalized with these concepts. The identity is a relatively simple one, and the concepts involved can be internalized in a suitable form by a young child. The identity as a Christian may take hold in the child at the height of a life crisis, such as the conflict and anxiety arising out of an infantile neurosis, or other life stress. In any event, basic personality structures are established—patterns of defense and instinctual expression—which last into adulthood. The earliness of the identity formation, its simplicity, and the generally absolutist conceptions of good and evil involved, indicate an identity with limited flexibility. This narrows the possibility of later changes and developments. Adolescence, then, is not a time of revision of identity. Identity may remain totalistic—simple and based on primitive structures and world views. The individual may be stressed in more complex social environments which require a more sophisticated, flexible identity. One unique avenue for personal development does remain open—the relationship with God. This is discussed below.

## 2. BAPTISM

In the modal pattern we are hypothesizing, the child is a member of a family which itself is a member of a relatively homogeneous community. Typically, the sense of a community of faithful, of the brethren, is relatively strong in close-knit conservative religious groups. An important part of life revolves around the church and the church community. A child officially becomes a member of the church and the community of Christians through the ritual of baptism. In Protestantism, baptism is voluntary. Infants are not baptized. A person is baptized when he is able to say and mean, "I take the Lord as my personal

Lord and Savior." This act and the attendant ritual mark a culmination of early stages of the child's development, and the guidelines are laid down for the most significant forms of subsequent development.

In almost any church service, opportunity is made for those who wish to "come forward" to express an act of commitment or some other feature or problem of their religious life. A child may announce his readiness for baptism by going forward at the appropriate time in the ceremony. Both this and the subsequent baptism are public acts and have social meaning within the community. The congregation, those who witness the rituals, is made up of family, friends, and the church community at large. Public ritual thus heightens and gives social meaning to whatever personal meanings the act of faith has for the child. To act other than as a follower of Christ is a departure not only in one's own eyes but in the eyes of the community.

## 3. REPRESSION AND ITS EFFECTS

In a typical case, the act of religious commitment occurs at the height of a childhood inner conflict. The affirmation of religious faith then sets in motion or finalizes defensive and restitutive processes which determine lifelong features of the character. Both the intense inner conflict and the more or less stern morality of the culture require relatively severe repression. There is a complementarity between the effects of the repression of the infantile conflict or neurosis and the values of the culture. This is exemplified in the partial rejection of sexuality, the passivity, the sense of brotherhood and tenderness to one's fellow man, and also, in some instances in the general moral rectitude of the faithful conservative Christian.

The early, severe repression may be expected to have extensive effects which take the form of limitations on ego development and functioning. These limitations seem "unnecessary" even for the given values of the culture and are actually in contradiction to some of them. In particular, early massive repression places severe limitations on the capacity for object relations, that is, on the capacity to love. Often enough this is cloaked in what can become a stereotyped and repetitive language and ceremony of Christian brotherhood. In addition there are other ego deficits or limitations which may be clearly indicated in projective materials. The Rorschach may reveal a surprising inhibition in cognitive functioning in a highly intelligent individual. Similarly, there may be an actual inability to perform the straightforward storytelling task of the Thematic Apperception Test. These are criteria of the rigidity of defenses and impoverishment of mental life attendant upon pervasive repression of fantasy and feeling. Examples of these effects are seen in Chelly and Pale.

The presence of the effects of massive repression in the personality functioning of these individuals raises the problem of the source of the repression. Is it a function of a particular form of superego structure—of an exceptionally severe conscience? There is reason to believe that other considerations are relevant here. The history of the kind of maternal relationship seen in the cases of Chelly and Pale (as well as projective material) suggests the presence of conflicts which may result in repressive or other ego-inhibiting defensive measures of an essentially self-preservative sort. Indulgence and frustration in a stimulating oedipal relationship help keep active the conflictful wish for and fear of fusion. These conflicts may demand repressive measures not so much because superego prohibitions are being transgressed but because of the threat of inundation of the ego by instinctual drives (cf. A. Freud, 1946).

## 4. PATTERNS OF NARCISSISM AND INSTINCTUAL EXPRESSION

While the religious belief system may have close ties with conscience, instinctual prohibitions, and superego functions generally, its functions in relation to aspects of self-image, narcissism, self-esteem, and the ego-ideal are in some ways much more important within the personality. The individual would not subscribe to instinctual prohibitions supported by a belief system which did not function actively to maintain a strong sense of self, self-esteem, and a life direction. In the case of some of the liberals discussed in later chapters, they are in conflict about their belief system around just such issues. They strongly feel pangs of conscience and sexual prohibitions; but these feelings are experienced as somewhat dystonic and misleading, arising as they do in relation to an old belief system only partially rejected and not in tune with newer beliefs themselves not fully established within the personality.

As to the narcissistic, restitutive, and ego-ideal functions of the belief system in the precocious identity formation, these are complex and multileveled; a number of illustrations are provided in the cases of Chelly and Pale. To summarize partially, the act of commitment crystallizes the child's definition of himself as a Christian in a community of Christians. It defines his ideals. It is a *good* act, makes him *feel* good, and tells him how to *be* good. It makes firm the inner personal relationship to Jesus Christ and/or God. The sense of loving and being loved and protected by the divine being heightens or reestablishes a variety of feelings of self-esteem. The inner relationship with the Deity preserves whatever feelings of being special, holy, or the chosen son which were part of the relationship to the mother. Identifying with Jesus has similar implications.

Patterns of instinctual expression will be heavily influenced by the strong early repression. As a result, the belief system will bear projective marks of those oral, anal, and oedipal conflicts that may have been central at the time the belief system crystallized in personality. Foremost in the child's consciousness at this time may be some experience, perhaps vague and diffuse, of guilt and the fear of death. The latter will have its source in fears of separation from and/or fusing with the mother, castration anxiety, or perhaps some other form of threat of the loss of self or ego boundaries. The act of commitment will help to relieve these anxieties.

Homosexual libido finds a number of sublimations in the culture and through the belief system. This is particularly important in those cases in which there is a marked identification with the mother. Generally, homosexual feelings and fantasies, and feminine submissive longings, can be channeled into the relationship with God. Various forms of "witnessing" and evangelizing, and also the love of one's "fellow man" (which sometimes seems not to include women), also are common channels for homosexual libido. The man's intense love for Jesus may be a homosexual, narcissistic object choice, sometimes overriding any other object choice in the individual's life (as in the case of Pale).

## 5. EXCLUSIVENESS

Some form of *exclusiveness* is inevitably a part of this pattern, and of great significance socially. Narrowly, "exclusiveness" refers to the practice of associating only with one's own kind of Christian. More broadly, it refers to those patterns of feeling and behavior which have to do with establishing the Christian—narrowly defined—as a member of the select and most holy community, one of those who is and does right, and, to the exclusion of all others, is most in the will of God. It is in his feelings of exclusiveness that the conservative Christian betrays that sense of being holy, special, and right that may be so intolerable to those who do not participate in his system. It is exclusiveness that allows an otherwise passive and mild individual to evangelize in an aggressive, even destructive way.

## 6. DOING THE WILL OF GOD

The purpose of life, in the context of conservative Protestantism, is to do the will of God. In the paradigm case of precocious identity formation, as we are formulating it, the effort to do God's will is given explicit and conscious place in the context of a personal relationship with God. Every major act and decision is considered or undertaken with the question in mind, "Is this act in God's will? What is God's will in this matter?" The sense of personal relationship with God and the constant effort to do God's will may extend even to the minutiae of everyday life—to asking God the whereabouts of a mislaid pencil, for example.

Where the effort to do God's will is a consistent, conscious orientation to life, it is a central part of the self and has profound implications for personality structure and the structure of the ego-identity. The constant effort to do God's will is an indication of how the individual experiences himself, and it is also a primary feature of his decision-making processes. Doing God's will externalizes central aspects of decision-making. In doing God's will, one is not doing one's own will. The relationship between the self and internal and external cues which provide the basis for decisions is changed when it is God's will that is done. Cues are to some degree dissociated from the self. They are attributed to

God. In this case, the cues—feelings, abilities, successes, failures, inclinations, whatever—are not internalized and used in the service of fuller definition of the self. On the other hand, as the example that follows will show, the attitude of doing God's will usually includes being open to perceiving God's will. This attitude of openness to God leaves the individual open to his own preconscious self and internally originating cues for action and decision. Also, while the self may not, in one sense, achieve fuller definition, through action the internally experienced relationship with God may be deepened and enriched. Nevertheless, major aspects of the self as active agent remain externalized. The individual is thereby partly relieved of anxieties attendant upon the sense of the self as an active agent responsible for its own fate. Extensive passivity within the personality may also be rationalized through the relinquishment of one's own will to God, and in some ways, the individual may never develop a very complete sense of the self. What inclinations exist within the person can be accepted, within limits, as God's will, and a trust in God and His purpose helps relieve anxiety about success and failure and the future in general. This orientation is exemplified clearly in the case of Pale.

The orientation to God's will as a way of dealing with major life decisions is also illustrated in the following dialogue. This subject[1] also follows the model of precocious identity formation. He was born and raised in a small, very conservative rural community in northern Maine. He also has an advanced degree in nuclear engineering from a distinguished university. He currently intends to become a missionary-teacher in Africa.

> Throughout this year—another thing that's been
> settled in my mind—so gradual that I didn't think
> too much about it as a question—I really feel now that
> God has showed me that I ought to work as a teacher
> instead of going into the ministry—I feel no leading
> to the ministry. I just don't think that's where
> God wants me. [Chuckles] I can't explain—it's hard
> to explain how—why you think what you do—it's just
> there—the thought that I don't feel God is leading me
> to the ministry . . .
>     Perhaps this is why God has given me all this training,

'cuz they are looking for people with this training in
Africa. So someday I'll be going across—God willing.
        One thing about me, I guess, that I've noticed
different from a lot of people is that—a lot of people
say that, you know, they're studying to *be* something—
they want to be a nurse, they want to be an engineer
or a professor, or they've got something in view that they
want to be. And I've never had that, I guess. When
I went in to college, I didn't know what I wanted to do.
When I got to X, I didn't know what I wanted to
study in physics or take in nuclear engineering. I've
never had a goal, in a sense, before me, except that I know
God is leading me somewhere. This is what has kept me
going in place of a goal, is—I think the strength of
God—knowing that he's leading me somewhere. He's
got something planned. [PH: Has it bothered you not
having a goal?] Mm—no—not really. Mm—I think I've
been a little more open in some respects not having
a goal—in that I can be led one way or the other.

We may agree with his last comment, that trust in God's
leading can leave one open to whatever possibilities come up.
In the case of an otherwise functioning ego, this life attitude may
be very effective. He continues:

So [in college] it came down to a choice, with me
anyway, between physics and mechanical engineering.
I didn't know which one. Somehow when the time came,
I chose physics—engineering physics. I can see now
that God was really having me make that choice, because
after I got into it, I found that that was *really* what I
liked to do. It was really—*fit* the way I liked to
do things. So I'm glad that God had me make that choice.

These last comments indicate the kind of criteria the individual may use for ascertaining that he *is* doing God's will: if
he likes what he is doing and is functioning effectively. However, those personal inclinations, likes and dislikes, successes
and failures, which provide the inner clues as to what God's will
is and whether one is doing it, are in some measure dissociated

from the self. They are attributed to God. They are not taken into the self and used as materials for defining self and identity, or for enriching the awareness of oneself. Thereby, one form of ultimate responsibility for what one *is* is partially avoided. "Responsibility" here does not mean only moral responsibility. It has to do with assuming the burdens of one's own identity, the inevitable anxieties involved in the knowledge and effort of the self-aware individual trying to fulfill and guide his own destiny.

## 7. ADOLESCENCE

There is, in one sense, no adolescence in the life of the individual who typifies the pattern of precocious identity formation. That is, adolescence is not a time for major reorganization of personality, reworking old conflicts, and finding new models, ideals, and life-style. The individual remains loyal to family and church in much the same way as in childhood. There may occur a tumultuous struggle with sexual fantasies and masturbation. The stirrings of impulse are not taken as intimations that a new way is to be found. On the contrary, lust is fought bitterly, and the intensity of the struggle gives the observer some indication of the energy that goes into establishing the suppression of adolescent sexuality (cf. the case of Joel).

No such struggle need occur, of course. In the case of Chelly, there were no such temptations. For him, the problem of whether or not to attend dancing school came up in the fifth grade. A large segment of the church community was against it. He, however, could see nothing sinful in it, and so, characteristically and with his family's backing, he went ahead and danced. As he makes perfectly clear, it was hardly an activity of lust. He feels however that, for others anyway, the problem takes on a different tone in high school, when people mature sexually. Morality is a large and important part of Christianity for him, and he paints a vivid picture of the temptations faced by motorized, drinking teen-agers, dancing with girls in low-cut gowns to dreamy music. (The projective quality is apparent in his description.) When asked if this were a problem for him at that time, his reply told the story: "No. I handled them in the fifth grade."

## 8. VOCATION

Since the primary identification lies in being a Christian, there may be relatively less need to find identity and fulfillment in another vocation. Where a vocation other than a churchly or a "full-time Christian" one is sought, it is likely to be seen as secondary to or a vehicle for witnessing, being a Christian, and doing God's will. Self-development and self-actualization are less likely to be sought in a profession and through professional development. Furthermore, the profession itself is not highly developed in the person of this type of conservative Christian.

Pale, for example, wanted to be a college teacher, and to use this position as one from which he could spread his Christian witness. He is an intelligent man, and he wished to bring to his conservative Southern Baptist community some understanding of the liberalism and current philosophical thought which he acquired in his Northern education. Throughout college, however, and into his first two years of seminary, he was not able to find a focus for his scientific and philosophical interests in one discipline. He remains a teacher without a subject, being in actuality overridingly preoccupied by his own religious quest.

# PART THREE

# The Resolution of Pervasive Doubt

# VII

# Electon: Resolution Through Conversion

Then psychology treats of behaviour, not of the soul?

What do psychologists record?—What do they observe? Isn't it the behaviour of human beings, in particular their utterances? But *these* are not about behaviour.

LUDWIG WITTGENSTEIN,
PHILOSOPHICAL INVESTIGATIONS, IIv

Doubt of the sort exemplified by Pale I have called "pervasive." It seems to pervade the entire belief system and the personality as well. The belief system is threatened at its core. The doubt is not a matter of a tension between firmly defined alternatives (as illustrated in the cases of Joel and Briting). The doubt is a disintegrative threat of an immediate sort, and the major boundaries of the belief system seem in imminent danger of being more or less completely lost. Other indications of identity diffusion may accompany this sort of doubt. It is also accompanied by a weakening of the defenses which are fragile and permeable. Finally, of special significance for the religious belief system, there are expressions of oceanic longings for a peaceful state of mergence with a transcendental object.

Electon and Mudge have both experienced periods of this sort of doubt, and their stories illustrate two different modes of resolving pervasive doubt. Electon became more conservative through a transforming conversion. Mudge became more liberal. In the process, Electon reorganized needs, defenses, and belief system around the concept of God, while Mudge redirected some of his basic needs away from religious relationships into the self-concept and the relationships of everyday life. The evidence indicates that during the periods in which, as conservatives, they doubted, they manifested the signs mentioned above—weakened defenses, oceanic longings, and other features of identity diffusion.

Neither Mudge nor Electon were raised in cultures as conservative as those of Chelly and Pale. They do not manifest the pattern of precocious identity formation. Mudge's identity as a Christian did not solidify until the middle of his college years; Electon's did not until he was about twenty-two. In terms of the concept of totalistic personality orientation, our three subjects—Pale, Mudge, and Electon—illustrate the different tensions of the three life-cycle crises which may precipitate such a personality organization. Pale is struggling with the earliest such crisis, the problem of whether the world is basically good or essentially evil. Mudge, at the end of his oedipal stage, set out to be absolutely good, perfect. Electon, after suffering the anxieties of identity diffusion, redefined himself in terms absolute enough to resolve finally a series of torturing ambiguities and tensions as to his own identity.

In spite of important differences between the three men, there are important similarities of character and life history. Some of these will be clearer in the course of discussing them individually. I wish to point out now, however, that there is a striking similarity in the family constellation of these three subjects, all of whom had periods of pervasive doubt. The similarity lies in their close and prolonged relationship to their mother, and the fact that the father, in comparison with the mother, was devalued. There is a strong identification with and idealization of the mother. The positively valued aspects of the life and character of the father are not integrated into the son's image of the father, until after the son becomes a young adult, if it occurs at all. These considerations will be developed further in the course of later discussion.

## 1. ORIGINS—FAMILY AND CHARACTER

Electon, twenty-three, is a twin. He and his twin brother were the only children. The father is a high-school industrial arts teacher and apparently an enthusiastic builder and craftsman. The children grew up in Vermont, living in "rinky-dink" little towns and going to two-room schoolhouses up to the fifth grade. Although there was clearly a religious tone to the home, Electon feels that a specifically Christian belief of a conservative sort did not matter to the parents. They did not talk about it, nor was there very much family ritual observance. There was an emphasis at home on living in a moral, pietistic way. Electon and his brother did, however, attend Sunday school and church from an early age. Through his college years Electon was skeptical, did not believe in God, and said that "the Christian faith had never meant that much to me; it hadn't been a part of my life."

There was an important religious influence of a different sort, however, in Electon's early years. His parents ran a summer camp attended by children of many faiths, Protestant, Catholic, Jewish, Muslim. The parents felt that a religious life of some sort was essential to the camp and seeking a religious expression that would be equally acceptable to such a diverse group, chose American Indian. Part of camp ritual, then, was worship of the Great Spirit, Wakandah. Although the source was alien, the feeling and sense of these rituals expressed the mother's religious feeling accurately and Electon responded deeply to them:

It was really, it was religious in the sense of giving
the youngsters a sense of the meaning of life and the
mystery of life and relationship to the beyond. It was
religious in this sense. This was the most meaningful
religious experience, I would say, which I had during my
growing-up years. . . . I have never had any mystical
experience or something of this sort, but I have, you know,
when you stand up there on the rock during the council
fire, and it's dark, and [you] look up at the stars
and sky and there's a camp fire and all—and then you
get up at the end of it and say the prayer of Wakandah
—you would get a real sense that—oh—it could be
defined as a religious experience, I suppose. But it was

something which the whole group entered into and participated in. It wasn't something which *I* had, which others didn't have. But it was really a *group* experience with the focus being—all the fellowship at the same time with this element.

In the last sentences of his description, Electon introduces his central conflict and central concern. This central concern, and the focus for his later conversion, was the necessity for something uniquely his and uniquely self-defining of him. The conflict is the conflictful wish to merge with a greater transcendental object, expressed here as his sense of fusion with the group. His later conversion was successful because it could combine the needs for uniqueness and also for submission and loss of self.

Mother, the dominant parent to the boys, was also the predominating religious influence in Electon's early life. He describes Mother as having a sensitive religious temperament, a religious sense, a sense of the mystery of life. She is a "great soul." He describes himself in similar terms, and as introversive. His response to the feeling tone, the mystery of life, expressed in the Indian ritual at camp is an early manifestation of his identification with her. The twin, B, apparently identified more with the father, although he too chose a religious vocation. Father and B are practical, do not have the religious temperament, and are not as sensitive, as Electon sees them.

The mother is the daughter of a minister. Electon's grandfather was a multi-talented, vigorous, charismatic figure whose "call" and active career took him from an Iowa farm to a Boston seminary and a romantic marriage. Not surprisingly, he has been an ideal to Electon, who identified with him through the mother. It was the image of the grandfather, in part, that first drew him to seminary at a time when he was completely uncertain about what he wanted to do in life. The active presence of the grandfather in Electon's constellation of identifications may also be taken as an indication of his identification with the mother and the likelihood that she repeated with Electon certain aspects of her own relationship with her father, Electon's grandfather.[1] Facilitating this complex of processes was the mother's close and partially unresolved tie with her own father, and of course her son's particularly close relationship with her. Electon's mother's spent five years at home, after graduating from high school, helping in her father's work. This is probably the period during which Electon said she was very religious. She is said to have had ecstatic experiences, dancing and singing by herself on New England hillsides.

Mother was talented musically, had a chance to go to a major music school, but turned it down because she did not like "big city society life," and went instead to a state teacher's college. Further, Mother herself was a minister for six years, starting when Electon was four or five. She took some correspondence courses from a reputable seminary and then took a small rural, part-time parish, where she preached and made calls. The family moved into the parsonage and Father commuted to work. There was one other woman minister in the state at the time. Electon spoke of Mother having an "emotional breakdown" during this period and having to stay in bed for a couple of weeks, although he does not report concrete memories of this.

In the face of Mother's varied interests and activities, her initiative and concern for the children, and the charisma of her father, Father seemed a pallid, less valued, somewhat passive figure in Electon's eyes. He feels that there were strains between Mother and Father because they were so different, their interests were different, and especially, Father was not particularly interested in religion. As to how Mother and Father got together, Electon comments:

> I would assume from looking at them—my mother took my father—married my father—not because he was A number-one, or the one she was waiting around for—but because she was getting on, you know. This is getting hypothetical, but I would—just from my looking at it—think that this might be the way it went.

Whether or not this is an accurate picture of the realities, it reflects Electon's comparative evaluation of the parents. He needed to be asked again about Mother's original interest in Father for one to learn that he is an extremely handsome man, an athlete, a person of integrity and honesty, and one who works well with young people. As with Pale, Electon's image of the mother remains over-idealized; he does not have insight into her character and the aspects of it that contributed to the family tensions. Further, he has not integrated into his image of his father the father's positive traits. It is only in the most recent years that he can admire and appreciate his father for his good qualities, and it is only recently that he can think to himself, when he visits home, "Oh God, Pop—why don't you do something—why do you let this woman run your life?" The implications for the character of "this woman" have not yet sunk in, however.

Electon feels that Mother was forced into assuming leadership and initiative in the family, whether she liked it or not, because of Father's passivity and lack of focused concern about the children's moral and religious training. He feels that Father was jealous of the boys and felt threatened by them because Mother held them in higher esteem than she did him. He feels that Mother saw in the boys a chance to relate closely to people who would share her interests and with whom she could grow. It is also significant for the family constellation that the mother interpreted the father to the boys and mediated their relationship with him. Not surprisingly, Electon's Rorschach imagery has a full complement of powerful, and also destructive, overwhelming, phallic female figures.

Electon, particularly now, resents his father for not providing him with a relationship in which he could have learned to be a man, take responsibility, and have confidence in himself. He attributes his profound sense of inadequacy in large measure to this lack. For example, his father did a lot of building, but it was an extremely unpleasant experience for the brothers to work with or for him. Father was always critical, annoyed, dissatisfied, and disappointed with their work. Electon is also critical of Father for not being highly motivated, enthusiastic, and idealistic. He is a "proletarian" personality, satisfied with doing a good job, and then coming home, reading the papers, and watching television. Father is quiet and not interested in ideas. It was the mother that Electon talked with, sharing many of his ideas and experiences. It is with her that he connects the warm memories of his childhood—every night she would come to the boys after they had gotten into bed, listen to their troubles and their prayers, and rub their backs. Electon says this gave him a feeling of peace and security, and he felt that the world was basically good and that he was loved by his parents.

Electon sees himself, as he was during his boyhood and adolescence, mirrored in his relationship with his twin brother. This, as he experienced it, was a torture, a burden, a constant humiliated subjugation and degradation before someone who seemed always to come out superior. There was constant tension and fighting, and it was all very upsetting to the mother. The boys would sometimes stand side to side, taking turns belting each other on the arm as hard as they could. B, as Electon describes him, is extroverted, active, sociable, popular, and an outstanding athlete. He overshadowed Electon, it seemed, and the latter felt insignificant in the shadow, even though he was superior academically and was supposed to be the more intelligent. The brother was demanding, insisting on his own way, and compelled Electon to practice baseball with him whenever he wanted to. A curious twist on all this is that, in wrestling, Electon could actually beat his brother, could pin him. However, the brother would never give in, no matter what. He was the persistent fighter, and Electon would finally give up just to end it.

Electon has been preoccupied for years with the pervasive, deep sense of inferiority and inadequacy which he locates above all in the torturous twin-relationship. In response to the feelings engendered therein, he withdrew, shunned relationships outside the family, and, retreating to his own room, threw himself into writing out the fantasies of his active inner life and painting. He would read up on the background of historical heroes and leaders, and then write about them, projecting himself into the role of hero. In fantasy, he would be the "leader who was masterful and dominating, and had his own way."

It should be noted that he has no illusions about this writing. He says that the stories were not too good, but "they were great when I was writing them, man!" He has perspective on this turn to books and fantasy and sees it as a compensatory outlet. It also, however, is probably the source of his intellectual interests in history, government, and politics.

He nevertheless conveys that one of his deepest experiences in his growing years was the sense of sadomasochistic subjugation which he locates as deriving from his relationship with his twin. His preoccupation with the issues of grandiose dominance and humiliated submission are clear from the above material. His projective protocols are pervaded with sadomasochistic imagery. An image of torture introduces the Rorschach protocol:

> Two witches [*laughing*] . . . dancing around a fire . . . [Anything else?] They are probably pretty gleeful— thinking about the evil work that they are going to do that night. A young child caught in their grasp—it looks like it might be a child hanging over the fire. [Inquiry.] Witches . . . they looked sort of dis-jaggled, you know, sharp, pointed . . . fire's usually associated with witches . . . funeral pyres . . . two small upstretched hands—crying for help, I suppose. (R*I*)

There is imagery in the Rorschach and TAT of sadistic, degrading mockery:

> A cow, looking me right in the face. Sort of an amusing figure, sort of sad, but sort of a funny sort of way. It's definitely a she-cow . . . bedraggled—she's gone through a rough experience. [Inquiry.] Maybe a trick played on her. Like she woke up in the morning, wasn't in a barnyard, but she was off in a mountain or something, on top of a railroad car—heading for a Chicago—meat-packing plant. (R*X*)

In the relationships described in the TAT stories, people are a burden and torture to one another and to themselves. Everyday situations and relationships are almost always seen in a perspective twisted in the direction of suffering and burden, and, in the course of fateful events, people are torturing one another emotionally. This theme is relieved by the theme of growth through suffering, another theme that played a dominant role in Electon's conversion.

Imagery of grandiose, aristocratic domination also appears on the Rorschach: "The coat of arms of the house of Romanov . . . [*after long thought, and looking off*] eagles wings out there" (R*IV*).

These themes all reappear in his conversion and its subsequent theological elaboration and in other areas of his life, to which we shall return. The projective imagery was introduced at this point to convey the centrality and depth of his experience with his brother and as an indication of the persistence in his contemporary life of the needs and themes first experienced there.

The question must arise: Why did the experience with the twin brother grip Electon so intensely and in this way? Electon himself was indignant when asked this question. The importance and meaning of the relationship to him was self-evident. B, Electon explained, was the only other child, and he himself had no other relationships outside the family, so of course the relationship with B was central. There must have been more to it, of course, for the question still remains not only why Electon focused so intensely on his twin but why that relationship took the peculiarly torturous turn it did. It is just these further elements in Electon's experience which apparently become obscured by the twin-relationship, even while they are the source of the involvement in that relationship. Now the twin-relationship is not an isolated one. It occurs within the matrix of the familial relationships—the parental relationship, each boy's relationship with each parent, and so on—and it must be understood within this context. The parents' dissatisfaction with one another, or perhaps more, Mother's devaluation of Father, undoubtedly was one source of the fuel feeding the fire of the rivalry between the twins. How this actually worked cannot be entirely known, although we do have Electon's account that Mother did turn to the boys for gratifications found lacking in relation to her husband. Perhaps Electon experienced this maternal interest more strongly than B for one or another reason.

As it turns out, the boys, as Electon reports it, had somewhat different relationships with the mother, although the relationship to Father was quite similar for both. B was fighting with Mother a lot of the time. To Electon, his criticism often seemed irrational.

> I never had a chance to fight. I never really fought with
> her—my mother. I sort of let him do the fighting, and I
> would sort of listen in and I tended to take my mother's
> side. I'd sort of stand in between—try to be a mediator,
> one who would listen. My mother would talk over
> her relationship with B to me.

Electon conveys a sense of never-expressed anger at his mother. But he also took her side and acted as mediator between her and his brother. The role of mediating one of Mother's important relationships carries with it a sense of specialness. There accrues from it a gain in secondary narcissism. In some sense it is a breach of the boundaries between the generations, a special mission to the son, and carries with it a sense of high reward. Further, Electon received consolation from Mother for his present desolation. She held before him hopes for a very promising future, telling him of society's great needs, of his potential, reassuring him that some people grew up more slowly than others, and that he need not worry. Perhaps she told him that he had something very special for the world and would one day be great. Electon alludes to this, but claims not to remember for sure if this, explicitly, was part of it all.

The relationship between the twins, then, must be understood in terms of its context in the family and especially in the maternal relationship. Electon's relation with Mother developed, in part, around assuaging the anguish he felt in relation to B. But more than that, lying behind both Electon's interest in being so assuaged and his preoccupation with his sibling in the first place can only be a great oedipal disappointment enhanced by the unavailability of Father. In addition, perhaps genetic determinants inclined Electon more toward introversion and passivity than his brother, and perhaps the fact that Electon is fair and B is dark had something to do with it. Whatever its sources, there is a psychological difference in the boys' relationship with their mother. Electon's relationship with her was two-edged. He sacrificed what B apparently retained, a phallic aggressiveness and the capacity to strike back at Mother and strike out on his own independently of her and the family. However, Electon gained a special relationship with her, a high ideal, a high sense of himself as one to fulfill that ideal with great hopes and expectations for the future. There was an heightening of the processes of idealization within himself and in his image of his mother. Conversely, it is probable that by focusing his conscious attention on the twin-relationship, he defended himself against the overwhelming engulfment which is the threat in this sort of mother-relationship.

Electon escaped the torturous entanglement with his brother

when he won a large enough scholarship to go to an Ivy League school, and B did not. In college, Electon was a seeker. He became obsessed with the problem of the meaning of life and read widely in all sorts of ideologies and religions. He majored in political science but was very attracted to psychology. He read the existentialists and became even more introspective. He had no plans at graduation and with his concern for problems of meaning, and with the image of the grandfather hovering in the background, he and his family felt a year at seminary would be a worthwhile experience. His brother had made the same decision independently, and the twins wound up roommates their first year at the seminary.

## 2. CONVERSION

Needless to say, Electon's first year at seminary was an unfulfilling one for him. Once again he fell under his brother's shadow. He did not find the answers he was seeking, and he was disappointed in himself because "something was going to happen to me at seminary" and nothing did. It was a difficult year. Isolated and introspective, he fell prey to that anxiety that besets young men suffering from a diffuse identity formation·in which the pervasive sense of inferiority, negative identity fragments, and hyper-self-criticalness, as well as the unorganized homosexual libido and feminine identity, all coalesce into the panicky fear, "Am I a homosexual?"

He decided to try the Peace Corps. He did well in the training program, but, as the program progressed, he felt he was hurtling himself into responsibilities and tasks for which he was ill prepared. Fate seemed to confirm his worst fear when, having developed a prostate infection, the examining physician asked him if he had had any heterosexual intercourse. The reply to this being negative, he asked Electon if he had had any homosexual intercourse. The question seemed like a statement to the frightened Electon. This, his fears, and having been approached homosexually a few times, all seemed to be pointing in the direction of a reality. He fled the Peace Corps, went home, and planned to return to seminary to give himself time to mature before trying further responsibilities in the world. His conversion occurred during this period at home, before returning to seminary. His description is worth citing with some completeness:

I left the program, returned home. Then—from there, I had a very strange—there before going back—had about three weeks . . . I had a strange experience—reading Karl Mannheim's *Utopia and Society*. I was—of course— when you've had a real setback like that—I took it—I felt real bad about it. I mean, there's—proved to me that Old—didn't amount to very much. Then I had a— the question was just was there any *meaning* to this, is this just another defeat, just another defeat, another setback, was that all there was? Maybe the question was in my mind: Did this mean anything? Could this be seen in terms of any ultimate meaning? . . . Reading Mannheim—he sees *ideas* as the end—the result of the conflict of different environments. The creative person is the kind of person who is a bundle of contradictions —or who filled with all these conflicting ideas and backgrounds and has to resolve them. And comes up with something new, and creative. And reading that book, I—it suddenly struck me how—how I was—was, you know, uniqueness, the idea of uniqueness, or my uniqueness—came home to me. That I was, because of my background, and so on, I was in many ways unique and I had a unique—perhaps a unique contribution to make, just simply by the fact of my being—my being a man of contradictions. And this idea stayed with me. And also—and it began as, I suppose, as I came back [to seminary] began to get sort of a theological twist, in that perhaps—I think it would have happened before I came back to seminary—that perhaps in this— in this very defeat, disappointment, there was meaning. There was rhyme and reason to this. If I could stick with it long—if I could endure it, and stick with it long enough then—then the meaning of this defeat —defeat on the surface would be—revealed to me—made known to me . . . all these contradictions. . . . Perhaps there was in this very fact of these feelings of inadequacy —perhaps they were what made me unique and made me different and made me perhaps one who could make a unique contribution to society, or to others. Precisely because I was a bundle of contradictions. And if I bore with it long enough, I'd see there was a *plan*, a pattern in all of this. Uh—so—I did—[PH: You did?] [*Laughs*] Well—so I did—I began to approach life with this point of view. And I've come to—come to believe that, in a real sense, God, uh, God is at work in my—*God is at work in my life*. There is a God who's active in there. He's a God who doesn't—there's nothing that's meaningless as long as you stick with it and bear through—and look for the meaning—for the meaning in the apparent meaningless*ness*.

Electon summarizes some of this as follows:

It came home to me that perhaps there was a God who wanted me to do something special in this—this my own work and had something for me to do which was—very important which I could do and nobody else could do. And this feeling—of God's *calling*. Calling—me, and calling out people—to do His work [is] a way of seeing God which is most meaningful to me—I can see that they [these views] *are* definitely a response—fill or set to my deepest need—this particular doctrine [of God's calling] that means most to me is one of the ones which *means*—means very much to me. I can see why it does.

In the last comments, Electon expresses his awareness of some psychological needs met by his belief system. The significance of his making these comments will be apparent shortly.

In this quite complete and remarkable account of Electon's, there are a number of distinguishable phenomenological elements each of which may be seen to have a distinctive psychological meaning. Each element is a manifestation of a complex psychodynamic process which varies in form, intensity, and salience for the whole. Woven all together, they form the living psychosocial tapestry which is the belief system. In our analysis we separate from this endlessly complex and rich fabric a few strands and fix them in the static conceptual medium, reminding ourselves that much of their essence is thereby lost.

First, Electon had suffered a profound humiliation. That he had certainly created it in large measure himself does not make the threat to the self any less. Compared with the high ideals, his real self was nothing. At the same time he suffered that poignant form of social anxiety called "homosexual panic." The self was totally threatened, to the extent that there must have been the threat of a kind of loss of self. Students of psychopathology will note the parallels in Electon's description to phenomenological descriptions of the early stages of some forms of paranoid schizophrenic episodes of previously adapted individuals. The restitutive grandiosity that appears in Electon's account also parallels the psychopathological experience. Electon did not have a psychosis, though, by any means. As he says, he bore the anxiety, he thought it through, and he looked at the experience for the meaning it carried for his life. He did not lose reality contact, and the restitution took a culturally valid form. The parallels to psychopathology are pointed out because they raise questions for ego psychology. There are many ego states which have not been described, and our theoretical knowledge of the ones that have been described is expanded by having the broader context of parallel but different states.

The next phase of the experience was the search for meaning within it. This set in motion the restitutive processes in which the sense of being unique and special was called up, given salience, and opposed to the profound sense of being nothing. His reading gave him an intellectual rationalization for interpreting his experience as he did. Now, the sense of being special was there from the start. It had played a role in his adolescent fantasies, and we may assume there were earlier forms too. A narcissistic wound of the sort Electon had suffered, a deep humiliation, requires for its healing that whatever affective forms of basic trust are available within the psyche be mobilized, called up, and reaffirmed. In going back to his sources in the maternal matrix, feelings of being special were the affective states available to Electon. These were some of the affective experiences which had made life livable for him and had been his source of inner conviction that he was somebody and somebody worthwhile.

Related to the feeling of being special were the feelings of being "unique" and being a "bundle of contradictions." These feelings must have many meanings. Some of the meanings, it may be inferred, relate to his experience in the twin-relationship. First of all, being unique is being the only one, someone distinguishable from others. The work he was being called to do was his *own* work; nobody else could do it. This would seem to express the effort and wish to separate himself as a distinct entity from the entanglement of the twin-relationship. In that relationship, he had not been a distinct entity, he had been one of an intertwined pair. Similarly, part of his feeling that he was a bundle of contradictions was his having *stood*, for many years, *in contradiction* to his brother. He defined himself to some extent by being the opposite of his brother. For example, Electon had considerable athletic ability himself, but would not develop it just because his brother developed his.

There are affective connections within Electon's personality between the meanings of being "special" and "unique" and being "a bundle of contradictions." If it is true that the former feeling derives from the maternal relationship and some features of the latter feelings derive from the twin-relationship, then this is further confirmation that the meaning of the twin-relationship must be understood in the context of the maternal relationship. There are other meanings to this feeling and idea of being a bundle of contradictions as well. It probably signifies the sense of being both male and female. It probably also expresses a multitude of deep-lying and long-standing ambivalences. And certainly feeling unique, special, and called by God is a feeling that stands in contradiction to feeling like nothing.

It is of particular interest that it was after the restitutive processes had been set in order and a compensatory secondary narcissism—feeling unique—had been called up that Electon gave the meaning of his experience a "theological twist." It is possible that before doing so, he tried out, in fantasy, other, nontheological, interpretations which he rejected for one reason or another, possibly because he recognized their tenuous reality connections. In any event, the theological interpretation of his experience—God calling him to do something special—put his interpretation of his experience within a consensually valid framework and was also such as to preserve the feeling of being special, having unique, highly important work to do, and so on.

The idea of "contradictions" appears in Electon's conception of God. God is "the One who stands over and against one,"

> . . . who speaks to you—who has a word to communicate.
> This is something which you can get your teeth into
> [in contrast with Tillich's conception of God]. . . . He's
> a God who's *active*—and who's continually reaching out
> to one, and calling one, and making demands, and
> insisting upon His way. This is God for Barth and
> Bruner.

Electon contrasts this idea of God with the Tillichian conception of God which he sees as passive. In Electon's conception, "God wanted me to do something." Now, we notice that he uses some of the same words to describe his experience of God as he uses to describe his experience with his brother—"making demands," "insisting on his way," "wanted me to do something." Part of the meaning of these expressions is that Electon takes his own meaning and self-definition from a transcendental object to which he submits. This meaning stands in contrast with his expressed wish to be unique, to be differentiated from a larger unit, to define himself. Herein lies his central developmental conflict, and it is this that provides one of the basic psychological conditions of his conversion experience.

The relationship to God expresses Electon's central conflict and is also an expression of the psychosexual level which permits the occurrence of a conversion experience of the sort he describes. On the one hand are the wishes and fears attendant upon merging with and taking meaning from a higher transcendental object. On the other hand are the wishes and fears attendant upon choosing one's own identity, defining oneself, and determining one's own fate. In terms of the relationship to God, on the one hand God is to tell Electon what to do, and on the other hand his calling is to be something that is unique, nobody else can do it. The demanding, insistent quality of Electon's conception suggests the sadomasochistic tinge apparent in the twin-relationship, in which the issues of separation and individuation were merged with those of dominance and submission. The psychosexual level is that one at the end of the first year of life and the beginning of the second during which awareness of separateness from the mother grows.

These issues find other forms of expression in Electon's life.

As we will see below, Electon insists on the prerogative of defining himself. The insistence itself is so persistent and only partially attuned to the realities of his social situation that we must assume that it contains the wish for the opposite. We also see the expression of the contrary wish in his desire to find some great cause in which he can lose himself.

Let us pick up one further strand in the conversion experience. Electon says that he found the idea that "perhaps in this very defeat, disappointment, there was meaning." That is, he found meaning in his suffering. Now it is noteworthy that he mentions thinking in these terms *after* giving the interpretation of his experience the theological twist. In any case, this idea is peculiarly Christian. That is, through suffering, one finds one's salvation. Later, Electon was to read Erikson's *Luther* and find in it and Luther parallels to his own experience. In spite of his distrust of psychology, he used Erikson's description of the late-maturing Luther overcoming inner emotional difficulties to shed light on his own experience and to give him assurance that there is meaning in suffering and that the outcome may be uniquely significant.

## 3. REAFFIRMATION

A year and a half or so after this initial conversion, Electon was tried again, and his faith was too. The experience and the outcome were quite similar. An account of it will highlight certain other central features in Electon's personality, especially the tendency to get into battles with people and groups and the tendency toward a totalistic identity formation. The experience also confirmed and deepened Electon's faith, and furthered the development and maturation of his personality.

The experience occurred during his summer psychological clinical training at a state mental hospital. With his supervisor, he had tried to discuss his anxiety over "homosexuality." He felt that this man responded by trying to make him confess that he really was homosexual or had homosexual feelings. Electon felt that he was pushed into confessing this in his small group meetings. He finally did, to the hushed silence, as he experienced it, of his colleagues. For a time he felt that perhaps he was going to have to run from the whole seminary training as he had from the Peace Corps. He girded himself to stick it out, telling himself

that God would be at work in his life even in this, and the way
and the meaning would be revealed. He had felt that the supervisor misunderstood his anxiety, had tried to force him into a
confession in the group, and that he, the supervisor, was trying
to define who he was. Electon finally resolved the issue in his
mind by deciding that he would be the one to say who and what
he was. He would not allow someone else to do it by some mis-
use of psychology.

The struggles over these issues occurred in a more general
context of an authority struggle. He felt that the supervisor was
after him in the group. The other group members seemed to side
with the leader, until the last day, when they sided with Electon.
Electon worked over in his own mind the question, What is the
reality? Was it as he defined it, or as others defined it? He felt
insights were coming from right and left, and wrote at length in
his diaries. He thought over the issues psychologically and theologically and tried to see the relationships between the two. He
felt he was doing thinking that had never been done before. His
criticisms of the group and the program were interpreted to him
as his "authority problem," and he could not see their point of
view, thinking they had replaced a defensive psychologism with
a concern for truth. He expressed fear about the letter of evaluation that would come from the supervisor, a fear by now clearly
justified by the mutual antagonism. This concern was interpreted
to him as a "psychotic" concern. Again, he seemed to be seeing
things one way and everybody else another way. What was reality? Once again his whole being was at stake.

Whatever really happened that summer, it is clear that Electon got himself into a struggle with authorities in which he felt
himself to be on the brink of a total humiliated submission and
despair. Uncertain of who he was, he felt they were trying to
force something on him that was not true of him, in particular,
that he was "homosexual." He roused himself into anger and for
the first time said to himself that *he* would decide who he was
and where he was going.

In his despair, he had turned again to his newfound faith,
and with help from it bore through and felt more deeply committed:

   . . . made me even more cling to this idea [that God is
   at work in his life] that in the *depths*, you know, the

depths of despair—there's *got* to be some meaning in this
and there's *got* to be—you know. Gotta. You know—gotta
—gotta make some sense out of it. And just what does
this all mean? . . . I've had the feeling, you know,
the *trust*—the trust that there was—that God could—that
God could work even in this ["homosexuality"], even
though it was this—and this sort of—sort of *pulled* me
through—pulled me through this very—very—very
difficult period.

Electon's words convey, better than any commentary, the threat
and anxiety he felt during this period. His further comments
help us to understand one way in which a person comes to have
greater certainty about a religious belief system.

I've become so committed and so assured of the validity
of this way of perceiving life—perceiving reality—through
these experiences that they've become *extremely* real to
me—inescapably real. That's why I'm a Christian,
basically; because at this very formative stage of my own
development and my own thinking, the Christian faith
—was—or my belief in God—or God—God met me, and
stayed with me and—stuck it through with me and made
me a success in that—I'm not a success—I'm still struggling
—but when I look at life in these terms, I have nothing to
fear. Come hell or high water, God'll be with me—working
out His purposes for me—and putting meaning where
there would—giving me meaning where there otherwise
would be complete meaninglessness. So I've become
convinced that the Christian faith—

His certainty became stronger because the belief system had protected him from a deep humiliation, the threat of loss of self,
the confirmation of his worst fears about himself, and a proof
that he could never live up to his high ideals and fulfill the dream
of a golden future.

We have seen the pattern of torturous struggle with the
constant threat of humiliated submission or definition of self
from outside appear in different areas of his life—brother, God,
work—and on different psychic levels—projective materials, the-

ology, action. It is not surprising that the battle during the clinical training was not without its gratifications. "It was great—I was fighting a battle." This pattern came home to me when I found that Electon's initial interest in participating in my research was to set straight the brush with psychology he was having in his training. There was a tendency to try to repeat a torturous struggle with me—and be confirmed in all his worst fears about himself. My impression was that the situation in his clinical training had been mishandled and misinterpreted, but my reassurance did not seem to matter much to him. A parallel trend is seen when, in speaking of his current search for a cause, he says that he has a need to "strike out" and to feel that large numbers of people are wrong and must be set straight.

"Psychology" came to play a distinctive role in Electon's thinking during this period. It came to represent an evil, the Other, the force opposing his positive growth and all his efforts to feel positively about himself. "I've seen psychology in terms of being one of those principalities and powers,[2] in a sense, which is a threat—a threat to my—to my being." Psychology became allied with those forces which coercively define one from the outside:

Modern psychology should let the person define what his problem is and not force problems down his throat.
This is how psychology is misused and why people are so afraid of it. It sort of forced these problems down on people.

Electon felt, for example, that his undergraduate psychology courses made him become too introspective and attribute all sorts of things to himself instead of allowing him to grow up naturally and unselfconsciously. His antagonism to psychology also represented the fear of determinism. Psychology said that one was determined, one was bound to one's past, stuck with one's limitations. One did not bring anything to life. One could only analyze the past to see what one was, and then work with it as best one could. The Gospel, in contrast, says that God gives to those who believe in Him the power to become anything. In the end, it came down to a choice between the Gospel or self-destruction. He had made an absolute, totalistic alignment between all that was positive within himself and all that was

negative, and he ascribed the latter to the realm of psychology
and the former to theology:

> Psychology can be a terribly destructive bit of knowledge.
> This is a place that I know that theological insight came
> in. Because I had to decide what was really real. And
> the alternative was between the Gospel account which
> said God can accomplish anything in those who believe
> Him, and Jesus Christ and His love and forgiveness and
> power to change one's life; then psychology, you know,
> over here. And I had the feeling that psychology said you
> were who you were and—work with it, sort of implying
> the impossibility of change, really, but simply being able to
> better work with your own problems. And I was faced
> with what is really real? What is really true about the
> nature of reality, and the nature of me, and I made the
> choice for the Gospel. . . . This is one of the insights
> which—really pulled me over. It was sort of a choice
> between faith—faith and self-destruction [laughs]. It was
> posed in that way: either this is really true or, man, I am
> just a goner, sort of that sort of a choice. So, rather
> than destroy myself, I said, it may be a lot of absurd parts
> to this Gospel and a lotta questions, but man—it's gotta
> be true. Sort of that sort of a feeling.

For the time, Electon had established a totalistically oriented identity. He had an ideology which had to be nearly absolutely correct, and he had one to which he could stand in
opposition and use to externalize and personify all those forces
of inner and outer evil which threatened him. Psychology "forced"
him to consider all those things about himself he saw as negative:
his sense of inferiority, the possibility that he was "homosexual,"
the difficulty of change, the presence within himself of destructive, egocentric motivations. It raised questions about his interpretation of his relationships with authorities that were not only
not flattering, but seemed to question his very sense of reality. It
suggested he look at his past, and this would possibly necessitate
a reinterpretation of his early years, especially an aggressive de-
idealization of the image of his mother. Psychology seemed so
much a confirmation of all the self-destructive criticism and hate

that he could possibly unleash against himself that we can take Electon literally when he says, "It was sort of a choice between faith and self-destruction." Onto psychology he could externalize his self-hate and negative identity fragments, and into theology he could project all his trust, hopes, and high expectations, indeed, his salvation.

Psychology posed the real possibility that his dreams of a golden future, his high expectations and ideals, were only—dreams. At the time he could not even conceive of the more ordinary sort of life exemplified to him by his father. Later he could conceive of it, but only to dismiss it. In our discussions he said he possibly could be happy as a high-school teacher, but this would not fulfill his destiny. He feels called to do and be something great and out of the ordinary. He can say now that perhaps these "wild dreams and imaginings" were planted in him by his mother, that is, maybe there is a psychological explanation for them. But that does not matter; this is how he is and this, he says, is how he will try to live.

## 4. SUMMARY: CONDITIONS FOR CONVERSION AND REAFFIRMATION OF FAITH

What are the psychological conditions that permitted Electon to undergo a radical reorganization of his religious belief system, from skeptical seeker to one who believed that an active, providential God had called him out for a special mission? His conversion was certainly first of all a response to a deep need. He was threatened with more or less complete loss of meaning and worth—a loss of his very self. He needed to feel that he was of some worth, that his life had some meaning—that he was not, literally, nothing.

What permitted restitution to proceed via the religious belief system? One basic psychological condition was the capacity to regress to the oral level at which there is a tendency and wish to merge with a superior transcendental object. This apparently occurred in Electon's case, and the wishes and fears attendant upon this psychosexual stage are still present and conflictful within his personality. This stage permits the personification and externalization of various aspects of the psychic contents into the concept of God. As we have seen, Electon's conception of

God contains elements that were central issues within his personality.

A second basic condition is the capacity to suspend partially and in certain areas critical reality-testing of one's feelings and ideas. Electon had always been skeptical about God's existence. He was now able to suspend this criticism of his wish to believe and set an arbitrary final form upon his belief system. A recurrent feature of his projective protocols is the idiosyncratic, somewhat arbitrary, specificity of certain of his percepts and conceptions. There is not a loss of reality. He gives reality a very specific interpretation and uncritically suspends an openness to the possibility of other interpretations. On occasion he explicitly insists on his own interpretation regardless of an awareness of evidence that might contradict it.

This second condition of his conversion is closely related to a characteristic of the faith of many believers and characteristic of Electon's description of the growth of his own certainty. That is, the *feeling of rightness* about a belief is accepted, without further criticism, as an indication of the truth of that belief. "The heart hath reasons that the mind knows not of," as Pascal says. This is sometimes quoted by divinity students in their questionnaires, and it expresses the idea that the sense of faith, of conviction, the *feeling* of truth and reality, are higher criteria for belief than the critical evaluation of reason. In this way faith is protected from intellectual doubt and reality-testing in general. An inner, emotional experience is accepted as the criterion for and definitional of an exterior and ultimate reality. The emotional experience and its symbolic interpretation are thereby preserved from critical reality-testing.[3]

These are two psychological conditions that permitted the sort of personality reorganization to occur that Electon experienced as a conversion, a coming to faith. It is clear, however, that although a relatively radical reorganization of personality occurred over a relatively brief span of time, the psychic elements which went into this reorganization had always been salient features of Electon's personality. The symbols of the religious belief system, the ideas of Christianity, had, for example, been a central feature of the family culture even though Electon had not attached central significance to them. However, the symbols of the religion served as the vehicle for the personality reorganization. The processes of ego synthesis occurred through this medium. Through the belief in God, for example, Electon achieved an exquisitely appropriate combining of both his profound sense of inferiority and also the sense of being special, his long-standing feeling that he was to fulfill a golden future, be dominant, and achieve something great. Both within Christianity and within modern depth psychology he found reason for believing that in his very suffering there was an ultimate meaning and a partial source of his potential greatness. The religious symbolism allowed both these features of his personality—the feeling of inferiority and the grandiosity—to come to fruition, achieve an active, motivational salience, and take a culturally valid, conscious form. Further, the relationship with God allowed him to externalize and experience in a form acceptable to himself the wishes and fears of submitting to a higher power. Being able to submit to God protects him, in some degree, from the tendency to do so in his power struggle with colleagues and superiors. In like manner, the symbolism of an active Father-God is a defense against the dangers of maternal engulfment which in Electon's case is affectively related to his power struggles. (The twin-relationship, it will be remembered, is to be understood in the context of the maternal relationship.)

The symbolism of Christianity had been salient during Electon's childhood and adolescence. If it had not been, and Electon had undergone a similar conversion, we would have had to say somewhat different things about his ego structure. Specifically, conversion to a more alien symbol system would necessitate an interpretation of reality somewhat more arbitrary and discontinuous with the past. This in turn, I would think, would require a greater relinquishment of critical thinking and reality-testing. In Electon's case, it was apparently possible for him to transfer the cosmic feelings, the spirituality, the religious sense, the sense of the mystery of life, and so on, which he associated with his mother and the Indian religion of the summer camp—to transfer all of this into his conception of Christianity. In this sense too, the religious symbolism served as a vehicle for ego synthesis, coming to condense and contain, as part of their meaning, these aspects also of his life and experience.

It is of the greatest significance also that Electon's belief system allowed him to bear a large burden of depressive anxiety and to experience consciously a relatively wide range of psychic contents. This is exactly the burden the ego has to bear—the anxiety of the individual's life. At two critical life periods, the belief system protected Electon from further loss of self-esteem and threatened loss of self. For this reason, his faith grew and his certainty about the belief system grew. Pale, in contrast, did not have a greater burden of anxiety to bear. In Pale's case, however, a fragile, precociously crystallized personality structure became threatened by disintegrative forces. Electon, as he himself correctly asserts, matured, in the sense of forming an identity, much later. He had already suffered humiliations and the threat of loss of self. Any source of healing that gave an increment in self-esteem could only be positively cathected and held closer. Pale, suffering, felt a fall from grace. Electon, suffering, found a new meaning in his suffering and salvation.

Both Pale and Electon had to deal with the complexities of a strong identification with an active, phallic mother in a family constellation which included a weaker, devalued father. In Pale's case, the ego was threatened by primitive, unintegrated impulse, affect, and imagery. This accrued from early, severe, partially effective superego prohibitions, contrastingly weak incest barriers within the family, and failure to separate the self from early object relations within the family. In Electon's case, the threat to the ego resulted from the lack of identity, the constant comparison with an exalted ideal, and the libidinous fixation on a form of object relationship involving torturous subjugation and humiliation.

The synthesizing power of the religious symbolism, in Pale's case, has been enfeebled by the experience and anxieties of his recent years. The symbolism could once again be an efficacious and powerful vehicle for ego synthesis if he were to undergo a totalistic reorientation of the sort Electon experienced. This would require some regressive revival of the trustful experience of his early years, a concomitant externalization and personification of certain psychic contents, and at least a partial relinquishment of critical reality-testing. In thought and feeling, some arbitrary limit would have to be set on an interpretation of reality, one which in his case would have to exclude finally as possibilities many of the liberal theological ideas he now considers. On the other hand, a liberalization of the belief system might also restore the synthesizing powers of the symbolism, and would place less of a psychological burden on the religious beliefs. Such a transition is illustrated by the case of Mudge, to which we now turn.

# VIII

## Mudge: Resolution Through Liberalization

> . . . several things dove-tailed in my mind, and at once it
> struck me what quality went to form a Man of
> Achievement, especially in Literature, and which
> Shakespeare possessed so enormously—I mean Negative
> Capability, that is, when a man is capable of being with
> uncertainties, mysteries, doubts, without any irritable
> reaching after fact and reason—Coleridge, for instance,
> would let go by a fine isolated verisimilitude caught from
> the Penetralium of mystery, from being incapable of
> remaining content with half-Knowledge.
>
> JOHN KEATS, LETTER TO HIS BROTHER, DECEMBER 21, 1817

Mudge illustrates the processes whereby pervasive doubt in a
conservative context is resolved through the individual becoming
more liberal in his beliefs. The questions we want to try to
answer in the case of Mudge are: What was liberalized? What
did liberalization consist in? And, what were the conditions
which allowed liberalization to take place? The first two questions we will understand as pertaining to characteristics of the
belief system, particularly the theology, and these questions are
therefore relatively easy to answer. The third question pertains to
underlying psychological processes, family constellation, and problems of development. This question is therefore very difficult to

answer, and as elsewhere the answer is partial and to some degree speculative.

## 1. MUDGE'S CHANGE IN OUTLOOK

In Mudge's questionnaire are expressions of pervasive doubt similar to Pale's. In response to one question he writes:

> I am seeking for needed answers, but I am far more seeking fulfillment for my needs of being loved and wanted, with a purpose coming from God. In God's will and purpose I can find meaning in life, but it is so difficult to know (a) what is God's will, and (b) how then do I choose to fulfill it. I lack faith and commitment because I am rather uncertain of what to believe and do.

Later in the questionnaire, he writes:

> Why doesn't God speak more clearly, reveal Himself more personally so that more men could see and believe and do His will.

These comments clearly express the oceanic longings, the wish for fusion with a transcendental object, the deep sense of abandonment, and the pervasive lack of personality integration expressed by Pale and by Electon before his conversion. The belief system was simply not meeting Mudge's needs at that time, nor could it carry the defensive and integrative burden that his personality functioning required. Also, in our use of the term, the quest for a personal relationship with God in which one is loved and protected and from which one finds exactly what to do in life is characteristically conservative.

Mudge wrote these answers as a second-year seminary student, and he participated in this project a year later, when he was concluding his studies. At this time he said he would not "denounce" anything that he had written a year earlier; it was still "underlying." He still asked why God did not "present himself in a way in which he could be realized more easy" [*sic*]. He also had the doubt that perhaps he still believed in God because he had to, that if he relinquished this belief he would "throw in the sponge" and die to the possibility of living a productive life. On the other hand, the idea of taking over his father's insurance agency looked very inviting, particularly as Father, both grandfathers, and a paternal great-grandfather were all successful in business enterprises in rural areas of Pennsylvania where Mudge grew up.

At the time he was interviewed, however, Mudge was no longer as preoccupied with the quest for the loving, protecting, direction-providing God. His sense of well-being no longer depended directly upon God conceived in this way, as it had during ups and downs during his first two seminary years. His theological conceptions had changed. His conception of God and how God was a part of men's lives had changed somewhat as follows. He found that when he discussed God, or tried to make another person aware of how he saw God, he would have to speak not in abstractions but in terms of the events and relationships of everyday life. In a sense, he did not "have God left." Similarly, in terms of action, he found he had to be able to go ahead and act without being certain about God's will. He had to trust that if he kept in mind an awareness of God, then his actions would be correct. Uncertainty had to be tolerated. He had also found that for him there was no alternative to the Christian way of life as he saw it, and he was able to use Jesus as a figure for identification in an everyday practical way. His conception of guilt had also changed. Whereas at one time he had struggled to maintain himself in a state of absolute purity, he now felt that guilt could only occur in respect to acts that affected other people. He did not feel guilty before God because of what he was, but he did feel guilt on those occasions when he felt he did not live up to a responsibility to some other person or group. He felt that men are imperfect, that they are made that way by God, and that they are not punished for this.

Mudge was clear about some of the psychological shifts which accompanied the theological ones. They are, of course, simply another side of the same changes, as he knew. From the effort to find answers and meanings in an abstractly conceived God, he had changed to finding new meaning in real interpersonal situations. He seeks satisfaction for his needs for love and dependency with other people. He learned that life is universally ambiguous and that one must act in the face of uncertainty, bear tension, and trust that with a good will, good will be done. The change in the conception of the nature of guilt betokens a change in the nature of the self-esteem system. Mudge relinquished, to some degree, the requirement of absolute personal purity, perfection, and holiness. He accepted human limitations and a conception of responsibility toward other people. Finally, being less dependent upon the religious symbol system in certain ways, he is now able to use it as a source for guidance in action and identity formation. The stories of the Old Testament, with which he was very familiar, and the figure of Jesus can serve as sources for models for everyday life.

Mudge attributed these changes to his experiences of the preceding year. He had had one more year of seminary, and he had led a confirmation class at a church. The latter had made him think through what he would *declare* as his basic beliefs. Also he had found a new source of love and esteem: a young woman who loved him and whose love he was gradually learning to accept. For someone as immediately focused on the need for an income of love as a basic source of self-worth as Mudge, this was most important.

Another event which occurred in the course of the year also altered Mudge's outlook. Its roots go deeper and Mudge is less aware of the part it played. This was the death of the beloved paternal grandfather who had played with Mudge and indulged him as a child. Like his fondness for his father, his fondness for the grandfather is suppressed in large measure. At the time of his death, Mudge had to realize that the grandfather did not measure up to his, Mudge's over-scrupulous demands for the observant Christian. He found, however, that he had no desire to judge the grandfather as he had judged many people. He learned then to "loosen up on my doctorine [*sic*] of judgment." "I sort of wonder how he is now, you know. What he's up to or how the battle's going." His love for his grandfather and the loss made him think through a judgmental outlook which had not been based on an emotional contact with people and insight into his own personality.

## 2. CONDITIONS FOR THE CHANGE— FAMILY CONSTELLATION

The foregoing gives a brief idea of the nature of the change in Mudge's belief system, and also suggests some of the immediate life experiences which facilitated and were the medium for the change. We will now examine the psychological substratum which permitted this change to occur and which allowed Mudge to find an accommodation in a more liberal belief system.

Although Mudge had tried hard during his last two years in high school and his first year and a half in college to be a fundamentalist, and considered himself to be such, it had simply never taken. Fundamentalism was not the religious orientation of the home nor of his family's community church. We will consider briefly the psychodynamic and developmental factors that inclined Mudge on the one hand to a more ardent conservatism than the one in which he had been raised and on the other finally led him into a doubting despair.

Religion in the home was largely in the service of a hyperscrupulous legalistic morality and sheer strict discipline. The source of both these and of the religious tone was Mother. A number of powerful forces within the home left Mudge feeling broken, crushed, unloved, and unworthy. On the other hand the same forces left him with a deep-seated stubbornness and a striving for absolute perfection and purity which a turn of narcissism convinced him were in his grasp.

Whatever else happened in Mudge's development, its context was a parental tension of which Mudge felt as often as not that he got the brunt. This had its source in the parents' characters, but also, specifically, in the events surrounding his birth. Mudge had always known that his birth had been problematic: he and his mother had both barely survived and he had been very "premature." What became clear in the course of the interviews was that Mudge had been conceived out of wedlock, a striking contradiction to all of Mother's moralizing. Mudge always had sufficient information to draw this conclusion and had even occasionally asked himself if his parents "had" to get married, but he was reluctant to bring this preconscious conclusion to full light. Further, Father continued to have extramarital relations with women, and would cover up this and late nights out at a bar with false stories. Mother took it upon herself to see that the son had the virtues of honesty and fidelity that the father did not.

The considerable strife between the parents frightened Mudge and had other effects on him. Father would come in late and Mother would strike out at him verbally. The small Mudge would awaken, become frightened, cry, and pray. When the par-

ents were in bad moods, Mudge would clear out, because nothing he could do would be right. In all of this was an apparent
focusing in on Mudge which had an effect in addition to making
him feel insecure, frightened, and unwanted.

> I had no brothers or sisters—no one to spread it out with
> —someone in the same boat with me—out in the country—
> nearest kid was a mile away. I just sort of took it and
> absorbed it all. You know, whatever they told me, I was
> —bad, naughty, rotten, or whatever—not sensing—not
> really thinking I was that—important.

Mudge was the only child and he did not understand that he
was really that important. Both meanings of this remark should
be taken seriously. The implication for Mudge's low self-esteem
are clear enough. In addition, a powerful feeling of importance,
being the center of things, accrues from actually being the center
of things—even in a negative way. Part of the message Mudge
got was that he, the only child, was the center of his parents' dis-
cord, and therefore responsible for it, and therefore very important. This is one source of the turn of narcissism that results in
the feeling of being special and the striving for perfection and
ideal attainments. It accompanies and compensates for the negative self feelings, but it also has a source that makes it more than
compensatory.

Another emotional quality accruing to the circumstances of
Mudge's birth was passed on to him and became another source
of his religious idealism. The birth was dangerous to the lives of
Mother and child, and Mother felt that both had survived through
prayer, as an act of grace. Mudge speculates that although she
never told him as much, Mother bore in mind, in his upbringing,
the story of Samuel.[1] That is, Mother dedicated him to God, and
tried to bring up Mudge "as best she could" out of the motive of
returning to God what God had given her through a special act
of grace. Whether or not Mother actually viewed things in this
light, there must have been some emotional aura in Mudge's relationship with his mother of which this would have been a symbolic reflection.

Mother trained Mudge to be good, to be obedient, to be-
have, to keep his nose clean, and not to poke into things. She was

a strict disciplinarian and Mudge feels she would have come down hard on him and broken him in any event. Closeness, physical and emotional, between Mother and child was extremely intense. Father was "a non-entity" and Mother was "both figures" —both father and mother to Mudge. Father had had a "nervous breakdown" the first year of Mudge's life, and then a second one. From Mother it was always, "Don't bother your father." Father, then, was weak and immoral, as Mother interpreted him to the son. As with Pale and Electon, Mother interpreted the father to the son, and the son has not integrated into his conception of him Father's strengths and successes. Mudge's father in fact seems to have done well in rural Pennsylvania at a number of business enterprises, yet Mother says Father "doesn't push it," and she says Father's family is "lazy." Father has indeed failed to create within his family a sense of his own male competence. To Mudge he is fragile and wounded. And yet Mudge's earliest memories are fond ones of touching father and son scenes.

Part of the training Mudge remembers is his toilet training:

> My mother said whenever I had to go to the bathroom
> —even when she was toilet-training me—I'd always go off
> to the corner and go in my pants. Then she'd get so
> mad at me. I remember one time she just got—scrubbed—
> the kitchen scrub brush out and she rubbed my ass till it
> was raw practically. I remember being mad over this for
> several days.

A whole cluster of character traits grew out of these stubborn anal battles, only a few of which will be touched on. One lasting effect is the continued mingling and confusion of imagery of the front and the rear, the behind. This occurs in his belief system where, for example, a confrontation with God is sometimes experienced as a feeling that someone is behind him. It also occurs at the basic level of body imagery, as will be shown below.

The relationship with Mother was in other respects warm and loving. One of his fondest memories is being read to before he went to sleep. Mother also used this means to instill a spiritual attitude. She read to him Biblical stories, mostly Old Testament ones, and this was almost a nightly occurrence. (Mudge felt a strong affinity with the Jews as a result of the long immersion in the Old Testament.) Mother also spent time with him every evening after her work. At the time of Father's first "breakdown," she had learned to be a beautician and worked at this continually thereafter. Mother and son were also in the habit, during one period, of wrestling with each other. This is probably one more source of a fusion with Mother which will be described below.

Mudge, nevertheless, was severely trained to be good. In retrospect he feels that perhaps his religious education was no more than being strictly trained to be an obedient, good boy, and a good pupil. The crowning symbol of all this was that Mudge attended Sunday school religiously (if we may play on the word) for fifteen years with a perfect attendance record. The other crowning result of his rigid training was that at the end of his childhood, when Mudge was about six, he was literally a bundle of nervous tics, twitches, and ritualistic mannerisms. He was the object of teasing from his peers, and his father was actually embarrassed to be seen with him in public. Mother told him that sometimes Father and she felt like leaving him in an orphanage and starting over. These symptoms were relieved only in junior high school when, in his rural school, he started doing well as a student and excelled in that way. He also found a circle of friends among the younger boys, who were not yet interested in girls.

The "perfect" Sunday school record and the collection of tics and ritualisms represented the same dominant trend: Mudge felt he had to be perfect. The Sunday school record was a perfection of a sort. The tics and rituals were features of the mechanisms whereby those sexual and aggressive thoughts that were incompatible with the idea of absolute goodness and purity were warded off. He took a dislike to all his bodily functions. Impulse contradicted the demand for perfection and also indicated mortality and limitedness.

Mudge's involvement with fundamentalism came through a Baptist church in the area of the family summer home. Mudge was sent there to preserve his perfect Sunday school record. He found the group congenial. They were warm, highly moralistic, there was no talk of sex among the young people, and so on. The beliefs were also compatible with, but more involving than, those of the comfortable conservatism of the home town. Mudge's enthusiasm took root, and he went off to college convinced that he was a fundamentalist.

### 3. DOUBT AND THE PSYCHODYNAMICS OF AN IDENTITY CRISIS

In college Mudge experienced a period of devastating doubt similar to Pale's and for very similar reasons. He felt like "a man without a country." For a time he considered giving up Christianity. The belief system did not protect him from and in life. He had a difficult time finding a major. He did not do well in science, and he could not bear the competition of pre-medicine. Psychology and determinism were threats, and the students majoring in the field disturbed him. At length he came to rest in the department of religion. This was noncompetitive, the people in it were warm and friendly, and they were conventionally moralistic, that is, they did not, like some of his fraternity brothers, drink and have sex.

In his junior year, Mudge had an experience which had the effect of finally rooting him again in the Christianity his mother had taught him. He considered it a mystical experience, and for the next four or five years it was something he fell back on when there seemed to be no other justification for his faith. He was ill at the time, and he was reading one of the books of Martin Buber, the Jewish philosopher. He was asking himself whether he had to be a Christian. Why not just believe in God? He had been putting off going to the college infirmary, but he finally gave in to his illness and crept over there with a high fever, still contemplating this problem. As he lay in the darkness of the infirmary, his mind focused intently on his preoccupation and he had a vivid hypnagogic-like experience:

> I remember seeing this black coffin—casket, traditional shape, pine box, black—had sort of—had a picture of just black—sort of like the universe or something—sky— just deep black, and then somehow—I don't know how this could have been visible then—black casket, somehow became visible—out of black—and on the casket as it got closer, I could see there was a cross—a gold cross sort of on top, you know; the casket was tilted. First it looked like it was on its side—that it was just tilted toward me—as it came closer—I could see that it was a gold cross—just against the coal black, and as it passed by, the cross

> stood up—and it became sort of a burning gold—I wouldn't
> say a reddish gold, you know—just shown shined or
> shown and the casket kept going by—sort of blatant [*sic*]
> shining gold cross.

Mudge took this experience to mean that he was to follow the
way of the cross.

> I took this to mean for me—this was the way I follow,
> the way of the cross. And I had—about a year or two,
> I knew a rationale for my Christian faith—particularly this.
> I'd somehow been told that this was the way.

The experience had the integrating effect of an identity crisis.
Mudge was perfectly aware that the imagery was in his own
mind.

What are some of the meanings of this simple but powerful
imagery? If we consider the cross (with its striking power of erec-
tion and its "blatant" colors) as a phallic symbol and the box
as a female symbol, we will find justifications for doing so not
only in the classical psychoanalytic framework but in other of
Mudge's imagery as well. He is inclined to mingle sexual and
religious imagery, as, for example, in this description of prayer:

> Some nights aware of what I call God—a presence beyond
> myself. I'll overextend my own limits. A swelling feeling.
> Maybe like when holding a girl in arms—a good
> overwhelming feeling.

In the hypnagogic imagery, the cross is fused with, rises up
out of, and lies on (is dependent upon), the black coffin. This
suggestion of a fusion of the imagery of male and female sexual
organs has clear parallels in Mudge's Rorschach imagery, even
though the latter was produced several years after the religious
experience we are analyzing. The Rorschach imagery suggests
the following themes: the fusion and confusion at the level of the
body image of male and female sexual organs and functions; the
fantasy that he possesses both male and female organs and that
he can give birth to a baby (via the anus); and the fantasy that
the penis is shared with the mother. There is considerable preoccupation with and confusion about sexual organs and functions

on the Rorschach, and homosexual fantasies are suggested in it and in the TAT. We find, for example:

> The first thing . . . was a kitten . . . then a phallus or male penis . . . running straight on through the female sex organs at the other end. . . . A tank-armored tank with a cannon . . . (RVI)

The phallus is joined with the female sex organs "at the other end." The qualification of the phallus as "male" immediately raises the question of the possibility in Mudge's mind of one that is female. The confusion of the image is sustained when Mudge later finds ovaries in the shading at the base of the phallus, a position which one might expect to be occupied by the testes. The phrase "the other end," particularly on one undifferentiated body, as Mudge has left it, suggests the "rear end," the nonsocial rectal area.

The mingling of male and female organs and functions is also sustained in a more symbolic way in his description of the armored tank which contains some unusual perceptual manipulations:

> The tank—this first baby—when I just looked at this mass and was trying to figure this whole thing a tank—(RVI)

(Notice that the blot is left one undifferentiated mass; and note the use of the colloquialism, "baby.")

> . . . this whole thing a tank—but this is the gun, the firing mechanism, but then I split it, and then I had two tanks upside down—bottoms joined—with the general shape of a tank . . . and this minor gun—the top projection is a minor gun—and the main cannon—the main firing cannon—the two tanks would share one cannon and—that isn't very good. (RVI)

This may be somewhat difficult to follow for someone not familiar with the Rorschach card (see figure 1). Both tank images Mudge finds are relatively satisfactory percepts. The shift from one tank to two joined at the "bottoms" is striking. The word "bottom" and the phrases referring to minor guns and main

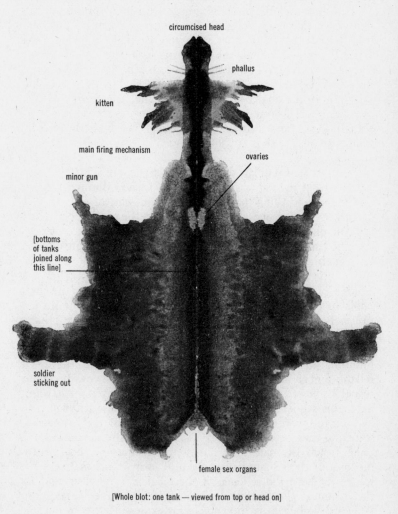

[Whole blot: one tank — viewed from top or head on]

[Two tanks — joined along bottoms and viewed from side]

cannons are all reminiscent of childish talk of the "bottom" and "number one" and "number two." The area of the card referred to as the "main cannon" is the same one perceived as the phallus. The resolution of the one tank image with its main cannon into two tanks sharing it suggests the fantasy of sharing the penis with the mother, "and that isn't very good." Mudge's feelings about the fate of the tanks is hardly dispassionate.

Mudge's description of the provocative incidents with Mother during the period of toilet training would lead us to expect libidinization of the anal zone. With this, the fusion with Mother at some level of body imagery, and the general confusion about sexual organs and functions pervading the body image, the fantasy of anal birth is not surprising:

> I must be Freudian today—my first thought was the
> lip—that the red was lipstick—that flashed through. And
> the second thing that flashed through—sort of a
> menstruation period—like this hole in the center being like
> the uh—oh, what's the hole—the hole in the spine where
> the baby's born through—which would leave the organs
> on either—[side] . . . (RII)

Mudge knows well enough that the vaginal opening is not a "hole in the spine." His description again obscures the distinction between male and female, and he suggests a "hole" that a male does possess. The idea of giving birth to a baby through that hole is explicit. The lipstick percept, positioned as it is surrounding an area of the card often seen as phallic, suggests a fellatio fantasy. In the TAT also there are expressions of homosexual feelings and fantasies. Coming as it does from a young man, this sequence of Rorschach imagery is most striking.

To return to the vivid religious imagery of the hypnagogic state, we may assume that it also symbolically condenses this same fusion of male and female body imagery through the medium of the religious symbolism. The maternal matrix is the source for both the salience of the religious symbolism and for the fusion at the level of body imagery with the female. The religious symbolism is the vehicle for expressing this fusion and also for the defense against it. As to the latter, we may consider another striking feature of Mudge's description of his religious experience. That is the repeated use of the word "black" and also the deathly connotations of the box coffin. Both suggest deep anxiety over personal and bodily intactness which may be assumed to derive from both the castrative upbringing and the wishes and fears attendant upon psychic fusion with the mother. Here is another instance of the masculine manifest content of the religious symbolism serving as a defense against its basic feminine source.

In Mudge's case the symbol of the cross seems to be a vehicle for preserving a sense of phallic intactness in the face of an otherwise overwhelming sense of being broken and scourged. His imagery in interviews and Rorschach is a clear illustration of the use of high ideals to preserve, at a fantasy level, a sense of phallic intactness.[2] Mudge occasionally gives expression to fantasies of phallic ascendancy like those of a little boy. An amusing example is a favorite analogy of his, that of comparing people with cars. Some people are like the family sedan: they are dependable, get where they are going, do not often break down, but they are not very fast. On the other hand, there are the racers. They can go very fast, are striking, and so on, but sometimes they break down, and then they do not go anywhere at all; then they need a good mechanic (to assuage their feelings, relieve depression, and so on). "I suppose I picture myself as one of the smaller racers." He has idealistic dreams of going fast and far.

## 4. CONDITIONS FOR LIBERALIZATION

We have described a psychic fusion with the mother and a family constellation bearing certain similarities to the cases of Pale and Electon. What are the differences which allowed Mudge to become more liberal in his beliefs? Pale struggles in this direction, but has not been able to find much emotional or theological relief in it, and Electon pursued just the opposite course. We have noted central factors already. Religion in the home was largely a vehicle for Mother's severe discipline and training. The church community of which Mudge was a part, while conservative, was lukewarm. However, there are more central psychological conditions and accompaniments to Mudge's liberalizing. He relinquished some of his conservative beliefs and became less totally dependent for a sense of well-being on religious belief and practice. These words suggest the central psychodynamic process in his liberalization: separation from the mother and giving up central psychological derivatives of the maternal matrix.

We may consider in more detail some aspects of this process and the conditions that allow it.

It is clear enough that Mudge has some distance on his moral and religious upbringing. In college, for example, he came to wonder if God were not simply a notion used for holding people in line. This question clearly reflects his own experience and training. He felt that perhaps his beliefs were a matter of his having been "brainwashed," another expression of the feeling that he had been vastly imposed upon to the extent of being broken in his early training. Also, he says that during his college period he hated his parents and particularly his mother. Psychological separation from the parents and an adult sense of independence require that a person be able to experience, to *feel*, the negative side of his ambivalence toward his parents, to whatever degree that is present. In the cases discussed previously, there was every indication that a negative feeling for the mother of considerable depth and strength was never allowed to see the light of day.

Part of Mudge's distance on his religious training consists in his awareness of the fact that to some degree it sprang from the tensions between the parents and also that it related to their personality characteristics, especially Mother's. He knew he was being trained to be good to make up for Father's being bad. He also knew that Mother's mother was an exceptionally cold, rigid, and compulsive person who was not able to give Mother very much love. The result was, Mudge felt, that Mother also was compelled to be overly strict, rigid, and scrupulously orderly and moralistic. Mudge attributes some of this also to the germanic, Pennsylvania Dutch, and Mennonite influence in the family background and the area in which he grew up.

Supporting these processes and Mudge's insights about them are psychologically deeper ones. The fusion with the mother that we have described is expressed in terms of body imagery deriving from anal and phallic stages of psychosexual development. There are two important implications of this. One is that this indicates a higher level of ego development than would be the case if the fusion were expressed in oral terms. Second, another result of the quality of interaction with the mother which resulted in this fusion is a great deal of body narcissism and narcissistic involvement with the self in general. To the degree that the system for the establishment and maintenance of self-esteem is not dependent upon projections involved in the concept of God, but is based upon the person himself, to that extent the person can be more easily independent of God. Mudge gives a considerable history of bodily preoccupation, from a long and elaborate concern with the bowels to an interest in body building. The preoccupation in the Rorschach with sexual and reproductive imagery is another indication of preoccupation with the body and an expression of body narcissism.

We find an interesting manifestation of this complex of trends in Mudge's long history of taking dietary supplements and laxatives. His mother had involved him in a way that for a long time allowed them both to continue sharing an interest in his eating and bowel habits. In recent years, with permission from the family physician, he rebelled and relinquished the pills and so on.

> That's what I needed—I wanted to for years—and I just
> needed assurance that I could do it if I wanted to, but
> then I talked to her. Funny she didn't want me to go to
> the doctor. She said, "Oh keep on taking these, they
> won't hurt you." I said, "Yeah—you'd feel a lot better
> if I gotta take 'em with you, wouldn't ya?"

Mudge hit the mark with that retort. He was telling his mother that he was no longer involved with her as he had once been, and he perceived and responded to her reluctance to let go of him in this respect.

We noted earlier that Mudge was able to relinquish a sense of guilt before God that had its existence only in the fantasy of personal perfection as something separate from social living. From this he went to a conception of personal growth. Certain things were good or bad for him because of their meanings to him and for his life, not because they were good or bad in terms of some absolute moral system. Now we noted in the case of Pale that a constant preoccupation with sin and guilt is actually a way of maintaining a sense of the self as exceptionally holy, special, and pure. Mudge was able to give up this source of self-esteem in some of its more exaggerated forms. Our hypothesis is that this was made possible by an underlying body narcissism and narcissistic involvement with the self. This made possible a more limited, realistic, and human morality and conception of personal growth.

A further factor enters that originates in some of the same experiences as those we have been discussing. Mudge, in spite of a considerable passivity and a strong need for a continual income of love, is also an extremely stubborn person. This manifested itself during his toilet training, as the incident we recounted indicates. In college and seminary he claimed he would never study. His basic stubbornness and rebelliousness were also something that allowed him to separate himself from the family matrix and establish an independent conception of things.

We may summarize as follows the basic psychological processes which are the conditions for the process of liberalization in the case of Mudge. The process of liberalization was attendant upon the process of psychological separation from his mother. This could occur because, although there was a psychological fusion with the mother, it is not expressed primarily in oral imagery. Ego development had proceeded far enough to sustain the experience of the negative side of ambivalence toward the mother. Further, in spite of a deep confusion at the level of body image, there is sufficient body narcissism to allow a narcissistic cathexis of the self. This is basis for a value system related to the idea of personal development, and it allows freedom from having to base the system for the establishment and maintenance of self-esteem upon a grandiosely conceived ego-ideal.

The impression should not be left that Mudge has made a clear and final shift from conservatism to liberalism. In the first place, he is not really one who is gifted in the intellectual expression of systematic theological ideas. His thinking is often muddled and seems to partake of fusions and confusions of the same sort that color his cognitive productions on the Rorschach. Second, his beliefs are really a mixture of the old and the new. While he at one moment gives expression to the most current liberal conceptions of God, he will in another moment express a traditional notion of immortality. His beliefs are in fact highly colored by wish fulfillment. He believes in immortality because he cannot conceive of his own death. He says that he finds this world too imperfect for it to be the final experience. There must be another chance to make right the imperfections, frustrations, and seemingly needless suffering that he has experienced. His beliefs in fact sometimes precisely parallel Freud's description in *The Future of an Illusion* of those burdens and seemingly unnecessary injustices of life that religion is supposed to correct. His productions on the TAT are pervasively characterized by wish-fulfilling fantasies very much like daydreams.

It is also interesting to note in this connection that in spite of having made a certain use of psychological ideas, Mudge, like Electon and others, holds Christianity and psychology in opposition. To him, psychology means that a person is trapped by his past; he is left with all the problems for which he resents his parents and upbringing. Determinism, which Mudge equates with psychology, also means that he may become something bad —in Mudge's case, a roué, like his father supposedly was. Christianity, on the other hand, means that one may change "overnight."

> To me—one of the greatest things, I think, in the Christian Gospel, for me—and you can see why—is . . . it says to me that I can change and become anything I want overnight. You know, it's the opposite of determinism. Just become a new person. Saying that you're not a slave to the past. One of the greatest things is that there is a power beyond yourself. If it were just me and the world, I would really be trapped. I would not feel I could do anything. But being able to believe in a reality, a power, more than myself, who if I will let it, will pick me up and carry me beyond—pick me up and put me down over here way beyond what I could be.

The belief system is a magical way to change in which one does not have to assume awareness of and responsibility for the factors in one's background which determine the quality of one's life. It expresses a deep passivity ("pick me up and carry me . . .") and relieves what would otherwise be a sense of helplessness and hopelessness.

# IX

# Ambivalent Faith

As if the world had not enough problems, we are confronted
with the task of finding out how those who have faith
in a Divine Being could have acquired it, and whence this
belief derives the enormous power that enables it to
overwhelm Reason and Science.

SIGMUND FREUD, MOSES AND MONOTHEISM

In this chapter, two cases, Joel and Briting, will be discussed.
The faith of both is characterized by a marked ambivalence. In
both individuals an alternative, competing belief system is maintained in more or less constant conscious opposition to the religious belief system or some basic feature of it. The competing
belief system is an expression of depression over the possibility
of the meaninglessness of the world and life. The meaninglessness, despair, and loss of hope compete as a viable alternative
to the hopefulness and meaning of faith. Barth's dark sayings
apply precisely to these two:

> Swaying and staggering, life in uncertainty and
> embarrassment about our very relationship to God's work
> and word—this corresponds all too closely to the
> ambivalence in which we here and now totally exist.
> (Barth, 1963, p. 125)

> . . . doubt does not mean denial or negation. Doubt
> only means swaying and staggering between Yes and No.

It is only an uncertainty, although such uncertainty can
be worse than negation itself. (Ibid., pp. 123–124)

Similarly, the cry that has followed the believer through the ages,
"My Lord, I believe, help Thou mine unbelief," might well be
heard from Joel and Briting.

Joel and Briting both have a deep faith and a deep commitment. Joel is considered the doubter not because he has more
doubt than Briting, but because the doubt he has occurs within
the context of a belief system which leaves less room for any
kind of doubt. His doubt is therefore more threatening to him.
The doubt, in both their cases, is experienced as intrusive and
external, as "ego-dystonic." It is experienced as alien, unwelcome,
and threatening, as something to master, control, and surmount
through greater faith. Nevertheless it is a constant companion
to their thought and feeling. It is in fact more in line with the
realities of their character structure to say that the religious belief
system contains and symbolizes a conflict by giving simultaneous
conscious, symbolic expression to two opposing, basic attitudes
toward God, the world, the self, and life. For example, life is
empty and meaningless, "a giant burying ground," as Briting
says, or on the other hand, it is out of this very apparent meaninglessness that ultimate and absolute meaning can be wrought
along with hope for everlasting life. Or, as Joel expresses it, either
his own experience gives him immediate irrefutable knowledge
of the presence of God, or, on the contrary, we are all haunted
by the "gray specter of skepticism" which demonstrates that we
have no certainty about anything whatsoever.

Ambivalent belief systems such as these represent a distinctive way of handling deep-lying ambivalences. Defensive mechanisms allow for the compartmentalization of affect or ideas such
that both sides of deep ambivalences can retain some form of
conscious symbolic expression and attain meaningfulness in the
life of the person. One typical way of managing this is to assign
different meanings to feeling and to thought. Joel, for example,
denigrates the meaningfulness of his merely intellectual doubts,
and assigns to feeling and immediate experience the capacity to
reveal ultimate reality. "The heart has its reasons the mind knows
not of," he writes on his questionnaire. In other cases, the actual
converse of this mechanism may hold, and the individual may
refuse the evidence of his own feelings while asserting the valid-

ity of a belief in God that is supposedly arrived at by purely
intellectual means (cf. the case of Strindge, chapter XII). Which-
ever of these mechanisms, along with supporting ego defenses, is
involved, it is only one facet of a life-style whose complexities are
partly determined by the tension of the ambivalent belief system.

## 1. *JOEL*[1]

Joel is thirty-two, married, and has children. Currently he is
attending graduate school and specializing in New Testament
studies. He is a highly intelligent man and stubbornly individu-
alistic in some of the particulars of his beliefs, especially ones pertaining to the church. A deep piety is revealed in his sense of the
constant presence of God in his life and in his relationship with
God. That relationship is so pervasive and personal that no detail
of his life is too small to exclude it.

> That is my life—I'm constantly in touch with God.
> And I talk to God all the time. Thinking and thought
> and every moment I have it [devotional] twenty-four
> hours [a day] in a broad sense. That is, the whole of my
> life is pervaded by a sense of the presence of God in
> everything that I do. People would think I'm nutty if they
> knew what I—I might ask the Lord where I left my
> pencil I'd forgotten. I would. I've done it.

Joel's belief system is characterized by the presence of clearly
defined beliefs which stand in tense opposition to each other.

> Well, I think that it's true—that I am not conscious of
> any deeper problem than the tenion that exists between
> these two points: one, the work that is demanded of me
> as a scientific historiographer in dealing with scripture.
> Two, my faith as a Christian—which, heretofore, at least,
> has been based on assumptions which now are questioned
> by methods of scientific historiography. And this raises
> a problem—leaves me doubting my own integrity . . .
> I ask myself am I really being honestly one or the other
> of these things? Am I really being an honest historian,
> if I cling to this faith? Or secondly, if I really cling to this
> faith, how can I have anything to do with the history?

Faith must have an absolute quality for Joel. The boundaries to the belief system must be clearly and rigidly marked, and there is no room for a compromise or even an intellectual amalgamation of the two positions which could result in a new belief system carrying with it a sense of wholeness and integrity. As it is, Joel feels torn and has to question his integrity. This quality of the belief system relates to an extremely rigid defensive system, and both reflect a long-standing battle for control of impulse. Consciously, this arose first for Joel in adolescence when his sexual impulses, which he felt contrary to all his Christian upbringing, nearly drove him to distraction, and he struggled to give up masturbation. That he was actually totally successful at this as the upshot of a profound religious experience when he was nineteen, gives an indication of the amount of energy that goes into control of instinct and defense generally. The price for such control is high, however. Affects seem strangulated and strange in his life, and there is a sharp quality about him, as if something were going to irrupt. The control of affect and impulse is such a pervasive feature of his character that it is one of the central themes of his intellectual and theological work. The control of emotion and "the spirit within us" is a theme that runs through several of his academic papers, which I read, covering nearly a ten-year span.

In the remarks just quoted, Joel says that "my faith . . . has been based on assumptions which now are questioned." From this and other similar comments, one would gather that Joel is undergoing a radical questioning of his whole faith. His explicit statement, however, particularly when this possibility is raised specifically, is that he does not have doubts about God, the heart of his faith:

> The notion of God, the reality of God in my experience,
> is such a deep-running fundamental keel to my whole
> being and life that I, I don't know that I've ever—I don't
> know that if I tried I can imagine, could imagine myself
> to live without—if I consciously said: Go to, now, I shall
> now be atheistic—in other words, that has never been
> to me an appealing option.

A Hamlet-like tentativeness seems to invade these comments, for some reason, and to weaken a potentially active, forceful expression of what Joel believes about ultimate reality. Although in other expressions of his faith, this tentativeness is entirely lacking, it is characteristic of Joel that it does always seem to hover in the background. Juxtaposed as it is in these comments against the core of his faith in God, his tentativeness serves to introduce another major theme of his belief system, skepticism.

Joel insists that the core of his belief system, the personally experienced relationship with God, remains untouched by doubts or tentativeness. The observer, however, often has the impression that doubt and skepticism do sometimes impinge upon and threaten this core. Joel is perfectly explicit, however, about experiencing a great deal of doubt and uncertainty in the sphere of intellectual formulations of theology, Biblical criticism, and other beliefs that surround this core. (Some aspects of this sphere have to do with the institutions of his denominational church, of which he is critical. This will be discussed below.) It is all too easy, for example, for him to envision attacks on his current stance coming from both sides of his conflict.

> I envision an opponent who could—who, if the issue were
> raised could say—well, two opponents, for that matter,
> one from either side. A Biblical critic could say to me,
> "Now look here, if you're going to hang on to a doctrine
> of inspired scripture some way, you can't really be a
> Biblical critic." And on the other hand, someone from
> my denomination could say, "If you make any concession
> to these Biblical critics, you can't really be a believer."

In this manner, any explicitly formulated, intellectual position can be utterly vitiated, leaving him with no position at all. Even the idea of a total renunciation of the supernatural components of his belief system could be vitiated. To renounce supernaturalism would mean to accept atheism and "naturalism," that is, some alternative, specific intellectual position. The thought of accepting such a position is not as disturbing to Joel as the intimation that it might be intellectually impossible for him to accept any position whatsoever.

> What is [a] far more devastating option than naturalism
> —is skepticism. In other words it would appear to me
> that the naturalist knows too much. I'd say to him: Man,

how can *you* make statements like that? How can *you*
be so sure about all these things? And the gray specter
that haunts me—is not naturalism but skepticism and that
is, How can anybody be certain about anything?
And the more so when you get into—to find the professors
disagreeing—the people who ought to know most about
what they're dealing with sometimes reach opposite
conclusions. The thing that threatens me is—maybe all
this isn't—there isn't anything to it all after all. That's
the specter. Not atheism—skepticism. I'd heard about
skepticism. But in the last few years . . . I have now
given myself time and now I know by experience what
skepticism is. And I'd like to be sure about certain things.
I would even like to have the certainty my friends have
about their theories on New Testament criticism. How
they can be so sure?

This is certainly—in Barth's words—a "swaying and staggering
between Yes and No . . . an uncertainty . . . worse than negation itself." And it is just in relation to Joel's wish "to be sure
about certain things" that the possibility that any positive stance
whatever can be called into question leaving one with nothing
evokes a haunting gray specter.

The final feature of Joel's belief system to be presented is
that aspect which protects it and him in this vulnerable position.
Although at the same time it protects, it also preserves the
specter and makes more difficult the evolving of a belief system
that would encompass old conflicts and ease the tensions. The
opposition between "the Biblical critic" and "the evangelical
believer" is resolved at the intellectual level by deciding "that
these are two kinds of knowledge."

Scientific history, like any scientific knowledge,
is tentative always. It's incapable of being anything
but tentative. Because it is achieved by evidence
and one never knows what new evidence may arise and
demand modification. On the other hand [in contrast to
scientific certainty] is [the] faith kind of certainty. In
religious faith there is a kind of immediacy in my
religious knowledge of God. There's an immediacy
—there is anything, in a sense, but tentativeness. . . .

Immediate certainty. In other words, it seems to me
that faith, to me, cannot, for its validity be subject to all
the variations and the tentativeness that this scientific
method demands of scripture.

By this device, the core of Joel's faith is insulated and protected from the doubts and uncertainties that arise from both
internal and external sources. It is an intellectualization and an
institutionalization of inner psychological processes whereby
certain affective experiences are separated from other cognitive
functions and the sense of reality that accompanies the affects is
accepted as valid. This "sense of reality" consists in the certitude that the emotional religious experiences and the experience
of the relationship with God are exactly, and in reality, what
Joel *calls* them.

Referring to this realm of experience, Joel uses expressions
such as, "at the heart of my life," "what is most real to me," "the
realm of the soul," and "the deep inner life." In psychological
terms, Joel is indeed describing the realm of the soul, the deep
inner, personal life of the individual. The sense of the relationship with God renews and reaffirms a basic sense of self, reality,
and self-worth. For Joel, in the moments when the sense of the
relationship with God is heightened, so is the sense of self.

I want to indicate that this is not a disappearance
of the self—doesn't involve cancellation of one's personal
existence, but it does involve a heightening, shall we say,
of one's awareness of the reality of God.

Some further idea of what God and the relationship with Him
means to Joel is contained in more of his description of the
moments when the God relationship is heightened:

For me, the biggest thing is—the ability to realize that
here's really something that counts. Here's reality.
Here's what's important. Here's something that's
inaccessible—to the scientific method, and therefore, not
in peril by tentativity. Here's reality. In the sphere of
personal existence it's dominantly [an] experience of joy—
not an experience of sorrow—not sadness. I don't know
how else to explain it.

The phrase "inaccessible to . . . scientific method" is a reflection of the insulation of this aspect of his experience from other experiences that might imperil it.

The quality of the relationship with God and "the deep inner life" indicates its roots lie in the early development of the sense of self and that it is a preservation and expression of these early experiences with the parents, particularly the mother. It is a reaffirmation that there is, in himself and his life, *some* source, *something*, that is valuable, real, true, and continuous (not tentative). These global, abstract words refer to a basic psychological experience, a nonverbal "sense" of the existence, value, reality, and continuity of the self. It is no accident, then, that Joel insists, and he does insist, that he does not lose his sense of individuality in these mystical experiences, that, on the contrary, they reaffirm his sense of self and individuality.

At the core of Joel's belief system is the experienced relationship with God. Surrounding this core are intellectual and institutional commitments which throw him into critical and intense conflicts. He has managed to protect the core, but it sometimes seems endangered. What are some of the further psychological meanings of this strikingly structured belief system, and how did it develop?

A fact worth noting at this point, and one to which we shall return, is that the description of the belief system, as we have developed it so far, has a striking parallel to the one early dream that Joel recalls.

The dream I remember as a kid—I don't know, have no
idea when this was—was being chased by some serpent of
some kind and got into the house and thought this
was all safety and I went out to look out the window
and all I could see was this big body—it had circled the
whole house. Was so large . . . saw the body of the
serpent around the house. Coiled all around the house.
But by that time he'd become so big that—that just.
one part of his body was big enough to shut the window—
I mean to embrace the whole window.

This dream did not occur repetitively, but Joel says that even up to the present time he can count on one dream a year that has to do with snakes. The parallel with the belief system, as I would draw it, consists in the fact that in the dream, too, an inner realm of safety and security is surrounded by dire threat. Joel relates the snake to the idea of the devil, Satan—that is, all that conflicts with what he values and holds most dear. The dream symbolism suggests, and evidence presented below supports, an oedipal interpretation of the dream. The great phallic Father is threatening Joel's sole "occupancy" of a safe retreat in the form of his relationship with Mother.

Further, the psychological meaning of God as the basis for reality, value, meaning, and continuity stands in emotional opposition to *the meaning of skepticism*, which implies the lack, or the threat of the lack, of all these. Joel's basic conflict is, in fact, this inner emotional one: the struggle to hold on to a basic sense of the self, its existence, value, reality, and continuity. The expression of a conflict between two intellectual positions such as that of the evangelical believer and the Biblical critic is a way of externalizing certain aspects of this conflict.

The quest for a sense of reality, value, and continuity arose consciously for Joel in late adolescence, and the turmoil of this period was expressed in just these terms (in addition to the struggle with sexuality).

> In the teen years, my question was: What counts in life? What's real? What can you depend on? What's worth the most? What is the highest value? This is the kind of question I was asking. And the thing that really, really— was after me is, What is it that really counts? How can I best make use of the life that's been given me? I just knew that I needed to get hold of reality.

There are actually two levels of emotional problems presented in these remarks. One has to do with the effort to reaffirm the basic sense of the reality, value, and continuity of the self. The other has to do with the questions that many serious adolescents ask having to do with resolving sexual identity, finding a vocation— the questions of identity in general.

The seeds of the solution to the turmoil of his teens and indications for a calling and a course in life arose out of the profound religious experience Joel had when he was nineteen. Some weeks before this, he had torn himself from home and wandered, hitchhiking across the country. Following an evangelical service one evening in Los Angeles, he was moved to tearful prayer and repentance, and he felt a new dedication and commitment to his Lord. He also felt that at least rough indications for his vocation were given by this commitment.

In describing the tears of this experience, Joel points out that he had not cried since, as a boy, he had been whipped by his father. The tears of this experience of submission to God reminded him of the tears he had shed when his father whipped him for boyhood transgressions. I wish to relate the embattled, ambivalent quality of the sphere of Joel's belief system that surrounds its inner core to the nature of the relationship and identification with his father. I will summarize the observations upon which this conclusion is based.

In Joel's family, it was the father who was the religious one and who represented and passed on to Joel his particular form of traditional conservative Protestantism. Now Joel's only sibling was born when he was two and a half. Many of his early memories are about this event and the early relationship with his brother. It was obviously a turning point in his life. The evidence suggests that it precipitated a displacement as the mother's only child and an identification with the father as aggressor. This latter left Joel with a deep sense of inferiority as well as a deep ambivalence to Father and, as a result, to his father's tradition. This was expressed in his adolescent questioning of the tradition, and it was resolved at that time in the same manner as it had been earlier: submission and identification, that is, commitment to the Lord. Some of the many ways in which this ambivalence to the tradition is still manifested in Joel's belief system will be mentioned below. However, the most significant psychological effect of these developments is the following.

The deepest psychological meaning to Joel of God and the God relationship lies in the preservation and expression of the basic sense of reality, value, and continuity of the self as these affective organizations are aroused in the earliest parental relationships, particularly with the mother. In fact, however, Joel derived the *idea* of God and the particular cultural tradition in which this idea is embedded from his father, so that these are bound also to bear the mark of vicissitudes of the relationship and identification with the father. The vehicle for the preservation and expression of the sense of basic trust, then, becomes the acceptance of the father's tradition and the identification with the father. To the extent that this "vehicle" is fragile and marked by an embattled ambivalence, the core belief in God will also stand endangered, although at the same time it will be that part of the belief system which Joel can affirm is not touched by doubt or uncertainty. Thus it is that Joel's belief system is metaphorically similar to his early dream: an inner core of safety and security is surrounded by a threatening monster.

Joel is, in fact, highly critical of his particular denomination, and he always has been. With an apt psychological preciseness he says, "I define my attitude toward my foundation in the words 'critical loyalty.'" The word "foundation" reflects the depth of the attitude he is describing, that is, his masculine identification with his father and his father's tradition. He did not use the word "church" or "denomination." The words "critical" and "loyal" both apply: Joel is as loyal as he is critical. He believes that it is his mission to carry out reforms of certain sorts within the denomination. He is, however, endangering himself denominationally at this point in his career by going to a graduate school where he studies the Bible from an historiographic point of view. This conflicts with the fundamentalist assumption of the inspiration of the scriptures. On the other hand, by equipping himself with modern scholarship and scholarly techniques, he arms himself for his battle within the denomination. Joel thus stands in potential conflict with his own church.

On the other hand, he feels he stands in potential conflict in his current academic surroundings, because he cannot entirely accept the historiographic approach to the Bible or the liberal theology of his teachers and some of his colleagues.

> I think this is a kind of silent, submerged, personal
> tension. When I came, I expected that there would perhaps
> be open theological combat. You are a conservative,
> we are liberals—kind of thing.

Further, in going to graduate school, he is consciously challenging himself. Disliking explicit disagreements of any sort, he nevertheless had one with a fellow minister before starting graduate school:

> He said, "You wouldn't last," or "You wouldn't stand
> true to the faith," or something like that. I said,

"If my faith can't stand to be examined, I don't want
it." He has preserved his faith by ignoring the difficulties
it raises. I have not chosen to do that. I felt, all right,
I'll bring it out into the open. And this is sort of the
attitude that I came [to graduate school] with. And
came ready to face anything that I could face, and that's
what I'm doing. And I must say at this particular time—
right now, are very very critical issues. And I've never
felt—more critical—to use the right word, of my particular
church. And they've been very very critical days for me.

Again, in these comments, one is strongly impressed that it is his
total faith that is being threatened, not simply some particulars
of the denominational statement of faith, as important as these
may be to Joel. To repeat my interpretation of what is happening
here: the criticism of his tradition that Joel is expressing in these
remarks is an intellectual displacement of the ambivalent feelings
for the father. He sounds as if he feels his whole faith is in danger, and I assume that it really does feel that way to him, that
the issues do feel that "critical." This is so because the symbolic
expressions he is critical toward are also the very ones which
carry the deepest realities that he wishes to affirm. The different
levels of meaning are so closely linked that a dire threat to the
more peripheral level feels as if all were in danger of being
destroyed.

There are, then, pervasive characterological effects of the
distinctive quality of the identification with the father. Joel seems
to stand embattled on all sides. His deep involvement in his
father's tradition is scarred by intellectual and institutional conflicts. Often actually challenging himself and his church, what he
experiences is being threatened, as if, on all sides, there were
powerful forces challenging *him*. The threat is perceived as originating in the very institutional forms of which he himself is so
critical. In addition, he feels the more general and pervasive
threat of the modern, scientific, objective, liberal world, of which
he has chosen to become more a part than in the past. In
contrast with this world, and by virtue of his estimate of his background and his identification with the early, first-century Christians, he feels like a hillbilly. He characterizes these early Christians as, "these ignorant Galileans . . . the Kentucky of the
Holy Land [Galilee] . . . the back woods—where the hillbillies

come from." Perceiving "Kentucky hillbilly hats" on the first Rorschach card indicates that these comments reveal a deeper feeling about himself than if he were simply giving a colorful characterization of a group for which he feels a certain fondness. In the face of it all, he feels weak and unable to defend himself. He derides his high intelligence, referring to himself as "an academic cripple" because of his estimate of his undergraduate schooling, and he says, sadly, "In terms of personal problems I have ability to see certain problems but not enough ability to adequately solve them." Much of all this was projected into the interview situation. He chose to express his feelings about this directly by describing them as his response to the blank TAT card:

> The interviewee [that is Joel himself—he refers to us both in the third person here] for reasons not known to himself—occasionally seems to feel—threatened by psychological investigation—as if maybe he would be told —as if maybe he would be provided with a mechanistic explanation for religious faith. So the end of the story is—interviewer becomes a successful renowned clinician, and the interviewee continues to have his existence threatened.

It may be noted that in terms of life-style, Joel's brother went in the apparently opposite direction from Joel, rebelling violently against the parental tradition. Joel uses the family storms and tensions that center around the brother as a primary mode of describing and explaining the family. In talking about his brother and the brother's tempestuous relationship with the parents, Joel seems to be describing his own "shadow personality" (Jung, 1951).

These qualities of Joel's life—feeling embattled, threatened, inferior—all fit the characterological pattern that would emerge from an identification with a father who was seen as a threat, the great snake of the early dream, an "aggressor," about whom Joel had markedly ambivalent feelings. The ambivalences, and the challenges and threats, become expressed in feelings about and reactions toward various aspects of the tradition Joel learned from his father. At the same time, the very symbol system which contains these conflicts and oppositions is the one which serves as the vehicle for a basic core faith in God. The relationship with God preserves and expresses the basic sense of the reality, value, and continuity of the self. These are affective organizations which would have arisen in the maternal relationship prior to the birth of Joel's brother. This organization had to be reorganized and subordinated to the identification with the father. If this is correct, then both developmentally and through the inherent logic of the symbol system, the core belief in God is closely related to an acceptance of the tradition as a whole. Conflict within the symbol system at any critical point would have the result of threatening the core. So it is that, although Joel always says explicitly that doubts do not impinge on the God relationship, a discussion of other central conflicts is overlaid with the tone of total threat, as if everything might be swept away. Hovering in the background is the sense that the heart of his life is endangered, a feeling that Joel inevitably conveys to the observer, but which he can with equal truthfulness deny when it is raised explicitly. The "gray specter of skepticism" represents the feeling of this impending vacuum—in which there is no unquestionable, untentative source of reality, value, and continuity.

The deepest source of the threat to Joel's existence remains the threat of the loss of a basic sense of the self, as this is expressed in the God relationship. In the case of Briting, to be discussed next, the polar oppositions that exist within the belief system are a more direct expression of this basic struggle. In Joel's case, this level of conflict is obscured by a complex of conflicts expressed in intellectual and institutional forms. It is possible that for Joel also these latter conflicts serve to mask the anxiety stemming from the more basic conflict which might have independent sources other than the one we have described.

## 2. BRITING

Briting considers himself a Barthian, and the superstructure of his theology does follow Barth in a rough way. He believes in the Bible as the Word of God, but not in a literalistic way, and he believes in the Resurrection of Christ and the Second Coming, but again not in a simple literal way. While his theology is basically conservative, he does not consider himself a fundamentalist. His religious belief system is not loaded down with the gamut of moral structures that is characteristic of most American fundamentalism.

The central and repeated theme of Briting's theology is his perception of the meaninglessness of life counterpointed by the antidote to this, the meaning that arises when "God comes into relationship in the Christ event." The meaninglessness of "life as it is" and the fullness of meaning *if* the Christ event is real are the two alternative views of reality which are contained within Briting's religious belief system. "Meaninglessness" for Briting is quickly seen to be based upon a sense of deprivation of oral supplies—nurturance, human contact, acceptance, support and protection for the self. The emptiness and lack of supplies that underlie his sense of meaninglessness are most graphically expressed in his response to card 16 of the TAT (the card empty of a picture):

> A man standing in a vast desert—in the middle of the
> desert—alone—complete solitude—complete quietness—
> complete nothingness—nothing but sand as far as you
> can see in every direction—and he's standing there by
> himself—there're no mountains—there're no mirages—
> just sand. . . . I make this symbolic of man—of myself
> —faced with the reality of—of his own existence—
> of the loneliness—of the stupidity of walking in any
> direction because there's no place to go except more sand
> —and faced with the decision whether to walk or not—
> sitting down and dying or to walk in the hopes of someday
> reaching the edge of the sand or a spring or—water
> . . . (T16)

The religious belief system, then, can be conceptualized as an antidote to oral deprivation. Briting, however, is a believer, and although he says that faith is "a journey of doubt," he is not living in anxiety in this doubt nor in the continuing sense of crisis that would arise from being constantly in the process of choosing the meaning of the "Christ event" over the meaninglessness of "life as it is." These themes of the belief system must therefore be put into context.

Briting's theology, as he presents it, does have a dramatic quality of crisis and immediacy. He says that his belief is based on "a leap of faith," and that out of his perception of the meaninglessness of life arises his need to "cling on to something," and "draw meaning from somewhere."

> Faith to me is—is only a journey of doubt. It's
> a leap. At a certain point I said I've got to hold on—I've
> got to cling on to something. And to me that thing was
> God. And from this first decision to do this, which is an
> act of the will—an act of the will just to say I have to
> accept something—I have to start somewhere . . .
> A man, to me, if he looks at existence, if he looks at life
> as it is, is impressed with its meaninglessness—at every
> turn, everywhere—it's pretty futile business. He has to
> draw his meaning from somewhere. Life is without
> meaning to me, if I look at life as it is. But this all changes,
> to me, if God comes into relationship—in the Christ
> event. And I draw all of my meaning from this Christ
> event, always saying *if* God did, then there *is* meaning,
> there's something *if* God did this in the Christ event.
> And the leap of faith is—just saying I think he did,
> and moving from that assumption, always knowing that
> it's just an "if.". . . The world, if we're honest about it,
> is only a giant burial ground. When you look at it
> honestly, what else is there left to say?

His primary task as a minister, as he sees it, is to draw people's attention to the meaninglessness, to "look at life as it is," and to proclaim the Christ event as the source of meaning and hope.

Briting's repeated use of the phrase "life as it is" raises the question as to what he understands by it. What is it about life that makes it appear to him so empty? Briting is twenty-four, married, and has a baby daughter. He points out that R, the baby, has not yet experienced the meaninglessness. He considers her life to embody all that is the antithesis of the meaninglessness of "life as it is." Specifically, as he describes it, the baby is shielded from "real life," fed, loved, made secure. She knows her parents will not leave her, she is not exposed to hostilities within the family walls. She is allowed to believe in wish-fulfilling fantasies such as Santa Claus and to have comforting stuffed toys. She is accepted and loved without having to prove herself. That is, the baby has a full complement of oral supplies. She is nurtured and protected within the family. "Life as it is," then, is being exposed to the possibility of deprivation of some or all of these supplies. In "life as it is" one has to prove oneself, meet demands, find one's own supplies, deal with fears of abandonment, and so on. For a child, "his problems don't extend beyond having an all-day sucker."

Another quality of Briting's interpersonal functioning, including his aims within his church, also speaks to the issue of oral dependence. Briting finds certain kinds of interpersonal demands and responsibilities very anxiety-provoking, and he has a tendency to avoid a task orientation with another person. The Rorschach protocol is filled with side remarks which take him away from the task, for example. He finds counseling the members of his parish a difficult responsibility and one he would rather not have. His aim is to go into evangelical work. This would be "a hit-and-run proposition." He could come on the scene, preach, proclaim the gospel, and then leave. Preaching, he says, "is kind of like the center of my life." The one dream he reported was an anxiety dream relating to his fears about preaching. "I never get into the pulpit that I'm not shaking all over. It scares me."

The centrality for him of preaching relates to an identity image having an oral basis. We may label this image "the Broadcaster." Briting earned his living through college as a radio announcer, and he has a rich, pleasant voice with a slight Southern accent. Before his broadcasting days he had given magic shows for children and led a dance band.

Briting's early family experience both sensitized him to and protected him from fears of deprivation and abandonment. Within a highly conflictful family situation he was able, with the parents' help, to remain fairly protected. Thus while deprivation and abandonment were always possible, they were kept at a remove from him, and he was able to take away from his early experience some inner equanimity. However, the security must have been basically tenuous, because to maintain it, Briting had to cling to the idea of the family as a haven of protection, a sanctuary from "real life." His experience of his early family life is still very much with him, and his own early marriage at twenty seems to be a relatively successful effort to re-create another, even safer, haven.

What is particularly noteworthy is that in talking about his early life, Briting gives no indication of an infantile neurosis. He does describe an intensely conflictful complementarity between the parents, however, from which they both made efforts to protect him and his brother, four years younger. It is as if the conflicts remained external to him, and he did not have to internalize them. Thus a great deal of conflictful material is not apparent in the projective tests, even around issues of orality or dependency. However, the projective materials do reveal the immediacy to him of family issues. By remaining a member of his family, he has saved himself the work of internalizing a number of conflicts and working out them and his independence.

In explaining his entry into the ministry, he immediately introduces the family complex:

> I have a—my family—I have a father who is an alcoholic,
> the mother who is quite religious—not fanatically so, but
> quite religious. And I guess being brought up in this
> context—and my mother, I imagine, is the predominant
> character in the family, I would think. Dad is gone a
> lot [drinking and on benders]. I imagine that this played
> a part in it. I would hope that this wasn't all.

This summary of the family background is introduced almost as a keystone to his identity and to the reasons why he went into the ministry. Needless to say, it does not carry its own explanation as clearly as Briting seems to indicate it might. The identification with the mother, viewed as the predominant parent, and her religiosity is indicated. A degradation of the father in the eyes of the son is implied, and is in fact present within the family, but this also was muted by the efforts of the mother not to run down the father in the eyes of his sons. The resulting confusion in sexual identity is nevertheless also present in Briting.

The question still remains why these circumstances led Briting into the ministry. Briting often uses the phrase "shattering" to indicate the most traumatic event that a person could experience. And, in fact, his early family life was constantly threatened with being shattered. The parents were locked into an embattled complementarity. Father, with deep feelings of inferiority, drank heavily and compulsively, did some running around and once or twice got the family into financial troubles through gambling. Although "mean as a snake" to Mother when drunk, he was vulnerably guilty when sober. Mother was puritanical, prudish, moralistic, taking the role of "suffering servant—a vocal one—but a suffering servant." Mother was able to play on Father's guilt, feeding into his conflicts in this way, and Father provided someone with whom Mother could live out the moralistic, martyred role. She assumed that she was "lily white," and that it was Father who brought trouble and conflict into the family.

> She's been able to say, "I stuck with him—even in the
> midst of all this he was doing." This'll probably become
> a real major thing in her life. And she's lived—she's
> lived for us—for the kids. And she's always felt like
> she's doing the right thing and he was doing the
> wrong . . .

Briting has some distance on this syndrome. He is able to see his mother's contribution to the parental neurotic complementarity.

> She can be piercing and really drive somebody. If you
> have an ego at all, she can just kill it, and—my
> father—by pushing him down and lowering the things
> he's trying to do—I'm sure this played a part in it.

Father was away from home a great deal. When he came home at night after drinking, there would be loud fighting and Briting and his younger brother and only sibling would huddle together for security. Father would threaten Mother with physical violence, and Mother would threaten to leave home. The family structure was thus constantly threatened with being shattered. The importance of religion in the family was heightened by virtue of its being "a stabilizing force" through the mother who was also "the stable one." Briting says, "At times it was the only thing in the family."

In spite of the parental conflict, Briting says that both his parents loved him. They apparently made consistent, strong efforts to protect him from their hates and angers and not to draw him into the middle of their battle. Discipline was firm, but he was allowed considerable freedom. All in all he speaks with a great deal of appreciation of his parents, understanding their problems, feeling he was given a great deal of love and security. He is grateful for their efforts to make a secure home in spite of their problems.

One would expect a fear of abandonment and loss of family security to arise, at least to some degree, within such a family structure. It can be assumed that such a fear does contribute to the sense of meaninglessness of real life that underlies Briting's theology. The degree of protection that Briting did receive from such fears within the family accounts for its muted quality and for the fact that the meaninglessness of life that stands in contradiction to the fullness of meaning of the Christ event has not become so overwhelming as to encroach upon the belief.

Characteristically, Briting expresses his feelings about abandonment most clearly when he talks about another person. Father's mother died when Father was a small boy, and a trip to the grave with Father is the most poignant childhood memory that Briting reported.

> I can remember one time—we went out there one day
> and had to walk up a long rutty road. We couldn't even
> drive the car up to the graveyard where his mother was
> buried. And my Dad very rarely cries. And I felt that—oh,
> I felt so—felt so bad that day for him. It was when he was
> young because he talks . . . I remember that being I
> guess one of the saddest things in—that I can remember
> ever happening to me is—him standing there—the
> graveyard was dilapidated—desolate lonely kind of a
> place and him standing there looking at the grave of
> his mother—boy it was sad.

This memory must provide substance to his feeling that, "The world . . . is only a giant burial ground."

Along with fear of abandonment, it might also be expected that a child in Briting's family might come to feel guilt arising from the assumption that the family turmoil was his responsibility. Briting says that he never felt this way, that this also was something from which the parents protected him. This fantasy does arise, however, in the TAT:

> [A doctor is using hypnosis with the boy on the couch who has psychological problems. The hypnosis will bring out "something that is hidden, that the boy can't bring out himself, that's too hurtful to talk about."]
> PH: What might it be?
> Briting: Maybe this boy has blocked out a part in his life. That he has guilt feelings about something he feels he's responsible for—the doctor—you want me to be more specific on that? He feels responsible perhaps for uh—uh—for a breakup in the family or a—in my own case this would—this works in—breakup in the family. . . . The fellow wants to pass over them . . .

The issues of abandonment, deprivation, and guilt in Briting's life which we have been discussing can be seen woven into his theology and the meanings for him of the ministerial role. However, the relationship between the family complex and its effects on Briting and his theology and the ministerial role can be spelled out somewhat more fully. Briting says that it is because of these family experiences, in part, that he went into the ministry. He first made this decision, in a naïve and childlike way, when he was twelve. It was a "growing thing" from then on. That is, while he did consider other professions, he always came back to the idea of the ministry, and that decision became more and more of a firm commitment.

The decision to become a minister can be seen as serving a number of purposes which take their meaning from the family context. It preserves the identification with the mother as the "predominant" parent, and it also internalizes for Briting the source of Mother's stability, religion. It also preserves and internalizes religion as the "stabilizing force," the force which "at times . . . was the only thing in the family." That is, if he became a minister, the family was more likely to remain whole. (Briting says that he wishes he could be *his* parents' minister and sit down with them to counsel them and to help them understand how their conflict got started.) Further, the ministerial role identifies Briting with Mother's side of the family battle. That is, Briting became good, a minister, rather than become like his father, a "hell-raiser," an epithet he uses to label a suppressed identity within his own personality.

Briting refers to himself as a "hell-raiser" a number of times. What is most frightening to him—death, the possibility of discovering his beliefs are all wrong—he speaks of as "scaring the hell out of me." It appears, in fact, that he had the hell scared out of him within the family. That is, out of fear and guilt he subordinated sexual, aggressive, and rebellious trends in the service of becoming good. In his early teens he joined a fundamentalist group and became too ardent even for his mother's tastes. This lasted for only a brief period.

The actual hell-raising to which he refers is innocuous and seems to have consisted in no more than cutting up in school. At other times the "hell-raising" obviously extended to the pleasure he found in playing in a dance band, petting, playing cards, smoking, and staying up late. These are all Father's pleasures, the ones which were morally condemned by Mother and which threatened the breakup of the family. Now, while Mother apparently did not run down Father indiscriminately in Briting's eyes, she did tell him not to be like his father:

> Lots of times she said, "People know about the way your father is." And she would say, "You don't have to feel this way about it. But hold your head up, and don't let people say, 'He's just like his father.'"

Considering the pervasiveness of Father's moral culpability, any aspect of Briting's masculine identity, including his sexuality, aggressiveness, wishes for egocentric pleasure, and so on, must have aroused a great deal of guilt and anxiety.

> Lots of times, with girls, I've come right to the point of having relations, and I've always backed off—always thinking—"Boy, you're going to go to hell," or, "You're really sinning, this is terrible, you shouldn't—you shouldn't do this."

Any such trends might be one more threat to the disruption of the family.

The hell-raiser identity lies in the shadow of Briting's identity as minister, mediator, counselor—all that lies in opposition, as a way of life, to Father's meaningless "hedonism." Briting's struggle with pride, what he would consider the sin of putting himself, rather than God, at the center of his effort to do good, indicates the depth and level of development within his personality of a basic core of this identity:

> Even my most righteous of acts, if I'm really honest—I guess that very rarely I am, because most of the time I feel pretty good when I do something good, you know, stay up all night with a drunk, or make so many hospital calls. I usually think, boy, you know, I'm really —I really did something good today. I'm usually pretty much in the center of that, and it was usually me. I didn't do it because the fellow needed me or that he was a drunk. I did it because—the woman who— his wife had asked me over to do this. What she would think of me—I'm always in the center pretty much. . . . I say, "That was really good, you know. I'm a pretty good person." I don't say this myself, but this is what I'm thinking. "I'm a good person, you know. I really love Christ. I have a God-centered life." And most times I say this without thinking, but sometimes I say to myself, "Now hold on a minute, why did you really make that hospital visit?"

What may be derived from these remarks and other sources is that the religionist's archetypal and final struggle with sin— pride—is an effort to come to terms with the fantasy that one is God. It is to be recognized as a mature development within this type of personality.

By identifying with Mother and her religiosity and by sustaining this identification through the development of his own identity as a minister, Briting was able to preserve within himself the security, love, and basic trust that were available to him within his family. The price of this type of characterological development for him was that it entailed a lack of separation from his family and difficulty in establishing his own masculine identity.

A particular quality of the sense of basic trust is the deepest emotional resource that Briting preserved from his early years, and this provides the source of his most profound religious experience. He says that he is learning to live with a constant sense of being in the presence of God, that he lives "in two worlds," or on "two levels."

> For me to live is Christ. I live in two worlds. I am in constant communication in prayer lots of times on one level. And the other level I'm talking and laughing and crying. But on the other level I'm always in a state of adoration—praise. . . . [PH: How specific a form of consciousness does it take?] No, it's not more specific and it's vaguer. It's praying without ceasing and it's being in the presence of God and knowing this, no matter what you're doing. . . . [PH: What kind of a feeling is it?] Peace—at oneness—wholeness—meaning. There's joy to it—a feeling of rightness—not righteousness but rightness.

The experience seems to be only partially subject to verbalization. Also it may be seen to be parallel to the experience of a small child, whose needs have been met, in a state of empathic communication with a loving mother. As such it stands as the antidotal counterpart to Briting's sense of the "meaninglessness" of life. The religious belief system preserves this sense of wholeness and meaning-confirming presence and allows it to take a conscious symbolic form that protects Briting from shattering despair and meaninglessness. It is interesting to note that as his religious commitment deepened, so did his sense of the meaninglessness of life. That is, involvement with and individuation through the mythic symbols allowed expression of the deeper layers of Briting's personality—the sense of deprivation and abandonment and the residue of basic trust that is a protection against those anxieties. Briting's identification with the mother and his later elaboration of the ministerial identity allowed him to preserve the trust, love, security, and sense of self that were threatened by the familial conflicts.

# X

# Summary to Parts
# Two and Three

. . . Just then she paid us the compliment of making
God male. But I think she knows as all intelligent women
do, that all profound definitions of God are essentially
definitions of the mother. Of giving things. Sometimes
the strangest gifts. Because the religious instinct is really
the instinct to define whatever gives each situation.

JOHN FOWLES, THE MAGUS

## 1. COMPARISONS AMONG THE
## SIX PRECEDING CASES

The six life studies presented in Parts Two and Three might be
seen as forming a matrix of the psychologically possible positions
of belief and doubt. We could imagine one person moving, at
different times and under different conditions, through each of
the different positions. Starting with the position of clear certainty (Chelly), the opposite position in the matrix is that of
pervasive doubt (Pale), while conversion (Electon) and liberalization (Mudge) represent alternative resolutions of pervasive
doubt, one moving back toward conservative certainty and the
other toward a new kind of belief. The variations of ambivalent
faith (Joel, Briting) stand between pervasive doubt and conservative certainty.

The case of Chelly illustrates the pattern of precocious identity formation, hypothesized as a modal pattern in the culture of the American conservative Protestant communities. He is the paradigm for the position of the conservative believer least troubled by doubt. He believes in the Virgin Birth, the Resurrection, and that he will join the believers in heaven on some final day. He remains placid in the face of "this recent heresy of disbelief" that surrounds him in his current environment. He is fully identified with and satisfied by his role of churchman and "official Christian." The doubts that he might allow himself to experience are focused into experiences or identity fragments that are isolated from the belief system. Doubts arise when he considers the possibility that his course in life was determined primarily by the influence of his mother and the grandmother who set him to preaching and giving the sacraments with water and sunshine biscuits when he was three years old. Some doubts also arise in connection with the real feelings about death that are let through when he examines the seemingly irrelevant "piece of theology" involved in "dead like Rover, dead all over." This bit of doggerel was taught him as a child, and it contains for him the reality of death. These sources of doubt, as clearly central as they are to Chelly's development and personality, have been quite removed from the belief system and his everyday life. The removal of sources of doubt is a feature of that "characterological barrier to experience" which buffers his belief system and himself.

The case of Pale also illustrates the pattern of precocious identity formation, and his case is the paradigm of pervasive doubt in the conservative believer. Doubt has eroded the core of his belief system, the personal relationship with his Lord. Doubt encroached upon Pale's beliefs through the very hallmark of the precocious identity formation in the conservative believer, the personal relationship with God and the constant effort to remain in and follow God's will in the least act of everyday life. In the years that followed his leaving home, Pale suffered the consequences of his long-standing lack of closure or diffuseness of identity—anxiety and stress, being overwhelmed by the necessity of life decisions, the disorganizing impact of his own sexuality. His experiences were so painful and disruptive for him that he could no longer consider himself as acting in the Lord's will. Such burdens and anxieties, he believed, could not be experienced by someone who was living in the Lord's will. Sexual impulses, for example, ran counter to his conception of himself as one who would remain "spotless." He no longer felt like "God's child," one who has "satisfaction in being an instrument—in being one who is rightly related in going through these experiences." The belief system, especially the personal relationship with God, is the keystone to the integrity of Pale's personality. With erosion of the core of the belief system, it no longer performed the necessary defensive, subliminatory, and integrative functions. As a result, Pale is left vulnerable to profound inner anxieties and disintegrative forces, and the external world is experienced as filled with evil, confusion, and malevolence. The defenses are permeable, and the ego tends to be flooded with primitive impulses, affects, and imagery. He is subject to preoccupations about eternity, death, and everlasting life. These are the conscious aspects of an archaic fantasy of union with the mother in death, in which there is a fusion of imagery pertaining to death, sex, aggression, and the mother. Pale yearns to return to the relationship with the Lord which nostalgic memory tells him he once possessed, and to feel the peace of relinquishing himself and responsibility for his own identity to a transcendental being. Pale's position, then, in the hypothetical matrix of belief and doubt, represents the archetypal plight of the conservative believer who loses his faith. His case illustrates the effects on a personality such as Chelly's when the belief system which formed the core of the precociously formulated identity is encroached upon by a total and pervasive doubt.

The cases of Electon and Mudge are paradigms of two opposing ways of resolving pervasive doubt. Electon resolved doubt by becoming, through a conversion experience, a conservative believer, and Mudge resolved doubt through the liberalization of his theology. Neither Electon nor Mudge illustrate the pattern of precocious identity formation. However, their periods of doubt are psychologically parallel to Pale's in basic ways. In each case there is a profound threat to the sense of self and a yearning to relinquish the self to a transcendental being who would provide meaning, definition, purpose, and comfort. The periods of doubt represent identity crises, and the changes that Electon and Mudge undergo involve major redefinitions of the self and reality. In addition to the emotional upset and anxiety of such a crisis, there is a general openness and lack of coherence to the personality most clearly represented in the oceanic longing to relinquish the sense of self to God.[1]

Electon had not been a believer before his conversion experience. He went from college to seminary still a seeker, still on the quest for identity. The conversion was precipitated by an experience which he interpreted initially as a demonstration of his utter worthlessness, and it was the response to his great need to find some meaning and some reaffirmation of himself in that experience. The conversion and subsequent reorganization of personality were permitted by at least three basic conditions: a regression to an ego state which allowed for the sense of partial fusion with a transcendental object; a partial relinquishment of critical reality-testing which would allow for a final, absolute, and to some degree arbitrary interpretation of reality; and the availability within himself and his past of the Christian symbol system which is capable of providing a totalistic definition of the self and reality. It is beautifully clear, in Electon's case, how elements which were already present in his personality were reorganized into a different *Gestalt* through the conversion. In particular, both his profound sense of humiliation and suffering and the great need for uniqueness and special mission are expressed in the meaning he found in the notion of God calling out people to do His work. The realization that perhaps his very uniqueness lies in his suffering is an elegant amalgamation of both his sense of utter worthlessness and the sense of being uniquely special. Similarly, his concept of God contained and condensed his early experience with the Indian religion and also the torturous experience with his twin.

It is interesting to compare the effects of life stresses on Electon and Pale. It was the stress of his first years away from home that precipitated the irruption of doubt and the weakening of faith in Pale. In the case of Electon, conversion and belief followed severe life stresses. There are clearly a number of factors at work here. While Pale never experienced one brief span of total threat to the self in the way in which Electon did, both suffered in these years as a result of long-standing lack of closure of the personality, fragile defensive and self-esteem systems, and inadequate coping mechanisms related to a problematic masculine identification. Electon's trauma following his Peace Corps efforts was so devastating that some violent restitutive effort was an absolute requirement. Because he had within him sufficient resources, the restitution was adaptive and consensually valid, and not psychotic. Pale has simply not been pushed that far. He was used to being "God's child" and, by virtue of relatively successful functioning in his social roles, used to feeling that he was in God's will. In the system he has for interpreting reality and his own experience, he could only understand his duress as an indication of not being in the Lord's will. This perception enfeebled the synthesizing powers of the symbol system. Electon, starting from the position of being without belief, groping for a solution to a devastating problem, found a new fit between his experience and the Christian gospel. This newfound solution brought him relief, so he continued to make use of it, and in this way the integrative power of the symbolism was strengthened. Further experience with the belief system under other trying circumstances added to the store of memories in which the belief system played an active functional role, and this also strengthened the ego-synthesizing powers of the belief system. Through such sustaining use of the symbol system in the individual's life experience, the personality is enabled to make more extensive use of the symbols of the belief system for condensing, expressing, and giving socially meaningful form to fundamental psychic contents. The heightening of the integrative effectiveness of the belief system will inevitably lead to the reaffirming of faith, establishing it more solidly within the personality, although such reaffirmation cannot occur without the initial decisive, willed "leap of faith."

The case of Mudge illuminates another aspect of pervasive doubt in the conservative believer by showing those processes whereby doubt is resolved through a liberalization of the belief system. Mudge had tried to adopt the fundamentalist Christianity to which he was exposed during summers in the years before college, and he had gone off to college believing he was a fundamentalist. This stance apparently did not hold up for very long. During most of his college years he felt like "a man without a country," and he even wondered if he should consider himself a Christian. This particular doubt was relieved by the hallucinatory-like vision of the "shining gold cross" on the "black coffin." This experience was an identity crisis, and he interpreted it to mean that he was to follow the way of the Cross, that he was to be a Christian. However, his questionnaire responses indicate that the following three years remained a period of pervasive doubt. He was still on the quest for the all-loving, protecting, direction- and meaning-providing God. He did not know what he believed, nor what he should do, and he, like Pale, was seeking the solution to these problems of identity by wishing that God would "speak more clearly, reveal Himself more personally." This is a passive stance which is based on emotional turmoil and a strong sense of helplessness. The individual in this state is simply lacking in a model or conception for the resolution of his own problems, and looks to a transcendental source outside of himself.

Mudge's liberalizing was precipitated by life experiences which, essentially, indicated to him that his needs could in fact be met through ordinary life. He found a woman to love him, he had the benefit of further training and the experience of teaching a confirmation class, and so on. The death of his grandfather, whom he loved, made him "loosen up on my doctorine of judgment," which "doctorine" then became a more realistic expression of his feelings about himself and others. He found, then, he could tolerate, accept, and make personal use of a more relative, reality-oriented, and human belief system. His conception of God shifted from the absolute, externalized God to a more relative, internalized conception. One explained God by talking about events and relationships of everyday human life. His conception of guilt and responsibility had been related to a need for absolute personal goodness and purity, which expressed little feeling for the relevance of moral action to personal relationship. This shifted from the absolute, externalized God to a more relative, responsibility to others. The relinquishment of an absolute conception of God was accompanied by a generally greater tolerance for the ambiguities and uncertainties of life. He was more ready to accept the teachings of Christianity and the figure of Jesus simply as models and precepts for human living.

Fundamentalism had never really taken with Mudge. However, there are deeper psychological conditions which made possible his liberalization. The basic psychological process in his liberalization was the emotional separation from his mother. He was able to separate from and give her up, and give up the wishes and needs that are met by the primary mother. A number of factors permitted this separation. He received real warmth and love from the mother, and he was able to experience the negative side of the ambivalence for the parents. He had a suspicion that his religious training was "brainwashing" to keep him in line, and that it came out of his mother's personal needs and the parental tensions. He felt that his early training had been harsh and that he had been "broken." The early toilet training also left him extremely stubborn. A good deal of body narcissism arose out of his early experience with his mother. This provides the basis for a cathexis of the self and thereby the formation of an ideology of self-development with less dependence on a grandiose ego-ideal. Perhaps this description of Mudge should be qualified by saying that the liberalization and the accompanying psychological conditions related to separation from the mother represent major trends rather than fully realized personality changes.

The pervasive doubt experienced by Pale, and by Electon and Mudge at different times, is an unstable condition which contains within itself the impetus to set in motion some sort of equilibratory process. Joel and Briting may be considered to represent a type of resolution, an equilibratory process, distinct from those of Electon or Mudge. They have stabilized in a position of ambivalence, "swaying and staggering between Yes and No." The belief system contains a clear expression of both the Yes and No of Barth's description of doubt.[2] Of the two, Joel is considered a doubter because he feels himself to be so at this point in his life, and because his doubt is a more powerful threat to the whole belief system.

Out of Pale's disintegrative conflicts arises a struggle between two archetypically opposing meanings of the world, one as evil, malevolent, the other as good, nurturing. The belief system of Joel and Briting find a parallel to Pale's in the sense that they also contain two profoundly opposing orientations to the self and reality. The important difference is that in the belief systems of Joel and Briting, both orientations to reality are given articulate expression and the tension between them, as well as the negative orientation itself, is tolerated, or at least sustained, by the personality. One of these orientations is most clearly and powerfully expressed in the strong sense of personal relationship with God which both Joel and Briting possess. It is worth noting that of the six conservative believers, only Joel and Briting have this active, central sense of personal relationship with God. It is possible that this is achieved only by somehow isolating the sense of relationship with God from all other experience, thereby engendering the kind of split which their belief systems manifest.

The relationship with God preserves and expresses a positive, hopeful sense of the self, its reality, value, and continuity and the significance of its social identity. This is one orientation contained within the belief system. Within this orientation there is a comparable attitude to the world, work, and interpersonal relationships, and a sense of the effectiveness of the self in these spheres. The opposing orientation receives its primary conscious articulation through feelings about the emptiness, meaninglessness, and confusion of a world without God. The profound sense of the world and people being pervaded by evil and malevolence potentially destructive to the self that Pale expresses so strongly receives equally clear but more controlled and qualified expression in both Joel and Briting. Joel feels embattled on all sides and feels his "existence threatened" by various aspects of the contemporary world. In Briting, there is a certain tendency to fly from people and to a view of the "meaninglessness of life" and the world as "a giant burial ground." Underlying these consciously articulated views are intimations of a powerfully negative view of the self, its worthlessness and evil, as well as a sense of helplessness, hopelessness, and ineffectiveness.

To sustain the tensions and anxieties of this type of belief system clearly requires a considerable degree of personal strength and integrity. The individual's early years must have provided resources sufficient to develop the necessary ego strengths. While this is obvious, we may make another more specific observation. Part of what allows Joel and Briting to sustain the ambivalence of their belief systems is what I am calling the institutionalization of certain psychological processes. In Joel's case, a number of psychological processes receive a final institutionalization in the intellectual conclusion that there are "two kinds of knowledge." For one thing, the emotional experience of the God relationship, with all its immediacy, is isolated and thereby protected from doubts which might arise from a variety of sources. For another, the reality of the religious interpretation of certain emotional experiences—which have carried their religious meanings since childhood—is never questioned; indeed, it is never considered an "interpretation." The conclusion that "there are two kinds of knowledge" may be seen as a direct representation of the isolation and protection of the experience of the God relationship from other affective and cognitive processes. As an intellectual conclusion, it is actually made possible by the psychologically prior process of isolation. However, as an intellectual conclusion, "there are two kinds of knowledge" may now participate in social or "institutional" processes such as theological debate. The whole process is now removed from the intrapsychic realm, projected into the social one, and while, for example, Joel debates the philosophical merits of his conclusion, the personal meaning of it, the preservation of the sense of the God relationship, remains untouched.

A similar process helps sustain the tensions within Briting's belief system. Briting speaks of being able to "segment his life." Even when his doubt was at its greatest, in college, he was not continually swept up by it and was quite able to go about his life in other ways. "Segmenting" his life, then, protects him from being overwhelmed or depressed by his sense of the meaninglessness of life. But being protected from these feelings, he is then able to use his feelings of emptiness, meaninglessness, and so on, to give meaning to and dramatize in his ministerial functions his belief in God and the Christ event. His depressive feelings are thereby no longer simply intrapsychic and personal but are institutionalized by virtue of coming to participate in social processes.

## 2. THE PSYCHODYNAMICS OF DOUBT

The general formulations concerning the origins and nature of religious doubt suggested and supported by the preceding six case studies will be presented in this section. There are three such formulations I wish to present. (1) Doubt *arises* when the religious belief system does not protect the individual in his life experiences and from its more painful stress. (2) The *experience* of the God relationship (the psychological meaning of the concept of God) is formed from *derivatives from* and is a *restitution for* the primary maternal relationship. (3) Religious doubt itself is an expression of the wish for and the dread of *fusion* with the primal mother. Some of the meanings of and inferences leading up to these formulations may be briefly summarized.

Pale may be considered a paradigm of the conservative religious doubter, for present purposes, although what is said here about his case will be considered to have a general significance. A conservative believer, such as Pale, is characteristically in search of the Lord's will in the most minute daily events. The irruption of doubt resulting from stress is particularly clear in such a case. An awareness of excessive stress is the criterion of not being in the Lord's will and initiates a sense of alienation from the personal relationship with the Lord which may continue until that relationship seems altogether lost. Of central significance, in the discussion of this development in Pale's case, was the relationship with the mother, its quality, intensity, duration, and its place in the family constellation. The intrapsychic processes and developmental experiences which arose from the maternal relationship are considered to be the conditions which allowed for the development of the sense of relationship with the Lord, its loss, and the intrusion of doubt. The mother's influence on Pale was particularly strong. In addition, Pale in some ways triumphed over his father, as he experienced it, in competition for the mother. The father's masculine and paternal roles within the family were devalued, and Pale describes himself as a better Christian (holier) and more sensitive to his mother's emotional needs. He was the religious one in the family to whom the others looked up; he was the firstborn son and also favored by virtue of being more gifted. It was the father, at one point, who thanked Pale for his influence on his, the father's, life.

Experiences of this sort within the family and the son's favored position within the family constellation in relation to the mother heighten the development of secondary narcissism and the ego-ideal. The son acquires a sense of being special, pure, holy, Christ-like, or whatever, and the ego-ideal holds out great expectations for a messianic mission in this life as well as in an afterlife. Where there has been a developmental problem in establishing basic trust or autonomy these experiences may be clung to all the harder. The ministerial role is a particularly apt one for giving social expression to these developments of secondary narcissism—that is, the sense of being a specially favored person.

The personal relationship with God and the personally meaningful theological elaborations that surround it can be viewed psychologically as the restitutions for the all-important primary maternal relationship. The relationship with God preserves and expresses not only the basic sense of the goodness, reality, and continuity of the self derived from the earliest maternal experience, but it also preserves and expresses that heightened sense of specialness that derives from the prolongation of the maternal relationship. We can assume, I believe, that trends emphasizing the developments of secondary narcissism within the personality are particularly likely to assume centrality when there also has been a major narcissistic wound, that is, when the sound establishment of self-esteem is severely problematic. Under these circumstances the sense of specialness and the high ideals also serve a compensatory function.

The sense of having a messianic mission, a special calling, can contribute to the onset of doubt as well as other regressive trends. While such a feeling may lead to an earnest seeking of one's real vocation in life, it also may place inordinate demands on the individual to do something extraordinarily unique. The individual is then measuring himself according to extremely demanding criteria and the occasions for falling short will be proportionately many. Under these circumstances, clearly shown in Pale's case, guilt and shame are continually being reactivated with an attendant general undermining of self-esteem. The continual generation of intense self-doubt, through a comparison of the self with a grandiose ego-ideal, can only prepare the way for the doubting of the belief system in which the ideals are embedded.

Restitutions for various aspects of the early maternal relationship and the development of the ego-ideal can be observed within any personality. They provide the individual with "protection in life" through what Erikson calls the sense of basic trust. This consists in a nonverbal, emotional assumption that underlies all of life that the world is basically good and that it is possible for the individual's basic needs to be met. This underlying "sense" allows the person to proceed in his life with hopefulness, trust, courage, and so on, even in the face of the real difficulties of life.

In Pale's case, the restitutions for the maternal relationship and therefore, in part, the sense of basic trust, rest in the projections involved in the relationship with God. To the degree that the restitutions are projected externally, they will be experienced as sources of protection and goodness external to the self. It was all the more likely, then, that when Pale met inordinate, apparently arbitrary stress in his life, stress brought on even by himself, he would call into question his basic assumptions about himself and the world. What was experienced as a source of protection and goodness is so no longer, and is therefore questioned.

New sources of goodness, nurturance, and protection are

bound to be sought when the old ones are felt to be lost. In Pale's case, with the erosion of the ego-ideal as well as the projected sources of protection, this quest, rooted as it is in early experience, inevitably had a regressive aspect. That is, in these circumstances, the ego will inevitably take a partly regressive, partly adaptive turn to its earliest sources of nurturance and goodness in the memories, derivatives, and affective residues of the primary maternal relationship.

It is the wish for fusion with the primary mother which most directly expresses these trends, and it is fusion with the maternal imago which most assuredly promises an ever-flowing supply of nurturance, goodness, and protection. Fusion implies becoming one with the sources of nurturance, the obliteration forever of separateness and alienation. It promises never-ending hopefulness and, not simply does it promise the complete absence of the threat of any loss of self, but it promises the opposite of that, the ever-continuing sense of the reality, continuity, and goodness of the self. The wish for fusion becomes expressed in the longing for a source of hopefulness, the wish to surrender to a transcendental object, the quest for the glorious cause.

The quest for new sources of protection, then, activates the wish for fusion with its hopeful promises. However, there are not only images of goodness associated with the maternal imago; images of evil are associated with it as well. The strength of these depends on many factors, but in general is associated with the intensity of ambivalence and hate aroused and not neutralized by mutual love in the early maternal relationship. In any case, at these primitive psychic levels, the negative imagery associated with the maternal imago holds the threat of evil and annihilation as powerful as the promise of goodness and hope associated with the positive imagery. Thus the wish for fusion arouses not only hope but also dread, the fear of the loss of self in a maternal engulfment. Dread of this sort receives its expression in the sense of evil malevolence pervading the world, and in the feelings of deep threat to the sense of self which may be precipitated in any situation in which shame, doubt, humiliation, failure, and so on, may be experienced.

In the paradigmatic case, then, pervasive religious doubt of the sort shown in Pale is the expression of the wish for and the dread of fusion with the primary mother. The quest for the renewal of hope and the longing for fusion are experienced in terms of the symbols of the religious belief system. Since both hope and dread are aroused, the religious symbolism comes to have attached to it both powerful positive and powerful negative meanings. The individual is then caught between, in doubt.

The life studies presented illustrate the various ways out of this dilemma. There are two basic ways. One way depends upon giving up the ambivalent source of good and evil, of letting go and facing the experience of loss, emptiness, and alienation that follows. Mudge comes closest to this paradigm. The other way depends upon evolving, in some manner or other, two distinct realms—one of good and the other of evil—by "splitting" the ambivalence. Electon as well as Joel and Briting have all managed this in their distinct ways. For Electon, psychology became one of the principalities and powers contrasted with the goodness of the gospel; for Joel, "two kinds of knowledge" represent part of his managing of this split; and in Briting, meaninglessness, emptiness, and the world as a giant burial ground contrast with the separate and separated level of the relationship with God. For Pale himself, the imagery of good and evil are still fused, and he is still pervaded by doubt.

In Pale (and our other subjects) the restitutive processes and the quest for hope receive symbolic expression in the religious belief system and the ministerial role. This is understandable in the light of the role that religion played in Pale's family in general, and in the relationship with the mother in particular. It was through the religion that Pale could deepen and preserve the attachment with the mother. By becoming especially religious, Pale could outshine his father and be particularly worthy of the love of his mother. Furthermore, the religious language helped serve as a defense against critical awareness of the pathological disruption of the family structure. It is perhaps only the claims to relationship with the divine and an everlasting life in heaven that can finally capture the mysteries, expectations, and nostalgically remembered paradise of the relationship with the primal mother.

It will be recalled that of the five other subjects discussed, four of them—Chelly, Electon, Mudge, and Briting—display a striking similarity in terms of family history and development and functions of the religious belief system. In all four cases there is not only a strong, prolonged relationship with the mother, but there is a quality to the relationship that gives it a very special aura. The father is not only more or less devalued, and this usually in terms related to the family religion, but he is in some manner and to some degree edged out by the son in relation to the mother. There are also a variety of other circumstances that add to the specialness of the mother-son relationship. Chelly and Mudge are only children; and in their cases the birth may have been particularly difficult. Other feelings that the parents have about the birth may linger and affect the child. In Mudge's case there is his prematurity and his feeling that his mother lived out with him the Samuel story. It seems clear that in the case of all four, the mothers turned to their sons for gratification that an absent or supposedly inadequate husband could not provide. The four sons were all trained in one way or another to have the virtues, emotional sensitivity, or whatever, that the husband did not have. To the sons, the predominant and most influential parent is the mother. The strongest identification is with the mother, and the sons become religious through their closeness and identification with her.

Considering that in Christianity God is God the Father, it would be tempting to conclude, in the light of the evidence, that religious doubts, as in Pale's case, for example, arise because of the "doubt" within the family about the masculine and paternal role of the father and because of the absence of the father's influence on his son. A more complex dynamic is indicated, however. To the extent that the son has a more or less well established masculine identity, there will be a stronger personality integration, greater capacity to cope in the world, and therefore less strain put on the belief system because of life stress. The affects within the personality that are related to the God relationship and the function of the God concept within the personality are more related to the qualities of the maternal relationship and derivatives from it than to the relationship with the father. The projection of God as a father serves in part as a defense against maternal engulfment, and this function parallels exactly one purpose of the son's identification with the father in the course of the resolution of the oedipal complex.

While Joel appears somewhat of an exception, he is one only on the surface. There is less evidence, in Joel's life, of the prolonged, special relationship with the mother that is seen in the other subjects. Indeed, there is a strong identification with his father. It is that identification, however, that gives Joel a somewhat different mission than the other five subjects. He is more concerned with the reform of his tradition and also with scholarship. (There is a parallel in his case in this respect with that of Jameson, in chapter XIII.) As to the meaning within his personality of the relationship with God, it has all the qualities that Briting's does and seems by these qualities to be a derivative of the maternal relationship.

Some qualifications to the conclusion that the psychological meanings of the concept of God derive from the early maternal relationship, and that doubt represents the dread of fusion with the maternal imago, are obviously called for. Faith and doubt certainly have other sources. Generally, faith is a structure with multiple psychic roots, depending upon the reasonably healthy integration of the personality. The latter derives from the more or less successful resolution of a whole series of maturational crises. In the preceding case studies, numerous emotionally mean-ingful and developmentally significant events other than the early maternal relationship have been discussed in their relation to the religious belief system. Some of these events were clearly inimical to or at least problematic for the wholesome synthesis of personality. A problematic crisis or unresolved developmental conflict of any sort can have an undermining influence on the structure of faith and be a focal source for the development of religious doubt. And "faith" in this context can be understood in the narrower sense of religious faith, or in the broader sense of faith in life. As examples, in the lives of the men just dis-cussed, two common sorts of problems that make the structure of faith problematic have been mentioned. A problematic mascu-line identification makes the integration of coping mechanisms more difficult (or involves, in Joel's case, the integration of an embattled stance) and the individual is inevitably subjected to life stress. Also, an ego-ideal that makes unrealistic demands on the individual (e.g., for absolute purity) and on the world (e.g., for a special mission) and is inflexible (not sufficiently modifiable by further life experience) also places the individual in an unten-able position and increases life stress. Stresses of these sorts can only make the continued maintenance of the structure of faith problematic.

It is partly just such continued stresses, however, that lead to the developments that make appropriate the emphasis, in the analysis of the personalities of these individuals, on the affective system relating to the early maternal relationship. Under stress, with the basic structure of faith coming into question, the individual seeks to regain, sometimes by a regressive turn (Pale, Electon), contact with the original sources of hope, meaning, and wholeness. This signifies a revival in the personality of the meanings and affects relating to the maternal imago. The lives of the men discussed are characterized by this cyclical or continuing process. It is above all through the concept of God and the God relationship that they have struggled to maintain the effects within themselves of their own original sources of the sense of the reality, continuity, and goodness of the self.

Faith in the sense we are talking about here derives from a healthy sense of the self and strong connections with individual and life energies in a variety of forms. As an overall structure it might be distinguished from the God relationship or the meaning of God for the individual that is supported by and within that structure. In this way, the psychological meanings of the concept of God may be seen as deriving from the early maternal relationship, while the structure of faith sustaining those meanings and sustained by them may be seen as deriving from and fostering the continued evolution of identity and the continued wholesome synthesis of a lifelong series of maturational developments. However, I hope such a formulation will be useful conceptually without being taken as an absolute description fitting each case.

# PART FOUR

# The Liberal Context

# XI

# Eyman: A Paradigm Liberal

> I hate, I despise your feasts, and I take no delight in
> your solemn assemblies.
> Even though you offer me your burnt offerings and cereal
> offerings, I will not accept them, and the peace offerings
> of your fatted beasts I will not look upon.
> Take away from me the noise of your songs; to the melody
> of your harps I will not listen.
> But let justice roll down like waters, and righteousness
> like an ever-flowing stream.      AMOS 5: 21–24

Eyman is the paradigm, for the purposes of this study, of the
liberal. His theology, conception of the ministerial role, and his
conception of the self, as well as the psychodynamic meanings
of these, will serve to illustrate the psychology of the liberal
"believer." Contrasts and parallels with the conservative cases
will also be elucidated.

Eyman is twenty-five, has been married for less than two
years, and has been minister in his first parish, a Unitarian Universalist church, for less than one year. His training and background are Unitarian Universalist. Eyman was born and raised
in a major Middle Atlantic states city. His only sibling, a sister,
was born when he was nine and a half, so that Eyman had the
status of only child for a number of years. His father is a quiet,
self-contained, gentle, but athletic and self-assured man who
made his living in the insurance business after an Ivy League
college education. Mother is described as emotionally labile,

rather irritable, and not as thoughtful as father. Ancestors in America on both sides of the family go back to the time of the Revolution.

## 1. THE LIBERAL BELIEF SYSTEM

Eyman appeared at his first interview fresh from a week in jail and a powerful experience in Selma, Alabama. Martin Luther King and the Southern Christian Leadership Conference were concentrating their civil rights efforts in Selma, and this first interview took place only a few weeks before Eyman's colleague, Reverend James Reeb, was killed in a civil rights demonstration. Eyman was filled with the experience, and it was an obvious culmination in action not only of his belief system but of his new maturity as a recently ordained minister. He had gone to Selma, lived with a Negro family, scouted out the city on his own, participated in a demonstration, been arrested, and spent a week in a jail.

The experience means many things to him and represents a number of aspects of the belief system. Eyman found that, before flying to the South, he had to face the possibility of his own death. He views the world in a "naturalistic" way, and does not believe in an afterlife. The idea of dying at twenty-five was shocking, but the only consolation was that it would be in the service of a meaningful cause. It would not be a meaningless death.

Further, and more generally, the Selma trip represents Eyman's conception of religion as "an activity of man" and a certain kind of concern with human life:

> The notion of religion is not simply thinking about God.
> It has to do with—it's better defined as an activity of man,
> what men do. This being concerned with men and the
> meaning of their existence, the carrying out of their lives.
> Also the notion of—you do not have to believe in God
> to be a religious person.

Action, when it is moral action and a response to others' needs, can be seen as a religious activity. Just as Eyman believes that one need not "believe in God" to be a religious person, so he himself can speak of being engaged in a "prophetic ministry," and lay claim to an inner sense which he expresses by saying that he is "called to do this form of witness." Eyman is actively involved with the major social and moral issues of today: civil rights, the plight of the urban areas, and the Vietnam War.

Another specific element that enters into Eyman's conception of the ministry which was influential in taking him to Selma is his sense of himself as a Southerner. He grew up more near the South than in it, but, as his ancestry is Southern, and for other reasons, he feels "very deeply embedded in the South."

> Because I do identify with the South, I also feel called
> upon to do everything I can to rid the South of the
> racist element in its mystique. I have, well, a certain feeling
> of responsibility—a man's responsibility for his brother
> —this sort of thing—which is part of what encouraged me
> to go down. But there are also very definitely overtones
> of guilt. The guilt of being white in a society that says,
> "If you're white, you're right; if you're black, stay back."

Eyman speaks of the experience as personally broadening and deepening. This reflects a central strand of the liberal belief system: the emphasis upon the development of the individual and the self. The tender-minded emphasis upon the self, the naturalistic view of the world, the concern with minority groups, the underdog, and pressing social issues, are all the traditional concerns of an ideology which often is labeled "naturalistic humanism." Eyman sometimes refers to his ideology by this name. In general, Eyman takes a tender-minded view of life, saying that he feels a "reverence for life," a sentiment he equates with Schweitzer's.

An additional element of this humanism is an explicit recognition of open-mindedness as a value. This consists in an effort to be flexible, open to new forms of experience, and a readiness to consider as viable possibilities views other than one's own.

Eyman says that for him, theological problems, "thinking about God," are secondary to an active involvement with human affairs. A world view does, however, underlie his actions. Seeing the world naturalistically means, for example, recognizing the reality of death and the fact that much in people's affairs turns out for ill rather than good and that this is a result either of their own doing or of impersonal natural forces. There is an explicit rejection of the conservative view of God in which God takes note of and even intervenes in human life. The rejection of conservatism must be seen as a part of the liberal belief system.

After struggling for quite some years to retain the notion of at least a deistic God, in order not to have to think of himself as an atheist, Eyman discovered an even more attenuated but, for him, meaningful use of that—as he views it—emotion-laden word. He believes that it makes sense to think of a "divine dimension in the universe," a somewhat vague and global concept which remains relatively undefined. It does however point to an essential part of the liberal religious belief system and is part of this sort of tender-minded view of the world. Eyman speaks of the divine dimension in these terms:

> I think that perhaps the notion of a divine dimension
> within the universe is useful . . . progressive creation *of*
> creation. It's what is brought into being through the action
> of sentient life in the world. And this would suggest
> to me a sort of progressive act of creation of creation in
> which we all take part. And to me this is a good description
> of what does seem to be going on, and I think that
> recognizing it as an ultimate part of the universe is worthy
> of finding a label [i.e., 'God'. P.H.] To me this *is* the
> divine—toward which we can strive and which is creative.
> In other words, sort of the alpha and omega which
> brings us into being and the goal toward which we should
> be moving.

One implication of this is that all men and all human activities participate in or are infused with the Godhead. The goal of human activity, then, is to try to recognize and enlarge on the divine within life.

Taking Eyman's belief system as the paradigm, we might list as major tenets of liberal belief the following:

(1) Rejection of conservatism.
(2) A very global, diffuse conception of God as a "dimension" of the universe and of human experience.
(3) Retention of a conception of the prophetic ministry.
(4) A naturalistic view of the world and life.
(5) A tender-minded emphasis upon the self and the development of the individual.

(6) A tender-minded interpersonal orientation and an active
   concern with moral and social issues.

The combination of some of these tenets (1, 2, 4, and 5)
represent, in comparison with the conservative belief system, a
major step in internalization. Within conservatism, an important
sector of action and experience is related not to the ego but to
God as a being external to the ego. Within Eyman's belief system all experience is the result of the ego's action, or interaction
with others, or of forces completely neutral and impersonal with
respect to human life. This is a major step in the development
and enrichment of the structure of personal identity.

Characterizing the liberal belief system, then, in a general
way, are the relativity of values, the tender-minded humanism,
and the presence of a major, global, unifying concept—God as a
"divine dimension."

## 2. CHILDHOOD AND FAMILY CONSTELLATION

Eyman grew up in a family in which there was a good deal of
stability and security and where the parental bond was strong.
Although there was also considerable tension at times, it was
contained within a stable structure and did not become overtly
disruptive. The presentation of the family picture will focus on
those emotional strands which contribute to the background and
development of Eyman's belief system. Until Eyman was about
twelve or thirteen, Father spent "perhaps one third or one quar-
ter of the time" in out-of-town travel, at times being away four
or five days. Eyman, alone at home with Mother during his first
decade, developed a close relationship with her:

> My mother and I would be at home on our own. And
> then later my mother and M and I would be at home.
> So it was—this actually developed into a fairly mature
> relationship fairly early—between my mother and me, I
> would think. She would treat me as a fairly mature person.
> She would sometimes feel free to relate problems or
> concerns of her own—which I don't think that most
> mothers would be willing to do.

In contrast, Eyman felt there was "some distance" between himself and his father when he was young. Father was away a certain

portion of time and was "concerned with the abstract," that is, social problems, and Socialist party and Urban League activities. Nevertheless Eyman also felt "tremendous respect and tremendous affection" for his father. The relationship with Father grew closer as Eyman grew into adolescence, and he speaks of admiration for his father as a person and as the masculine figure in the family:

> He's an interesting fellow—my father. He's very gentle,
> and I think that this is something that has impressed
> itself on me. His gentleness, his quietness. Those very
> desirable and admirable qualities. Quietness—not in a sense
> of absence of thought or conviction, but in conviction
> that doesn't need to be shouted. Because it's secure.
> Haven't got to prove it to yourself.

Eyman found Father's reasonable, calm, deliberate thoughtfulness worthy of emulation, but Father's slowness to take action sometimes irritated the more emotionally labile and expressive mother. Father controlled his feelings strongly, and Eyman describes him as "withdrawn," saying he is like his father in these respects. Eyman describes himself as very similar to Father in temperament and says they get along extremely well together. Physically, Eyman describes himself and Father as "virtual twins." Eyman is quite tall, lanky, slow and deliberate in his talk and movements. He is extremely serious in talking, always bringing in his ethical and humanistic concerns. At the same time he speaks with a twinkle in his eye, and conveys the feeling that he is sharing something quite personal in an atmosphere of rather cozy intimacy, and one feels that this quality derives more from his history of confidences with the mother.

Eyman had, then, a particularly close relationship with his mother. It was with her, for example, that he discussed his first questions about the meaning of life and death, even though Father was the philosophic one, and Mother's ideas were "still almost sloganary." Two other factors heightened the closeness of the maternal relationship. When he was a child Eyman suffered a good deal from allergenic illnesses. As a result he "spent an unusually great amount of time in bed requiring attention." The problem with allergies lasted into the first few years of elementary school. Minor illnesses "plagued" him into junior high, and while this susceptibility passed, he was still, he says, never a strong person.

The other factor that heightened the closeness of the maternal relationship was Mother's practice of confiding to Eyman her complaints about her husband. The confiding occurred particularly in the period just before and after the birth of M, Eyman's sister.

> This meant I did go through a certain period in which my father was a little bit low on the scale. I felt that he was—not doing everything he should.

Thus Eyman shared a relationship with his mother from which, in part, Father was excluded and in which there was a partial devaluation of Father. Eyman's relationship to his father was mediated through the maternal relationship, apparently, up until his early teens.

Eyman characterizes Mother's complaints about Father:

> She happens to be the type of person who manages to get irritated fairly easily, and when she does get irritated, generally lets it be known. My father on the other hand is relatively imperturbable, so they make a good pair [*laughs*]. But my mother would state that my father thus-and-such and I wish he hadn't or I wish he'd done something else. And so I guess I became accustomed to hearing this fairly early on and accustomed to taking it with a grain of salt fairly early on because I learned in most instances that a day later, it'll be forgotten. This same sort of business that later came up with me: "He should have done thus-and-such; he should have known thus-and-such." It's awfully difficult to cope with. I think that my father has coped with it better since that time. I think he's grown.

These remarks convey the impression that Mother was somewhat demanding and infantile in the expression of her needs and in dealing with frustration. It seems to be the father who developed a self-discipline for the parental couple and took a paternal attitude to his wife in certain respects. On the other hand, Eyman points out that Father was an only child, very attached to his own parents, and did not always provide Mother with the absolute fidelity and attention she required.

In discussing these aspects of the family constellation, Eyman called to mind an important series of incidents from his early adolescence—he was about fifteen—in which Father had not taken charge in the family, but he, Eyman, had and had acted as the family mediator. For a time, each Sunday morning, in the process of getting off to church, tensions, irritability, and tears were set off, focused particularly between Mother and M. Here too the tension was of the sort that arises between people highly sensitive to and involved with others' feelings. The particulars are less important than the fact of somewhat irritable sensitivities vulnerable to minor aggravations. In any event, it was Eyman who took the initiative in making the family confront tensions he felt to be unnecessary and unreasonable.

> I told my mother quite frankly that I simply saw no point in our going to church if it was always going to be this unpleasantness and we were always going to be upset with each other when we went down. As I say, I think the situation improved after that.

This incident is important for two reasons. First, Eyman's sequence of associations at the point he brings it up indicates that, to him, his taking initiative in the matter showed that Father was not acting as he should.

> I suppose it is peculiar, though, that I was the one who finally spoke up about it. I think that my father and I *had* talked about it too. And he was as unhappy as I was.

These remarks also indicate a remnant of the feeling that Father is "a little bit low on the scale." Second, we have seen in the previous cases that for the son to act as a mediator in the family, particularly in the context of a close maternal relationship, encourages the development of a sense of specialness and mission—feelings which find expression in the ministerial role.

Eyman acted as mediator in the family in another way too. It was he who, in seventh grade, got the family to first become involved with the church. This accomplishment is very important to him.

Eyman admired his father for his traits of character and, later, for the idealistic social and political concerns of his early adulthood. Eyman was not particularly impressed, however, with the business life, and he found the customary parental dinner-table talk of details of the day's insurance business "undefined to me and not anything very exciting." He expresses some regrets that Father did not follow up on any of his earlier social concerns which were very similar to those currently important to Eyman. In this way too, then, the paternal image was, if not particularly devalued, not particularly enhanced.

Striking parallels are already apparent between salient features of the childhood and family constellation of Eyman and those of the earlier cases: the closeness and quality of the maternal relationship; some special shared intimacy with the mother which excluded the father and related to some degree of devaluation of the father; the son as mediator in the family. Eyman's family differs from all the conservative cases in other respects. Religion and specifically religious language were not a central feature of the family culture. Ideological concerns were important, however, but they and the ideology of the family, political and child-rearing, were liberal and tender-minded. The family was stable, and, while there were tensions, the level of individual and group integration and coping was high. The family structure did not require its members to establish a totalistic personality formation.

Eyman feels that the quality of his upbringing is a major basis for his current outlook:

One factor which I think is probably important in my upbringing is the fact that my parents, while being very gentle about the whole thing, did expect a fairly high standard of behavior. Particularly they expected me to take care of my things and of people—to care for people. Without punishing me very often—spanking or making me go up to my room and close the door—they made it clear that one should take care of things. In fact, this has carried over to the point where sometimes I husband things that are *made* for *use*. I nurse along a supply of something because I don't want to use it all up. This has given me a very strong feeling for, well, reverence for the world—I think that approximating Schweitzer's notion of reverence for life.

Discipline was in the form of fairly mild reproof, usually provided by Mother who "was the one I was with and also she was the one who was temperamentally more suited to it." Two or three spankings by Father were experienced mainly as outrageous infringements.

Eyman seems to have been under some pressure, within the family, to make an early relinquishment of childish ways. He says that his mother treated him as a "mature person" and that the relationship with her was mature. There is more than one indication, however, that Mother used the relationship with Eyman in the service of her own narcissistic needs. While she confided to Eyman her discontents, Eyman was the passive listener, and he himself remained reticent and somewhat secretive and withdrawn. Similarly, he learned to deal with Mother's irritability by holding on to his own feelings and letting things cool down until they could be dealt with in a more reasonable way.

An interesting facet of his "precocious adulthood" is the manner in which he responded to the birth of a sibling. Asked if there were other children at home, Eyman first responded "No."

> No—I was an only child until I was nine and a half,
> when my sister was born, so well—I was well on the way
> to being grown by that time—had been through a major
> portion of childhood—was verging on—well, was within
> a few years of adolescence. So I used to say jokingly
> that M almost had three parents instead of two parents
> and a brother. Because by the time she *was* born, I was
> old enough to take some responsibility in caring for her and
> minor discipline and so on.

And Eyman adds:

> And I'm quite sure that that played a role in the way in
> which my parents brought me up. Because all of their
> attention could be focused for those nine and a half years
> on raising one child.

Eyman certainly exaggerates his advancement in years at the time of his sister's birth. He seems to have facilitated a denial that she was competition as a sibling, or a displacement of him, by relinquishing claim to a child-role and becoming the "third parent" in the family.

A number of factors, then, led to a highly developed sensitivity to the feelings of others and of himself. The pressures to maturity, the high standards of behavior set by the parents, the maternal closeness and confiding, and, we may add, the need to learn to read the signs in a mother whose irritation was apt to flare up easily. Much of this, and further reactions of Eyman to it, are summarized in this delicate preschool memory:

> And I can recall feeling very guilty about—well,
> as I recall my mother had said something to me. I'd been
> noisy, and she was tired and irritable, and so she said
> something very cross to me. And then that made me mad,
> and so I wanted to get back at her, and I took a little
> figurine that she had and which she was fairly fond of and
> I think I took it out and buried it under some sand in
> my sandbox. And in the process, or in the process of
> recovering it, I broke it. I broke a little piece off it. And
> I recall feeling *extremely* guilty about this, because I'd
> harmed this thing.

Eyman "got back" at Mother, but in a very indirect, controlled way, which left him more guilty than ever and the anger not catharted. There are indications that the desire to "get back" is still present.

The patterns and emotional currents in Eyman's life which we have so far drawn out are all relatively peaceful, benevolent, and conducive to the growth of a sensitive, thoughtful person. Another current ran more covertly through Eyman's childhood, one less benevolent and one which Eyman conspired to keep to himself. In early childhood, he developed a phobic fantasy which frightened him but in which he also indulged as a kind of anxious game. Eyman places this experience in his "preschool years"; this and developmental considerations would lead us to expect that it probably was around the age of four. He describes the fantasy as follows:

I don't remember anything about an origin for it, but
I do remember having it. I don't recall ever verbalizing
it to anybody, which meant that I didn't want to have
to explain this to someone. But on the other hand, I
wanted to maintain it. So I imagine I had some fun times
moving away from the window without being obvious
about it. As I recall, as I constructed this fantasy,
well, there was—I believe I referred to him as "Killer-
Man" who was on this bus going by the house. And he
would—I think that I thought he would kill me if I was
visible to the bus through the front windows. This
would mean that there'd be two or three different windows
in a room looking out on the street. Or perhaps I'd have
to move across the room to be not visible from the
bus. This all depends. Sometimes when there were
other people in the room, I decided it would look silly—
"Okay, I'm not playing now."

Eyman minimizes the anxiety associated with the Killer-
Man fantasy, and he did seem to have under control any compulsive demand it exerted. However, such childhood fantasies,
even when voluntarily indulged, carry their own malevolency.
Beyond this, however, the Killer-Man fantasy was a specifically
and concretely symbolized manifestation of a more diffuse, in-
voluntary feeling that "beneath a nice, placid surface, where
things were basically fairly nice, there was something diabolical
going on."

As a matter of fact, I do recall that several times,
even up into early teens, I guess, it occurred to me quite
consciously that it would be possible that the world was
a façade put there—all the people with whom I came
in contact, merely acting out a role, all built up to fool me.

The Killer-Man fantasy and the fear of something diabolical
beneath a placid façade indicate an emotional trend of enough
power to require us to seek further meanings of the childhood
experiences already described. These meanings will be elucidated in conjunction with the interpretation of Eyman's belief
system below.

In discussing the Killer-Man fantasy, Eyman also relates inventing pretend playmates. He spent a large amount of time alone, as a result of his childhood illnesses, and having few real playmates resorted to pretend ones. The isolation and inactivity enforced by illness, then, facilitated in Eyman an active fantasy life. In addition to the fantasies mentioned, it could be expected that, consciously and unconsciously, he also elaborated on the meanings of his family relationships, heightening changing and coloring trends already present.

## 3. DEVELOPMENT OF THE RELIGIOUS INTEREST AND VOCATION

It was in seventh or eighth grade that a religious interest first became a consciously central strand in Eyman's life, and he started to become involved in church matters. At this time he says, "I did develop an interest in understanding the world—what made it tick the way it did tick—how we fitted into it." This somewhat diffuse quest for a unifying ideology took a more specific form in a question which he put to himself: "What is God like?"

How did this curiously specific question arise, and why did it take this form? The form of the question seems to assume an object, albeit one whose qualities remain to be determined.

Eyman had had little explicitly religious instruction, certainly little in the home. He had been exposed to the rather conservative Protestantism that filtered into the schools by means of Bible-reading and, in the seventh grade, a "period of silent prayer." While this source cannot be considered determinative, it is worth noting its influence. The period of silent prayer posed a problem for Eyman.

> Being a good little conformist, I was faced with the problem of what do I do during these—this minute or two of silent prayer? Who is there to pray *to*? And what sort of thing can one pray *about*? I suspect that this was a good bit of what really pushed the question over the threshold—at that time.

Eyman's question "What is God like?" and his more general concern with how the world ticks are other expressions of the emotional trends which gave rise to the Killer-Man fantasy and the fear of the diabolical beneath the placid surface. The two sets of mental contents were, and still are, deliberately kept separate, but they are directly related. This becomes clear when Eyman's various remarks on these matters are simply sorted out. For example, Eyman entertained primarily two conceptions of God—a deistic and a theistic one. The theistic God is one who is able to intervene directly in one's life; the deistic God set the world working in an orderly manner and then "keeps hands off." The deistic God, "just got things started and set up this wonderful system and that is the great force, the great organizing principle, and it keeps hands off. So it was always a rather distant deity." Eyman says that there were only odd moments at which he considered as a viable possibility a theistic God which he describes as follows:

> . . . a providential God, a deity caring for me personally . . . actually capable of interfering with natural processes. . . . A deity who could do something for me or to me . . . a personal but somewhat abstracted force that looks out for me if I placate him.

It was the deistic conception that Eyman primarily developed throughout his junior and senior high-school years. However, it is of the greatest interest that the moments at which he considered the possibility of a theistic God were those moments at which he was more at the mercy of his phobic concerns:

> I think that there were probably some earlier beliefs in which—at odd moments, although I don't think I ever consistently wondered about God doing something to or for me . . . [beliefs in] a deity who could do something for me or to me. [PH: At moments you say?] Well, moments of tension at which particular worries . . . the world wasn't all against me . . . a superstition in a fairly technical sense of the term . . . [Eyman goes on to describe the Killer-Man fantasy.]

Eyman makes further connections at another point. He says that the question "What is God like?" is "tied up with this whole question of what the world is like." And this question in turn had to do with "natural versus supernatural; whether this is a bifurcated universe—a natural layer and then a supernatural . . ." Further yet, a "supernatural layer" to the universe would make way for the existence of "this underlying evil." "This underlying evil would occupy that level—it would be underlying supernatural evil."

A deistic conception of God and, later, Eyman's liberal humanism, were not only alternatives to a theistic conception of God, but also an antidote to supernaturalism and the phobic conception of the world that would, for Eyman, accompany supernaturalism. The theistic God seemed most viable to Eyman when he was most subject to his phobic anxieties. Conversely, opting for a belief in a supernatural God would have reinforced the strength of the belief in supernatural evil, the diabolical evil that lies beneath the placid façade. By thinking through the two alternative conceptions of God, Eyman was reality-testing the Killer-Man fantasy and the fear of the diabolical. It is as if in asking "What is God like?" he were also asking about himself, home, and the world: Is there really someone on the bus who is out to harm me; and is the world really a façade put there to fool me? The deism, and later the humanism, defend Eyman against the effects of the phobic anxieties and the totalistic personality organization the phobia has the power to bring about. And ultimately, it is as if Eyman maintained an unconscious belief in a supernatural, theistic God, who, like the God of Barth and Chelly and the others, is all too capable of intervening in the affairs of men; so that the liberal's rejection of conservatism may, in part, represent his defense against his own underlying conservatism and the form of personality organization that would entail.

Eyman's quest soon led him and his family into an involvement with the liberal church. Eyman found here, over the course of the rest of his high-school years, a number of important experiences which allowed him to mature personally and to reach tentative solutions to his religious questions. Activities with the church youth group also provided a vehicle which allowed him gradually to develop a notion of the ministry as a realistic vocational option to which he could bring a number of proven interests and competencies. The development of an interest in the ministry meant a shift from a somewhat romanticized and more vaguely formulated goal of going into nuclear physics. The latter also represented Eyman's need to find a unifying view of the world, but he was finding himself more interested in people and their doings than in impersonal matter. These trends also had deeper emotional meanings which we will comment on below.

College saw a continuation and maturation of the same trends. Eyman was active in the church group, and here and in group discussions with peers he continued to find a satisfying and meaningful path. A course in the Old Testament also moved him, and he found in some of the Old Testament prophets a "call to righteousness" which he could integrate into his own version of the "prophetic ministry": "But let justice roll down like waters, and righteousness like an ever-flowing stream" (Amos 5:24). In college as well as high school, Eyman had assumed a leadership role in the church groups he was affiliated with.

Eyman's vocational development provides a contrast with that of the conservatives discussed earlier. His vocational development was gradual and based on a realistic evolution of interests and competencies over a long period. A final consolidation of a conception of the ministry as a vocation occurred during later adolescence and the college years. Under these circumstances, the development of the vocational identity occurs as an integral part of the development of self-identity. This contrasts with the rather premature vocational conception evidenced in Chelly's case, and also with a vocational conception driven by the effort to stave off a sense of nothingness, as in Electon's case.

Eyman's religious interest was clearly related to his childhood neurosis, and the development of these interests represented an aspect of the defensive process of the neurosis. However, the vocational and religious interests also resulted in an integration of the neurotic trends which provided a realistic basis for coping and identity formation. Eyman had considered other career possibilities which would have given expression to social concerns now current, but he chose the ministry as the vocation with the most openness, flexibility, and freedom of self-determination. There thus seems to be a degree of freedom and flexibility in the area of vocational activity not present in any of the conservatives.

In general, then, the relationship between the religious belief system and the defensive processes seems to be more flexible and open to change in Eyman's case than for the conservatives. Indeed, Eyman's belief system explicitly includes a high value on openness, flexibility, and change. Eyman's personality does, however, still bear a heavy burden of defensive processes, as we shall see below. It would be possible, however, for Eyman to deal with his defenses against affect and impulse and early object loss with little trouble to the belief system. In the case of the conservatives, any realignment of defenses would almost immediately bring into question the validity of major aspects of the belief system. This is one of the characteristics of the totalistic personality organization. This is not to say that it would not be possible for one of our conservatives to make a major personality change and still retain a conservative belief system. The question here is how inexorably and inflexibly the belief system is aligned with and mistaken for major defensive processes. In the cases of conservatism we have studied, the functions of the belief system are *relatively* less separated from those of defense, and both are in the service of maintaining rigid and oversimplified—totalistic—ego boundaries.

## 4. PSYCHODYNAMICS OF THE BELIEF SYSTEM

Eyman's early maternal relationship was intense and prolonged. A number of factors contributed: Father's absence, Eyman's childhood illness, Eyman being the only child for nearly a decade, and of course the mother's character. Mother was clearly someone who, out of her own needs, both infantile and mature, would cultivate in her son a close, highly sensitive, and highly sensitized relationship. The effects of the early maternal relationship pervade Eyman's belief system and his character at all levels.

The concept of God, for example, as a "divine dimension of the universe" may be seen as a symbolization which preserves and expresses the tender, hopeful aspects of the maternal relationship as well as the wish for fusion with the mother. Some of Eyman's imagery actually suggests quite directly an image of a primordial matrix from which we emerged and to which we wish to return, a kind of archetypal female-mother principle: "sort of the alpha and omega which brings us into being and the goal toward which we should be moving"; "progressive creation *of* creation," and so on. Further, the concept is global, diffuse, and all-encompassing, suggesting its derivation from and preservation of the time in which one relationship *is* the world, is all-encompassing. In the primary maternal relationship, the sense of goodness and well-being, when it is there, is all-encompassing; then the world is good. Similarly, Eyman's concept of the divine dimension unifies, brings together within one symbol, the essence of all that is good, valuable, and meaningful within the universe. It tends thereby to focus and re-create that original sense of global hopefulness and oppose it to all the possibilities for opposition, hopelessness.

Eyman arrived at this concept—or chose it from available theological notions—after a fairly long intellectual development. The intellectual development of his theology allowed a particular piece of emotional work to be accomplished. Eyman was able to separate out the "good" elements in the maternal introject and symbolize them separately in his concept of God. The symbol "God" represents the "divine," without contamination. He is then able to consider separately, at another more realistic level, "evil" in the world, human unhappiness. Then, at an abstract level again, he can also speak of the forces of opposition, "the force of impersonality . . . forces which assail him," with which he must struggle as a minister.

The Killer-Man fantasy and the notion of the world as a façade hiding the diabolical may be seen as responses to the intense conflicted feelings and ambivalences arising for Eyman within his familial relationships. The particular quality and details of Eyman's imagery may, however, be elucidated in such a way as to specifically suggest its deeper roots in the maternal relationship. When asked about the origins of the fantasy of the Killer-Man, Eyman's associations were of his calm, peaceful father considering registering as a conscientious objector at the time of World War II. This, and the image of the Killer-Man doing physical harm to little Eyman, at an age of approximately four or five, suggest that the fantasy was a response to "castration anxiety." That is, at a time when Eyman was competing avidly and aggressively with his father for his mother's attentions, it may have been less painful to create, by a series of projections, a retaliative figure outside the house than to see Father aroused to angry retaliation within it.[1]

Castration anxiety is expressed in one strand of the fantasy. However, there is more to the imagery than an evil male figure harming Eyman. The fantasy has a broader context. In describing the fantasy, the picture Eyman conveys is of himself scampering about *in the house,* in front of windows, looking out. Similarly, the Killer-Man himself is enclosed, as it were, in a large, moving, house-like vehicle, the bus, presumably viewing Eyman through the bus's windows. I take the imagery of the house, the sense of enclosed space, and looking out at the world from an enclosed, protected space as having a maternal source. Further, it was Mother who impressed upon Eyman the danger of the bus which passed in front of their home, sometimes getting too close to the pedestrians who were forced to walk in the street. There is a sense, then, in which the Killer-Man is feminized by being placed in the maternal context, and the danger to Eyman arises when he is at home, inside, where he spent so much time with Mother. The way in which the imagery of physical threat from the Killer-Man is embedded in the apparently maternal imagery suggests that Eyman responded to his anxiety about his phallic competition with Father by withdrawing from that competition and renewing his investment in the maternal relationship and its corollaries. This trend and its significance for Eyman's development and life-style are supported by other evidence.[2]

Curiously enough, the image of Eyman gazing out of the windows arose again in an interview when he spoke of thinking about his question, "What is God like?"

> I recall when—one afternoon, I was sitting at my desk
> in my room on the second floor of the house—my desk was
> right in front of a window—the windows—the window
> looks out the front of the house.

The house, being enclosed in the house, looking out, often being in the house with an illness, being cared for by Mother—this is the foundation of Eyman's early experience. "My mother and I would be at home on our own." His earliest memory is this tender scene:

> One thing that sticks in my mind as being fairly
> early, I remember my mother being in the living
> room with me—or I was with her actually. She was
> wearing a dress that I particularly liked. It was a very pretty
> plaid—very lovely shade of brown that particularly—

really especially liked. Then I recall the general area in
the living room that she was in. I don't recall what she
was doing or what I was doing. I think she'd been watering
flowers or straightening a stack of magazines or
something as momentous as that.

Eyman says that he does not recall what either he or Mother
were doing. But that does not matter, since the most important
thing they were doing, for Eyman, is recalled: being together.
These early experiences are the basis for nostalgically cathected
memory. The vivid and current appreciation of the beauty of
Mother's dress we must assume to be a representation of the
stronger affects involved in other real experiences which have
been repressed and screened.[3]

The Killer-Man fantasy has a broader context also in the
sense of being a part of the more global and diffuse fear that the
world is a façade and beneath a calm surface is something diabolical. This type of concern, whether the world as a whole is
friendly or inimical, has an origin somewhat different from
castration anxiety. It derives from anxieties and ambivalences
which arise in the relationship that makes up "the world," for
Eyman, the maternal relationship.

Since Eyman's liberalism is directly connected with the
phobic concerns we have been discussing, it too participates in
the preservation, integration, and defense against various aspects
of the maternal relationship. These connections have been mentioned previously. They begin with the observation that the
supernaturalism Eyman considered from time to time when he
was younger was a symbolization of certain features of his phobic
concerns. The supernaturalism would allow Eyman to deal with
anxiety by providing presumably real external objects in the universe to be anxious about, to seek help from, and so on. Liberalism became not only the alternative but the antidote to the
supernaturalism deriving from the phobic fantasies.

Eyman's belief system and life-style are centrally oriented
to "men and the . . . carrying out of their lives." Ideologically,
he places interpersonal relationships and social activism higher
than "thinking about God." His upbringing and his parents'
expectations for him taught him to be sensitively concerned with
people. It is clear also that in the close relationship with Mother

he learned to be highly sensitive and responsive to feelings. Eyman's Rorschach protocol gives other information in this area, and the results will be summarized without going into a technical review of the Rorschach protocol itself.

One of the strongest pieces of information to be derived from Eyman's Rorschach is the dominating use of repression in his current personality organization. There is an extreme sensitivity in the Rorschach responses to color and shading whose effects are likely to be the predominant determinants of the percepts. Emotional lability is suppressed, however, by highly developed cognitive controls. Thus Eyman is aware of and can speak about his emotional responses to the cards, and his feelings in general, with great sensitivity and perceptiveness. The powerful presence of repression is also indicated by a rather limited and bland array of contents of the percepts, notable particularly in someone as intelligent as Eyman. More generally, Eyman's thinking and theologizing do not show particular originality, but what he does perceive and describe, while they are the current issues and ideas, he responds to with great sensitivity, personal and moral. Characteristic also of the predominating use of repression is the occasional peeping through, as it were, of highly loaded sexual or aggressive issues. These, however, remain allusions.

A number of factors intensified the maternal relationship in Eyman's case, and other factors led Eyman to a strong and important involvement with his fantasy life. There is every reason to believe that a central strand of his early fantasies implicated Mother and various aspects of his relationship with her. Repression, then, we must assume, was instigated to lessen the effect of these fantasies as maturation proceeded. Other features of the Rorschach also indicate that this is the case, and that the qualities of character in Eyman now being described also developed out of the maternal relationship and Eyman's identification with his mother. For example, in three percepts, there is a feminization of areas of the blot that are likely, by virtue of their actual shape, to evoke phallic percepts. (The feminization in these instances bears a similarity to what was earlier called the feminization of the Killer-Man figure.) Another quality of the Rorschach that represents a preservation of the maternal relationship is more interesting.

A sequence of percepts demonstrates Eyman's keenly developed empathic capacities:

> . . . dancers or . . . women standing over a tub washing clothes or—perhaps grinding corn. . . . Actually I suppose the figures—depending on what feature one looks at—could be men with erect penises rather than women . . . (R*III*)

Initially perceiving the female and then shifting to the perception of an erotic male figure could, of course, be taken as an indication of Eyman's feminine identification. However, what is more interesting and unique is the shift itself. Now the reality of the inkblot gives equal support to perceiving the figure as male or female. Subjects sometimes have difficulty making the choice and select one. Eyman has with some sensitivity elaborated two well-distinguished and defined percepts. He is able to shift his point of view, "depending on what feature one looks at," from the female to the male, and speak of both with some accuracy. Recalling Eyman's description of his early memory shows us another example of this sort of empathic shift. He says, "I remember my mother being in the living room with me—or I was with her actually." Here too he shifts points of view, in a sense. From whose point of view should he speak—his or Mother's—or are the two one unit?

There is one kind of intimate dyadic situation in which this kind of shifting of point of view occurs and is very useful. That is where irritation arises between two people who are very close. Eyman was very familiar with this, of course, in his experience with his mother. It was in this kind of situation that he learned to "hold on" to his feelings, mulling them over, nursing his own irritation and waiting for things to calm down. The complex and developed cognitive controls over feeling and impulse displayed by the Rorschach are related, we may assume, to this aspect of Eyman's relationship with his mother. Eyman was far from crushed in these encounters. Part of his reaction when Mother, or anyone, became irritated with him was a sense of indignation, outrage, and the feeling that no one had any right to be angry with him. However, he did try to understand the other person's side and to assess carefully his own response.

Many of the Rorschach percepts reveal that they have undergone just such a careful scrutiny.

The origins of Eyman's tender-minded interpersonal sensitivity can be seen in the maternal relationship. Interpersonal responsiveness has a high place in his scale of values as does social and moral responsiveness. Living out these values, then, becomes another way of preserving a central quality of the maternal relationship. One qualification must be added to this picture. Eyman also has a marked underlying disposition to view people with a certain degree of contempt, as if he too were quite ready to find others irritating. This comes out in a variety of ways in the interviews and projective protocols. It is a trend that remains covert in his interpersonal relationships, although it must effect the way he experiences other people. He does not seem to view with much admiration the ordinary kind of life that most people live. In the TAT stories are a number of male figures who are in "business" or a profession. They are depicted as living quite drab lives, without much creativity or imagination—as if in some way they did not participate so fully in that "progressive act of creation of creation."

Two other complex trends in Eyman's personality organization and their expression in the belief system will now be discussed. They are the development of the ego-ideal and of the sense of self, and Eyman's sense of struggling with opposing forces in the world and his conception of action. These trends may be approached by first considering a remarkable TAT story:

> By way of prologue, let me say that—the name of the gentleman here in the foreground, and—not because of Genesis, but for the same reason that the name is used in Genesis—namely that in Hebrew, this means "man"—[is] Adam. And I guess I sort of think that this is somewhat archtypical. Adam came into the world —a whole and remarkably self-reliant being. After all, he had been growing for nine months—and within a short time after birth, he could fend for himself. Finding food where his parents had put it for him, defending himself from such enemies as he could imagine—his entire experience was of growth—of increased power. He was born with certain capabilities—and all of these grew as he grew. And he thought he could increase forever

in stature and in strength and in understanding.
And he tried to establish—firmly a symbol of his power
—his supremacy over the world. A scepter to go with his
kingship, so to speak. But when he challenged the
world in this way, it struck him down and he failed.
He failed because he thought he was the all-in-all.
And yet he was only within the world—part of the world,
and not its ruler. He was impaled by the painful
realization of the partiality of this power and he was
burned by the realization of the relatively immense power
of the rest of the world compared to his meager strength.
In shame and humiliation, he clung to what he had—
his own—concrete symbolization of his arrogance—a
monument to his own ego and self-assurance. Someday
he will mature and his monuments will not be material.
They will not be to himself, but to the world.
And the greatest monument will be himself—which he
will fashion largely after the world. And yet not wholly
because his gift to the creation will be just that—the
ability to be different. To be in and of himself challenging.
And so he will—while not maintaining or proclaiming his
absolute uniqueness, which he will know he doesn't
have—will maintain a unique self-consciousness and
consciousness of the whole, an ability to criticize both
himself and the whole—the world. (TIV)

The theme of the story is that a withdrawal to and cathexis
of the self and the development of the self in certain ways are
to be the manner of dealing with object loss, narcissistic injury,
and external opposition to desire and omnipotent wishes. The
original omnipotence and narcissistic perfection is lost but will
be regained by developing the self along ideal lines and in accordance with conditions external to the self. The self will once
again incorporate or make up the whole world by containing
a conception of "the whole." In addition the conception of the
whole will be one which includes unique qualities and ideal
conceptions which will allow the self to be the basis for moral
evaluation.

The form of the story itself is an example of the ideal functions of the self Eyman describes. The story has the quality of

personal experience, of memory, translated into mythic form. Eyman makes a translation of, "I am a man and this is my experience," to "I am Man and this is his experience." The self becomes the standard and guide for all men.

The idea of the self as standard is expressed elsewhere in Eyman's protocol and is integrated into his conception of the ministry.

> Jim had attempted—was attempting to be a minister to men and to the world. He stands—himself, pleading, mute because there is no higher court of appeal than the self and he—unlike the woman with the babe knows this—knows that he himself must find his answers— even if someone else offers, he must find that which is offered, before it can become his and can become meaningful. (TV)

The ideas of prophecy and the prophetic ministry and Eyman's identification with the Old Testament prophets are also integrated with this sense of the uniqueness of the self:

> I can't come up with a good proper-seeming name for the young man down here on the left—so I'll get around it by using the first person: Sometimes as I ponder on the sterile repetitive religion of the mosque, I wonder if I don't have within my mind, within my heart the keys to a better religion. I think back to those times when I felt like one of the prophets—a man growing out of the soil of his people, their traditions—but rising above them —proclaiming the great, simple verities that undergird life. (TII)

Eyman's Adam story (TIV) is presented as a developmental sequence. As such it is remarkably parallel to Freud's description of the development of the ego-ideal in "On Narcissism" (Freud, 1914). Eyman was not familiar with this paper. While we may be more inclined to interpret the story in terms of a contemporary dynamic than a developmental sequence, the dynamic itself points, according to our theoretical notions, to an inferred development very like the one Eyman describes in the story. Further, the fact that the story is presented as a developmental sequence is an interesting and important formal characteristic of the story. There is not only a series of psychologically related stages in the story, but the story itself encompasses a relatively long time span. A very broad time span is characteristic of several of Eyman's TAT stories. Eyman is inclined to see any particular event as a stage or as one passing moment in a more universal, comprehensive life span. A broad outlook of this sort provides a kind of philosophical perspective on things which is a fitting part of Eyman's religious liberalism. The time perspective is also part of the defensive system. It is a way of binding tension, conflict, and frustration, as well as of protecting against a sense of nostalgia and loss. The use of extremely global concepts, such as "consciousness of the whole," "divine dimension of the universe," and so on, has similar functions. Some reasons were given earlier for also considering the diffuse, global quality of the concept of a divine dimension of the universe as an expression, in part, of the wish for fusion, and these same reasons would apply to considering Eyman's broad time perspective in this light also.

The wish for fusion with the mother is expressed in another interesting way within the Adam story. Indeed, the whole story is a fantasy of fusion. The Adam of the story, as Eyman presents him, is quite a bit more than "remarkably self-reliant." Adam is a kind of completely self-contained unit. He is not presented as being in relation to others, including the others who would be caring for what would be, presumably, a neonate. He cares for himself, feeds himself, defends himself. He is the king of his whole world, and somehow he contains within himself his whole world. The fantasy is one in which the ego contains the maternal, caring-for functions. The feelings—"he could increase forever in stature and in strength and in understanding"—are feelings of omnipotence which accompany the imagined union with the maternal source. In the story, then, Eyman *assumes* the maternal functions and implicitly incorporates them into the Adam figure. This allows Eyman to sustain the denial that separation from the mother has occurred and in this way the fantasy of fusion is maintained. The fantasy of the incorporation of the maternal matrix into the ego is repeated precisely in the notion that the presumably mature Adam will include within himself a "consciousness of the whole."

Eyman's story of Adam contains parallels to the Biblical story of Adam and Eve. As J. N. Rosen points out, the Adam of the Bible also incorporates the functions of the woman:

> In the biblical story of Adam and Eve, part one, we find the striking notion of man giving birth to a woman . . . we may suspect that the unconscious purpose of this story of "creation" was to usurp for man the creative function of woman. Adam appears symbolically as the "mother" of the human race. (Rosen, 1964)

The broad time perspective is part of a complex of trends which preserve the sense of union or express the wish for reunion with the mother. Two other of Eyman's TAT stories have a sense of timelessness and capture affective states which express fusion in a somewhat different way. The following story also has the quality of a dimly perceived nostalgic memory:

> Don had always liked the soft green lushness of springtime and grass under a weeping willow tree. The sun was warm and yet its rays were broken by the thickly hanging leaves and the grass was often cool and vaguely moist underneath. . . . And yet he was fortunate, because he would be one of those who could always return to the soft moist spring ground under a willow tree and look up and be a person. (TVI)

This part of the story, with little change, could be the experience of a child being held on his mother's lap, looking up, and being "a person" through the reflection of his mother's gaze. Eyman describes the experience as a kind of internal retreat; he can return to this emotional state for restoration and relief from the pressures of the workaday world.

The tender-minded emphasis upon the self and the development of the self within Eyman's belief system is a direct representation, then, of a deep and complex trend within his personality. The turning to and cathexis of the self and the development of the self according to an ideal allow for the integration, maintenance of, and defense against the wish for reunion, fusion, with the mother. The emphasis on the self also protects Eyman against the feelings of loss arising in the face of the reality of having to relinquish the happy state of having only to "look up [at mother to] be a person."

In the Killer-Man fantasy we noted some evidence that Eyman had made a renewed investment in the maternal relationship partly to protect himself against castration anxiety. There is evidence for this trend in the Adam story as well. "He tried to establish . . . a scepter to go with his kingship, so to speak," the world "struck him down," and he withdrew his interest to the self and the maternal matrix. Throughout Eyman's TAT stories the heroes are presented as either struggling against opposing external forces or living as if they were held down and controlled by some inner pressures. Some comments on this trend will elucidate other aspects of the psychodynamics of the belief system.

The feelings of struggling against opposing forces are expressed in two ways, differing with the context. In the context of the religious belief system, Eyman sees certain abstract social forces as inimical to human life and therefore as objects for his concerns as a minister. In an autobiographical sketch written at the time of applying to theological school he wrote:

> Essentially it comes down to this: there is a crying need
> for men who are able and eager to free their fellow
> men from the deadening shackles of superficiality of
> belief, creedalism, and supernaturalism.

And in a current TAT story he says:

> Jim had attempted to be a minister to men and to the
> world. He was just beginning to understand the full import
> of what this task might be. On the one hand was the
> power and might of the world—the force of impersonality,
> the force of entrenched ways, the force of thoughts that
> have been enshrined and made sacrosanct. . . . He will
> be able to stand—to stand up before the forces which
> challenge him and will continue to challenge him, but only
> to challenge and not to defeat. (TV)

The impersonal threatening forces which now play a kind of implicit role in his belief system, alongside the explicit rejection of conservatism, can easily be seen to be the heirs of the earlier feeling of diabolical evil beneath a placid surface. One TAT story makes this connection clear:

> David, ever since the first day he had been led by the hand to the strange, red brick building with more people than he had ever seen in one place and told that this was the first day of school, had been afraid of institutions of power. He saw them as façades—façades with an air of unreality. He found them shadowed, veiled, and yet casting a large shadow of themselves across his every waking moment. Their threat was so great that there didn't even appear to be any way he could rid himself—rid the world of them. . . . He began to grow, not more powerful, but more capable. And rather than warring with institutions, he began slowly but surely to learn how in the future he would work with them, so that together, they could help to guide toward a better future. (*TIII*)

The feelings of dread and unreality projected into "institutions of power" is an expression of the dread of fusion. In turning away from phallic competition and the father's world, Eyman seeks the hopefulness of the maternal relationship, but is there confronted with another kind of dread.

Given another context, that of mundane daily life, the life of the business or professional man, the oppositional forces manifest themselves differently.

> Albert was about thirty-five years old. An engineer of moderate abilities—certainly not capable of great creations. Any such capability that he'd had had never come forth. Rather quiet person, not very assertive, still a bachelor. . . . Between the ages of twenty-five and twenty-eight or twenty-nine he stopped going out with any great frequency. He lived with his mother . . . (*T6BM*)

This character is presented as simply bogged down, tied to his mother, drab, and having little inner life-force. Two other TAT "heroes" are presented in the same light, held down, struggling, frustrated by their slow professional progress but frightened of too quick a progress. Further, looking at it from the outside, Eyman views professional life as depersonalizing and isolating:

> Yet now, sitting underneath the tree and looking up
> into its branches and thinking—other places came to
> mind—other times and memories not as pleasant. There
> were buildings—buildings with chimney pots—buildings
> with water tanks on top with company names painted
> on the sides, tall towers with clocks—steeples. . . . These
> were the sorts of things that would come to indicate
> for him a dying—a constriction of the spirit, a spiritual
> kind of death, isolating. (TVI)

This is the image that contrasts with the idyllic posture in the sun beneath the weeping willow. Eyman seems to be saying here that to be a man in the men's world is to become isolated, depersonalized, out of touch with all that is warm, nurturing, meaningful. Here too is an expression of turning from an identification with the masculine world of his father to a more maternal style. A similar shift is depicted in Eyman's first TAT story:

> George dislikes intensely practicing on the violin. He's
> really not very good at playing it. Right now he's feeling
> that—although he can't say this to himself—he's feeling,
> perhaps if he puts it off a little bit more—if he works
> up his anger, his rage at this instrument that he can't
> play very well, can't manipulate adequately, perhaps then
> he won't have to practice on it. . . . His mother's gonna
> come upstairs to check. He will take out his anger—his
> frustration by showing anger. . . . He wanted to attain
> this sort of mastery, yet when faced with the actual
> demands set before him, he was unwilling, almost afraid,
> to expend the necessary energy and time. (T1BM)

Anxiety over an issue of mastery is dealt with by fantasy emotional discharge or by turning to a relationship, in this case the mother, and venting the tension there. This general trend in Eyman's life is seen in its specific form in his shift in interest in high school from nuclear physics to working with people and social problems that eventually led him into the ministry.

In a religious or moral context, action is viewed quite differently from the way it is viewed in the context of the professional life. It is as if Eyman has two concepts of action. Action is possible in the religious context, even in the face of opposing forces. Indeed, struggle against inimical social forces is the essence of the activity of the minister, of religious activity, and Eyman feels able to "stand up before the forces which challenge him and will continue to challenge him." It is in the context of the professional ministry and the more realistic struggle of day-to-day dealings with institutional life that Eyman feels that frustration, difficulty in acting, and foreboding of potential drabness and failure that he depicts so vividly in his stories. Both concepts of action are operative in Eyman's own life. However, it is by making action religious and moral that acting becomes hopeful, meaningful, and exciting for Eyman.

The sense of struggling against opposing internal and external forces is an heir of the period of the infantile neurosis. The religious belief system allows an integration of these trends which permits Eyman to confront them and, through a meaningful social path, oppose them and act. A number of interwoven roots of the internal emotional currents which result in Eyman's sense of oppression have been suggested. One is castration anxiety. The second is the ambivalences that were aroused at various stages in the maternal relationship, including the dread of fusion. And a third source has to do with specific qualities of the interaction with the mother. Eyman seems to have been overburdened with stimulation in childhood by the closeness of the mother combined with a good deal of childhood illness. At the same time, he was the one who had to learn to take an early responsibility for controlling affective expression within that relationship. These two circumstances led to a strong, excessive control of emotional and instinctual expression, to a potentially stifling degree. Such a high degree of control of one's own expression of life-forces is likely to be experienced as an oppression, and, when the control is partially automatic and unconscious, an external oppression.

## 5. SUMMARY

Eyman's belief system provides a vehicle for the complex integration of a number of major personality trends. The roots of the belief system lie in the infantile neurosis. The choice of a belief in a deistic God and the gradual development of liberalism serve as an antidote to the inimical psychic trends that would have been institutionalized through a belief in supernaturalism. The infantile neurosis is a response to castration anxiety by a renewed investment in the maternal relationship. Central aspects of the belief system express the wish for reunion, fusion with the mother, and secondary responses to that wish: the emphasis upon the ideal development of the self; the global, diffuse concept of God as "creation of creation"; and the tender-minded view of the universe and human life. There is a rejection of the masculine professional world represented by Father. Eyman lives out in his professional and social concerns the tender-minded, highly empathic, sensitive style of interpersonal relations that characterized his relationship with his mother. A certain covert tendency to view daily life and daily people with contempt represents both his rejection of his father's life-style and his ambivalence toward his mother.

In the infantile neurosis, the negative aspects of the parental introjects were externalized in the Killer-Man fantasy and the notion that under a placid façade there was something diabolical in the world. These trends were reality-tested through Eyman's early religious questioning and were eventually integrated and contained by an anti-supernaturalistic belief system as forces in the world that mankind and Eyman, as a minister, must struggle against. However, these same trends are present in Eyman's defense system as an excessive control of impulse and affect and a resulting stultification of action. Action becomes most possible and meaningful through religious or moral pathways—all action becomes religious action, and therefore sanctioned. It is thus possible for Eyman to challenge face to face the forces that oppose him.

Eyman is not a doubter, and he has also developed a belief system which, although currently not in flux, could potentially sustain a good deal of self-questioning of different kinds. Indeed, an overall characteristic of his personality is a strong integrative trend. This trend is manifested in his history of a quest for a unifying world view. An inference is suggested by this datum, in conjunction with the evidence for the unconscious wish for reunion with the mother. Under favorable circumstances, the wish for fusion with the mother is put to the service of adaptation and coping by just such a transformation into a powerful integrative trend in the personality. An integrative trend of this sort is manifested by an ideology which tends to unify and make sense of life as a whole and by ideology-related work which is a deep expression of the individual's personality.

What allowed the wish for fusion in Eyman to become transformed sufficiently into an integrative trend to foster development of a coherent belief system and pattern of coping? If Eyman had tried to develop a supernaturalistic belief system, it would have given more power, within his personality, to aspects of the parental introjects which would have undermined his capacity to adapt, or at least changed radically that capacity. Eyman, of course, is still reacting unconsciously to these trends, and it is as if he had an unconscious belief in a supernatural God of the sort he rejects consciously. His battle against this unconscious belief in a supernatural God is represented in his belief system by the "crying need . . . to free [his] fellow men from the deadening shackles of superficiality of belief, creedalism, and supernaturalism." Now, there was very little, within the culture of the family, that would have supported a conservative religious belief. This fact no doubt helped Eyman sustain his quest for an alternative more in keeping with the family culture. Father himself had a liberal socialistic political ideology, and this served Eyman in his adolescence as a fulcrum for identifying with his father and developing a relationship with Father. Further, Eyman's anxiety, even at its worst, had apparently never gotten to the point where a conservative projective system was a constant necessity. So, for example, he did not follow through on a very brief encounter with a Presbyterian group in early adolescence.

Eyman did in fact gain a great deal from his early years in the way of a solid basis for self-esteem. The parents' firm, high, and apparently consistent standards were imposed gently and with consideration for the child as an individual. This form of discipline and training helps a child develop sound controls and self-discipline, and this is a source of security. We described Eyman as turning, in the face of early object loss, to the self and the development of the self. Through the maternal relationship and his position in the family, there was a valued self to turn to and develop. Further, while Eyman in some ways rejects an identification with a childhood picture of his father, he was able to build a later appreciation of his father which helped ameliorate a potentially destructive superego or conscience. Thus Eyman feels he can stand, face, and challenge the external forces that oppose him. He does not feel defeated or harassed or punished. As we shall see, it is in just this respect that Strindge (chapter XII) differs from Eyman. Strindge feels harassed and burdened by his own superego in a way which he finds nearly impossible to deal with.

The outcome, then, of a number of experiences during Eyman's early years within the family left him with more than adequate intrapsychic resources to deal with potentially undermining aspects of early parental relationships and introjects.

Eyman's choice against supernaturalism protected him against a totalistic personality organization which he still experiences as a threat. In the culture of the conservative theological student, of course, the choice of a supernaturalistic belief system is supported, and therefore, implicitly, the totalistic personality organization is supported. In both cases, the belief system protects the individual from some aspects of the infantile neurosis. The liberal belief system, however, permits enormous steps to be taken in the way of internalizing within the personality psychic trends which are externalized and institutionalized in the symbolic objects of the conservative belief system. One effect of this difference is that Eyman, for example, talks far more realistically and with greater emotional differentiation about the people in his life than do the conservative subjects. Another effect is that a realistic view of death is taken, and no grandiose claims are made on the universe in the form of expectations for personal survival of death. Further, in Eyman's case there is a more flexible relationship between the defensive structure and the belief system. Open-endedness is institutionalized as a value within Eyman's belief system, and this allows for a greater degree of emotional change and growth. Finally, without a precocious formation of a totalistic personality organization, vocational development, in Eyman's case, proceeded in steps appropriate to his position in the life cycle and on the basis of the development of real interests and competencies.

These differences between Eyman, as a paradigm liberal, and our conservative cases are set against striking major parallels. Particularly striking in Eyman's belief system and world view is a use of imagery of good and evil—the divine dimension compared with the "deadening shackles," "force of impersonality," and so on—similar in its cosmic, ultimate quality to that of Pale,

Electon, and others. This imagery is considered an expression of the splitting of the hopeful, positive side of the wish for fusion from the dread of fusion. The major roots of Eyman's belief system, as in previous cases, can be traced back to the maternal relationship and especially to an unconscious wish for reunion with the mother. The conception of self and the development of the ego-ideal which find expression in the religious life and ministerial role in Eyman's case, as in the case of the conservatives, arise out of a family constellation in which the son has a special relationship with the mother, in which there is some devaluation of father, and in which the son acts as a mediator in the family. Eyman's family constellation and its effects on him are precisely parallel to the conservative cases in these regards. The resulting secondary narcissism is integrated and developed differently.

The case of Strindge, which follows, will continue similar parallels and contrasts and will show where the liberal belief system is psychologically vulnerable to corrosive doubt.

# XII

# Strindge: A Liberal Doubter

This is man; and because this is man, there is religion and
law. The law of religion is the great attempt of man to
overcome his anxiety and restlessness and despair, to
close the gap within himself, and to reach immortality,
spirituality and perfection. So he labors and toils under
the religious law in thought and in act.

The religious law demands that he accept ideas
and dogma, that he believe in doctrines and traditions, the
acceptance of which is the condition of his salvation from
anxiety, despair and death. So he tries to accept them,
although they may have become strange or doubtful to
him. He labors and toils under the religious demand to
believe things he cannot believe. Finally he tries to
escape the law of religion. He tries to cast away the heavy
yoke of the doctrinal law imposed on him by Church
authorities, orthodox teachers, pious parents, and fixed
traditions.

PAUL TILLICH, "THE YOKE OF RELIGION," IN
THE SHAKING OF THE FOUNDATIONS

## 1. INTRODUCTION

Strindge—the name is meant to convey the fine, agonizing edge
upon which he lives—is presented as the paradigm case of a liberal doubter. Intelligent, introspective, and sensitive, he is twenty-
five, single, and has just finished his second year of seminary. His

mild manner and tender-minded concerns provide an immediate contrast with the sturdy, muscular frame of Midwestern farm life.

Although Strindge's origins lie in a culture conservative enough for him to refer to it as fundamentalist, he comes through on his questionnaire as distinctly liberal. His scores on the scales of liberalism and conservatism[1] are nearly the same as Eyman's. Also, on the Rejection of Doubt Scale,[2] he was one of the two out of one hundred and seven who received the lowest possible score, indicating the least possible ideological rejection of doubt as a part of the religious belief system. The low Rejection of Doubt score was one among other scale indicators of intense, tumultuous doubts. On a scale measuring the presence of a number of dilemmas typical of theological students[3] he received the highest score of all the respondents. On another brief scale measuring the belief that suffering is an essential ingredient in religious life,[4] his was one of the two highest scores.

Strindge's belief system does retain a core of conservatism. He believes, "intellectually," as he would say, that God is not only a spirit but a personal spirit, one which people can experience. He himself has not experienced God, although occasionally he believes that he possibly has. He also believes that a minister should be someone who does have a relational experience of God, and for this, among other reasons, he does not think that he can or will be a minister. In fact, at the time he applied to the seminary he felt himself to be essentially without beliefs. His purpose in applying was to clear up the confusions that surrounded the area of religion. However, his trend was, and potentially still is, to develop a more internalized conception of God. This is the area where the doubt lies.

Other aspects of the current belief system are more typically liberal, as defined in the previous chapter. He is interested in the secularization of the church—the breaking down of traditional church services and organizations and the sharing of religious interests and concerns among small groups of lay people in a broader life context. "There are no holy places or everything is a holy place." Similarly, he has discarded the notion that God calls only ministers—anyone can be called, any human activity can be a calling. Also, he does not see Jesus as a Savior. He sees Jesus as "just a person who responded in a very obedient and faithful way."

Strindge is struggling to transform within himself his religious tradition so that it will become a vehicle of genuine self-expression. Although he has been able to do this only partially so far, this trend is also characteristically liberal—the emphasis on the development of the self. As a tool to help him achieve such a transformation, he adopted Jesus's words, "I am the way." Strindge, at one point, took this as a justification for saying of himself that *he* is *a* way—that is, he as himself is acceptable as he is, and his religious quest could proceed from there. A similar use was made, at different times, of psychology and of a conscious effort at interpersonal honesty and openness—these trends again being congruent with the emphasis in the liberal belief system on the development of the self.

## 2. THE NATURE OF LIBERAL DOUBT

The liberal belief system, in contrast with the conservative, is characterized structurally by a higher degree of internalization. Projected images of ultimate good and ultimate evil are either eliminated or attenuated and depersonalized. Eyman's belief system is not entirely free of projected objects. He speaks of God as a "divine dimension of the universe," and he speaks of forces within society inimical to human life against which he must struggle as a minister. However, these concepts are not seen particularly as external objects to which one relates on a personal basis. They tend to be seen as qualities of human life; they become a way of looking at the world. By and large, in the case of the liberal believer, the fantasies and feelings which, in the case of the conservative, fill up the images of God, evil, and the supernatural realm are related to specific objects and events of daily life.

It will be recalled, however, that Eyman went through a period in which the process of internalization was not complete. He vacillated between a world view which included a supernatural realm and one which did not. This gives us a clue to a basic vulnerability to which the liberal believer is subject. When the process of internalization is incomplete and in competition with a projective system, there is a profound ambiguity as to very basic interpretations of everyday personal experience. Strindge is caught in just such an ambiguity. For example, in regard to crucial experiences he has such a question as, "Am I experiencing God or am I simply experiencing an irrational guilt?"

The structural vulnerability of the liberal belief system, then, is the profound ambiguity that arises as to the basic interpretation of experience when there is competition between a projective belief system and an internalized one.

A psychodynamic vulnerability may be pinpointed which is also a direct outgrowth of the processes involved in internalization.

Using Eyman as the example again, we noted that in his case a more totalistic personality organization would have accompanied a belief in a supernatural realm. The totalistic personality organization would have had to incorporate persecutory objects, the latter being manifested in Eyman's phobic fantasies about Killer-Man and so on. Similarly, the belief system, if the personality had continued to be organized along conservative lines, would have had to incorporate in some developed way ideas derivative from the persecutory objects. If, for present purposes, we identify the persecutory objects with superego formation, the possibility that exists in such a case is that the belief system will institutionalize a superego which is punitive and persecutory to a degree intolerable to the individual. Strindge displays just such a development. His belief system, we will say, does not protect him from his own superego. Even in the case of Eyman, we noted that abstract forces of opposition were manifestations of internal energies which he turned against himself and which made action problematic.

The liberal believer, then, is subject to the possibility of doubt when his belief system institutionalizes a superego so punitive that the belief system itself does not protect the individual from internally originating persecution, self-punishment, and harsh self-judgment. The belief system does not protect the individual from his own superego. This is the psychodynamic vulnerability of the liberal belief system.

## 3. A NAGGING GOD

The phenomenology of Strindge's decision to enroll in a seminary for ministerial training is an eloquent statement of his personality organization and the emotional status of his belief system as an aspect of his personality. Strindge not only did not want at that time to be a minister, but he was passionately, vehemently, against it. The decision to go to seminary was a desperate concession, an effort by Strindge to rid himself of a chronic feeling which he understood as God nagging him.

> I can remember once walking down the street and thinking sort of in terms like, "Okay, God, if you won't let me alone, I'll go to the seminary, but I don't like it *at all*. If I do a poor job, it's not my fault." And in these terms, you know, sort of saying that very disgustedly and unhappy about the whole thing. . . . I think it was just kind of desperate. He was really bugging me. I think it was sort of, you know, I was going to give God guilt feelings then. Sort of, "Okay, I'll do it, but I don't like it, and it's not my fault, and I don't know why you pick on me. Why don't you pick on somebody else." Kind of thinking if I could say all this, he'd feel sorry for me and let me go or something. I didn't really want to go, you know. I was agin it, and He was sort of nagging me and forcing me, and He ought to be ashamed of Himself. I didn't want to be a minister. It was more you know, saying all this perhaps to get the Good Old Almighty off my back, you know. Let me alone, get away, and—I'm not sure if He was really willing to or not.

Strindge is describing here an experience of being picked on, nagged, and victimized by his own superego. More than this, however, the experience seems also to be a perpetuation of an internalized anal battle. God is bugging him, and he is trying to get God off his back. Strindge does not experience a face-to-face confrontation with God, one which he can stand up to, as it were. God's approach is from the rear. There is a contrast here with Eyman's case. Eyman experienced the forces which opposed him as forces to confront and fight against, stand up to. Further, Strindge's tactics with God are characteristically anal. He will concede to God, he will be obedient; however, he will undermine and sabotage God's directive by being a failure, or threatening to be. Through acting unhappily in the letter but not the spirit of the directive and by passively attacking God—giving Him guilt feelings—Strindge provokes further attack, further nagging on the part of God. Such tactics, of course, keep the battle going, they do not provide a resolution.

Strindge is caught in an internalized anal conflict with his own superego. While the superego imagoes may derive from both parents, Strindge relates to the punishment with passive, feminine wishes. The conflict is eroticized. A whole syndrome of feelings about the self results from this conflict and the intensity of the passive wishes: feeling castrated, torn up inside, held down and held in; feeling isolated and yearning for release through violation, or trying to make contact by fighting; feeling confused and—Strindge's most characteristic word—"agonized."

This syndrome is clearly and graphically documented in the Rorschach protocol.

> Headless woman reaching up to see if her head's there.
> With lots of foggy or confusing area . . . a conflict.
> Sort of two opposing things . . . almost a hopeless type
> of thing because—seems like—not only will they never
> shake hands, they won't even be able to get close enough
> to fight. (RI)

> Two rabbits . . . laying on their side with their feet
> together. They've just been in bloody battle. . . . Very
> abstract quality of a something contained an' working
> to force its way out, to break loose—to kind of burst
> forth . . . proved fruitless or undesirable or too agonizing,
> too fearful. . . . Also a symbolic picture of a woman
> who has just been raped and mutilated and—specifically
> sexual areas of breast and vagina are inflamed and—a red
> glow of violence and—misuse. (RII)

> The gorilla—uh—that's been impaled on a—candle.
> [PH: Where was it impaled?] Where—things are normally
> impaled. Right up the old bunghole. (RIV)

His own feelings are given an anal interpretation, regarded as if they were feces. This is suggested by the "abstract quality . . . working to force its way out, break loose," as well as by many other remarks. He says, speaking of his feelings, "I hold this in," "I handled all the stuff within me," and so on. He also has the feeling that inside—himself or other people—is something dirty.

> Something disgusting. Disgusting and vulgar. Like
> someone responding to something. . . . Kind of like a

> good front or a pretty front—but the thing has sort
> of—seen a little deeper and gets kind of like a ugly or
> gross or nauseating feeling . . . like a cloak and—pretty
> paint on a building when inside is grubbiness. (RIX)

The feeling that his own responses are dirty makes him distrust his "good" emotional responses; he distrusts his own sublimations and moral judgments, as if they were really cloaks for something fecal.

Now, the fact of the matter is that Strindge takes every opportunity in the Rorschach procedure to find an "agonized" percept and to express, at the expense of reality, some aspect of his inner suffering. The insistent return to themes of suffering indicates the presence of the passive wishes. Also indicated is an active, libidinized use of fantasy in the psychic economy. Strindge is not unaware of this:

> So I'm afraid my fantasy is probably, I would still say
> pretty large, because there's more to it—I'm not sure
> —I'm probably not willing to go into it any more. Fantasy
> is still a big thing with me. Although I don't mean to
> just hold it into a sexual realm, because it expanded
> much more than that. But it continued through high school
> and college. And even now it's been such a thing—I'm
> into it sometimes—just daydreaming away. A need
> fulfillment fantasy.

The turn from reality to fantasy heightens the sense of isolation, and may also be regarded as an aspect of the anal syndrome. Fantasizing assumes a masturbatory quality and is equated with playing with feces.

To anticipate a later conclusion, we may speculate that the withdrawal to fantasy is an expression of Strindge's reaction to a feeling of loss experienced in regard to his mother. In the current personality organization, however, it has other structural concomitants whose further effects can only increase doubt and confusion. The experience of the nagging God, as well as a kind of fear of social censure, are indications of an unintegrated and externalized superego. Inner controls over and direction of instinct and impulse are therefore poorly developed. Strindge experiences an overall kind of prohibition against which he yearns to rebel. Similarly, the ego-ideal remains immature, and fantasy gratifications and fulfillments take the place of or distract from engagement with the world which could result in real gratification. A direct result of the immature and unintegrated inner controls is that archaic fantasies surrounding Strindge's primary objects—mother, father, church, religious belief system—still invade the ego.

> He sees himself standing there on a hilltop in front of this very large building, and he looks at this building, and it is more or less beckoning to him. . . . He feels compelled to go into it and yet he hesitates. . . . The doorway is very dark and very threatening . . . just a black hole, and he doesn't know its mystery, maybe evil. . . . The shadows are very dark, threatening . . . a tree there—yet not a leaf on it. . . . Here's this building which says, "I am the most important" and which dominates his whole view . . . yet something's funny . . . this point of utter confusion. (*TIII*)

In this fantasy, archaic feelings about the primal mother are projected onto the ecclesiastical building. Also, there are more explicit thoughts of an incestuous reunion with the mother:

> This is a young, young man named Daniel and he is very, very young, young man. And he's strong, muscular, very handsome man—and—had this vision—and this vision was that he was—there beside his mother—and his mother was holding a child which was her child yet of which he was the father . . . (*TV*)

The erotic submissive attachment to the father also receives direct expression:

> This young man, Raphael, is remembering this scene, from his dream. He's clutching onto a pole, he's turned his head away from an arrow with fire at the end of it. And in between is figure of his father. . . . He suddenly found himself naked—before his father who—a very pious, moralistic man, who in a sense stripped his son all the time. Yet all he ever stripped him of was the exteriors.

And inside, the son is just loaded with feelings which he can never express. He can't speak to them, can't let them out. And on this night he is stripped naked by his father again. And he has run. . . . There's this huge arrow. . . . He is strong enough to take [it] and wield. It's the very thing he could use and he has the urge to take it and run it through his father's guts. . . . And this has happened so much, that he cannot turn his eyes and look at his father or the spear which he might use to kill his father. (TIV)

Not surprising then are also fears of death:

He saw a skeleton, the symbol of death—and death was after him. Here he was a young boy about eleven years old, and death was after him. And this didn't make sense. He was so terror-struck. And he thought there's only one thing to do. There's only one way for me to escape. And beginning the next day, he would always go to church. . . . Just doing everything that there was to do in hopes that this might free him from death—take death away from him—get death off his trail. And this Tony did for the rest of his life. This agonizing terror filled life from twelve to fifty-two when he finally died. He took many sleeping pills. He killed himself. (TVI)

Strindge takes some distance on the four TAT stories just quoted by having the story heroes fantasize, dream, or envision them. This technique is also a manifestation of the fact that Strindge is currently making the effort to understand himself further by introspection. The pursuit of self-knowledge is made more difficult for him, however, by the fact that it tends to become simply another form of rumination. Rumination helps keep the inner conflict alive. And the archaic fantasies and feelings that are stirred up can only make an appraisal of people, institutions, and beliefs more difficult and shrouded in unresolvable ambiguities.

At the time Strindge said, "Okay, God, I'll go but I don't like it," he held a very conservative view of the ministry. A minister was the son of God; only the minister was called to serve God. The minister had a special relationship with God, was or should be extremely good, and the congregation watched him to make sure.

> . . . a minister being something special and something holy and pure and perfect and this sort of thing. And that, you know, he's really won. He's with the Old Boy, and he's got it. I don't know. It's just a very white picture. He's really a good guy and special and special relationship with God and all this. In opposition to the rest of the people, you know, in the congregation. And they don't have to be this. He has to be, and they watch to make sure he's that way kind of.

That Strindge would be more than reluctant to go to the seminary yet would grudgingly do so is now understandable. The religious culture of the family had been integrated into, become the assumed expression of, Strindge's own poorly integrated, punitive superego. That congregation watching the minister to make sure he is pure is an all too graphic representation of a partially integrated internal self-judgmental process. To go to the seminary, to be a minister, then, meant giving in to the passive, submissive wishes to yield to the castrating father. "He's with the Old Boy and he's got it." While he may derive the father's power in this manner, this is achieved through the erotic feminine wishes for the father and a kind of relinquishment of the self.

Strindge currently remains caught up in and confused by the same conflict. He feels deeply uncertain what to do and, in basic ways, what to believe; he feels agonized and nagged at; and he longs for release—the expression of feeling, of himself—and a feeling of real contact with others. And just where God enters the picture, other than as an intellectual assertion, remains a confusion.

> And as far as, perhaps I could say meaning in life in this sense, or purpose, I would be at a loss to in a sense formulate any such thing. The only justification really I have is just that the Almighty has put me here, and this belief, this justification by faith, as I suppose it would sort of come down to, is an intellectual assertion. It's not an experiential thing, a personal being type of thing, although

I would if asked to formulate my viewpoint on this, I would also say that the Lord of the universe is a personal being or perhaps personal spirit. I'm not sure just how I would play with those words at this point. . . . When I did fill out the questionnaire, it was just more of a state of uncertainty and doubt that I had, was in, and have been in and still am in—but without this: perhaps I should at this point say to myself that maybe this is what life is, even though I don't particularly want it. It's difficult, it's uneasy, it's uncertain, it's agonizing at times, it's unstable. It's self-concerning to the point where I cannot see what is really there. Perhaps if my focus is more straight ahead for what this world is or more focused on this world that maybe then I'd've broken down the barrier of self. . . . What I think now and will for a while anyway is perhaps there really is something more, and that I probably will not be able to gain this more fulfilling feeling or . . . Anyway—I do not feel that emotionally I am able to release myself. Inside I feel that I don't really open up to a person when I'm talking to him. So this always raises up to me, you know, if I weren't—if I didn't have this wall at this point, if I would really be willing to open up and say "I do trust," if I really would trust, that maybe this very barrier which I use to keep people out is also keeping out the Lord. And this is why I can't really say this is what life is because I still see myself as having this wall which may be stopping me from seeing it in a fuller sense.

In the last of these comments, Strindge indicates his uncertainty about how he should understand the nagging feeling. Perhaps he does not experience himself as if he were loved by God (in some sense acceptable to him intellectually) because of his own distrust and inadequacies; that is, maybe there is something wrong with him such that he deserves to be nagged and unloved. Later, he expressed just these thoughts:

I think all the more this is sort of why the nagging is there. I had not fully, fully searched for God. I haven't really loved or I don't really love. So maybe I am holding back, maybe that's what's nagging me. I haven't really

searched or I haven't really gone to the depths or whatever.
I haven't really loved. I haven't done what I should which
I think kind of goes along with my self-hostility or
self-anger and inadequacy. So I would blame myself.
I haven't as much as I am able as a person fulfilled my
human role or being one who is open, one who loves.
And this I think nags me for having again failed for being
weak or worthless. At least I would say that the nagging
at me is for somewheres having done something that
I shouldn't have done. Whether it be by mistake or by
not having done it.

But these feelings only add fuel to the fire, a fact of which
Strindge remains unaware. By blaming himself for being confused, held in, and nagged at, he only sides with that part of
himself which does the nagging. This, of course, intensifies not
only the experience of being nagged, but the mixed wishes to
submit and rebel.

The final question for Strindge remains how to interpret the
experience of being nagged, and the answer to this question remains a basic ambiguity:

[PH: Why was He nagging you?] I don't think, I think,
this, now, as I look back on it anyway, it was me and
my guilt feelings, and I don't know if they were guilt
feelings. My religious attitude, thinking that I should be a
minister, you know . . . [PH: The nagging was guilt
feelings?] Well, I don't know exactly what I would make
of it now. I think much of it, yes. Whether I was being
called or not, this I haven't—I don't even know. My
more rationalistic self would say—or psychological self—it's
just feelings you had and guilt feelings, and your kind
of a need for being religious or something like that. But
this part of it, you know, may really have been legit. I was
really being in a sense or experiencing God or whatever;
whatever words I might choose but perhaps that would
be better—experiencing. Or a call . . . I said guilt, but I
don't know if I should [have] used that or not. Guilt
may have been pushing me at that point. The fact that
I was fighting—fighting the ministry, or fighting listening
to God or whatever.

These remarks are clear manifestation of a partial internalization competing with a partial externalization. Should the nagging be interpreted psychologically as feelings of guilt arising from within for various reasons? Or should the nagging be understood as deriving from the externalized religious object? Or is there some compromise which would retain both possibilities, such as the nagging is from guilt, but the guilt is the result of not responding to an externalized religious object? This conflict leaves a deep rift within the individual and a deep ambiguity as to the meaning of important personal experiences.

To interpret the nagging consistently in psychological terms would bring Strindge into a more direct and useful confrontation with his tradition. As things stand, he feels subjected to and held down by the conservative tradition he grew up with; but he also sees the religious tradition as a possible way for his own meaningful self-expression. His struggle is to turn the religion into a vehicle for self-expression without either he smashing it, in a sense, or it destroying him:

> He's a young lad who has been given a rather expensive,
> traditionally important violin. . . . Finally he got to the
> point where the excitement is in conflict with the desire
> not to play the violin. . . . He'd sort of like to smash
> the doggone thing and yet he's really proud to have it . . .
> real conflict. . . . And this was a gift from his parents.
> So this is an extra concern in a sense. Even his impulse
> to smash it is, is held back a little bit. . . . It becomes
> a creative expression . . . but [he] keeps it as a source of
> expression . . . he wasn't able to use [it] for a vocational
> interest but just as his own free expression of idea
> and spirit. (T1BM)

## 4. THE WHOLE WORLD WITHIN

We have understood Strindge's experience of a nagging God essentially as an outgrowth of a poorly integrated, castrating father introject, to which Strindge relates with passive, feminine wishes in accordance with an anal organization of feelings and instinct. Is Strindge then an exception to the pattern that has been suggested in all our other cases in which the concept of God was a derivation of basic qualities of the maternal relationship? No; there is evidence in the data already examined and in other data to be presented that the wishes underlying Strindge's religious quest derive from the early maternal relationship.

The passive feminine wishes lived out in relationship with the nagging God are, in part, an indication of an identification with the mother. Further, Strindge is looking for an emotional experience—a release, a sense of contact with others—not for a work; this is also a feminine orientation. He speaks of not having "fulfilled my human role of being one who is open, one who loves." Further, the wish to love and be loved, the yearning for contact that will break through the isolation and loneliness, all seem to be based on a model which is a fantasy of mother-child love. He says, "I see myself as having this wall," which keeps him from opening up and having contact with others. The "wall" he speaks of must be understood, in part, as his own ego boundaries which he would like to break down in the service of reviving a fusion with the maternal matrix. The model for contact is not based on relationships between two differentiated, bounded adults where contact at any one moment is always partial.

In the Rorschach he expresses a complementary idea, a kind of reluctance or resistance to developing his own differentiated ego boundaries:

> . . . many different elements, varieties, shapes . . .
> stronger center . . . two very dominant elements that are
> growing sort of coming together. And yet when they do
> combine it's in a kind of a gray, not really positive way.
> On the fringe of the dominant elements both outside
> and inside are sort of strange, unknown, uncertain things;
> they're not too distinctive. . . . And going out from them
> are just sort of a solid rod which sort of suggests harmony.
> It seems incongruous because the progression of the
> picture is in that direction like it's come together into
> this rod, all these mixed elements. Yet it's inconceivable
> that all could be contained within. That is, it would
> almost seem that much of it had been wiped out and
> only a small element remained. And went from ugliness
> and anger into a kind of a solid, cold metal rod, in a
> sense, no, no warmth. (RX)

This description of the Rorschach card is an introspective account of the subjective impression created by the card. Strindge seems to be making reference to "mixed elements" within himself. And he seems to be saying that he does not see how it is possible for such a variety of inner trends to cohere into one solid, perhaps masculine, identity. Such a development would entail destruction of some aspects of himself, and the result would leave him alone or without warmth. In one sense Strindge is quite correct: to develop his own identity would entail limiting and controlling his extensive fantasy life, and it would entail a process of emotional separation from his primary objects, especially Mother. The reluctance to experience such a separation is the basis for his reluctance to see the mixed elements within himself integrated into one identity.

While Strindge's nagging God is not particularly maternal in His basic relationship with Strindge, one quality is apparently distinctively maternal. It was Mother who, at times, was the nag. The following incident is the only one Strindge remembers of overt disagreement between himself and his mother:

> I remember once—I don't know, I must have been about
> a junior in high school—and my mother was telling me
> something, I don't remember what it was. But I said,
> "Nag, nag, nag, all the time, nag," and this really hurt
> her. She didn't really say too much. She just sort of said,
> "If that's the way you feel." She wasn't angry or anything
> like that. Just, you know, "Get off my back," or
> something. And it really cut pretty deep as far as she was
> concerned. Her reaction to it, you know, kind of cut me
> to the core and really made me feel bad.

The episode indicates a highly sensitive relationship, in which overt anger could have little play. Father's commands, in contrast, could not be dallied over:

> Much more fear by all of us of my father, though, than
> my mother. Whatever he said, you know, that was it.
> Zoom. My mother—a little more lenience and a little
> more chance of persuading her. It wasn't quite so
> important to get right after it right then. Take your time
> a little bit more.

Although Strindge is the fourth of six children, a quirk in the family structure gave him a special place with Mother. One brother is a little less than two years older than Strindge, and another brother is a little less than two years younger. Strindge had little time of being the only baby in the family. However, when he was born, Father took over care of the older brother, and that alignment remained throughout Strindge's childhood. A similar alignment was somehow made with the younger brother and the father. These two boys were "more the worker and the farmer than I was." Strindge says that he was the "good boy, the one—my mother never worried about me. She didn't have to worry about me. I wouldn't do anything wrong." Strindge was his mother's son. He stayed close to her, staying in the house with her. In addition, when Strindge was a small child, Father drove trucks and this would take him away "for a pretty good section of time."

Strindge identified strongly with his mother's somewhat degraded position within the family. Emotional communications within the family were apparently minimal and subdued. "My father—I don't know—never really talked that much. Never really opened up that much." When minor things did not go right in the family, Father felt a need to blame somebody, often Mother. In addition, there was a certain amount of ridiculing of women on the part of the men in the family,

> Sort of superiority in the family, in a sense. Kind of a constant quipping amongst my brothers and my father about women, and "Ach—no—gee, they—yeah, they just—", you know. Picking on them and this sort of thing. Even amongst ourselves when none were around.

While Strindge may have joined in, he had other feelings about it:

> I sort of felt like with my older brother . . . I think perhaps my father too, that they weren't really treating their wives as wives, you know, in this sense. Giving them the full respect or full equality that they might have. So this sort of thing bothered me too. . . . I often thought when I get married it's not going to be, I'm not going to be like that. I mean not necessarily me

having to rule all the time. But that there can be a little more dialogue going on here than is evident in these cases.

Strindge is identifying here with the wives. He was very angry at his father for a long time:

> For a long time I was extremely hostile toward my father. Really angry. Hateful in a sense. 'Cuz I remember it wasn't his side that I took most of the time. In fact I don't know if I ever did.

A number of elements, then, in the family structure provided conditions the developmental outcome of which we have seen in Strindge—a castrating paternal introject to which Strindge relates on a passive feminine basis. These elements are: the alignment with Mother; Mother's partially degraded position in the household; Strindge's intense anger at Father; Father's periodic absence; and the minimal emotional communication within the family, especially on the part of Father, which would have made him all the more remote and susceptible to Strindge's fantasy distortions.

For ease of reference we shall speak of the "nagging God syndrome" to refer to the conflictful personality organization we have described so far and which did result in Strindge's experience of being nagged at by God. The syndrome was both an effort on Strindge's part to deal with the presence of the father in the family and, more, to deal with the loss of the primary relationship with the mother. Just beneath the surface of the passive-aggressive conflict are yearnings for love. "I sure had the desire in a sense to rush to someone's arms." Also just below the surface are feelings of isolation and loneliness arising out of a sense of abandonment.

> A young man . . . got a beard, kind of long hair . . . finished high school—was in college for a while and dropped out. Has bummed around. Had lots of friends, known lots of people. Through all this always felt alone, unable to really have a feeling that he was with anybody or knew anybody—just sort of lonely type all the time . . . develops a real need for [heroin]. . . . Finally ends up in a hospital. He collapsed . . . through a period

of just agony, and he's off the drugs. Finally gets out but
isn't really able to make any contacts at all. Somehow
just isn't even able to open up to anybody kind of. Kind
of lonely and alone and finally is back on drugs again.
And then one night decides that—just too much. He's
taken some drugs and feels pretty high but somehow it
isn't much good and he jumps off a bridge and commits
suicide. (T16)

This person, Ambrose, has been very, oh—everything's
been very screwed up for him. He's been in agony and
turmoil and confusion. . . . And it was wintry, cold,
and this Ambrose went out and was walking down the
street. It was to him this cold world he was walking in.
And this really fit his feeling that night. It was cold.
He was bound by it. He couldn't express himself—be free
as a bird to fly and float around. He walked on. (TI)

The internal conflict with God and the passive-rebellious struggle
with his religious tradition must be seen as ways to deal with the
loss of the mother. As we shall see below, Strindge *felt* most religious and most himself when he could relinquish that conflict
partially and experience within himself more of the basic self-
acceptance and sense of self that would have derived from the
early maternal relationship.

The central core of the nagging God syndrome apparently
developed when Strindge was very young. His childhood was
painfully lonely, by his account.

Somewheres in there though I was more and more the
loner in a sense. More and more by myself. Somewheres
around seven, I began to be—sort of, you know, the
whole world in me. I would handle my own feelings, or
repress them, or keep them within rather than sharing
them.

Estranged from Father by the family alignments and, inevitably
limited in his entitlements to Mother, Strindge turned to himself
and fantasy. He discovered masturbation early and used this and
associated fantasies as a kind of release. "I can remember being
very young, you know, and attempting to masturbate. This car-

ried on and was a big thing, something that I attempted very often, very regularly." Strindge felt it was bad and that insanity might result. A range of fantasies were associated with it, some explicitly around mother, father, and God:

> Sexually, quite a high fantasy associated with this. . . .
> Apparently I was religious at this age too [ten, eleven,
> or twelve. PH.], saying to God, send—just send a beautiful
> girl down here just so I can see what sex is like. Half
> expecting that perhaps it just might happen. . . .
> Also I had pretty strong in Freudian terms oedipal
> feelings, thinking sexually in terms of my mother quite
> strongly. Rationalizing this fairly well. If my mother
> could have sexual relations with me it would be very
> good education for me. I never recall consciously feeling
> particularly guilty about it. . . . I can remember at an
> early age, it would be grade school, probably fourth and
> fifth or sixth, but this would be more an estimate, I
> can remember my wishing my father would play with my
> penis and this sort of thing.

Other fantasies of being a hero, important, a leader, and so on, characteristically symbolic of phallic competence and greatness, were conscious throughout adolescence, and still remain so.

> . . . just anything . . . What I really desired to be but
> feared greatly and my fantasy world fulfilled it. I became
> that which I kind of would like to be. Important . . . I
> think of the attempt by me to fulfill my feelings of
> inadequacy. Inability really to be outgoing, to be leader,
> yet wanting to. And I think what happened is that
> fulfilled needs which was my way of trying to say this is
> really you and you're okay, you're adequate, you're
> acceptable, or whatever.

The sexual and heroic fantasies were efforts to ameliorate his isolation and loneliness. Especially they were to be a salve to obliterate and overcome his deep sense of inferiority, the damage to his self-esteem, and his painful lack of feelings of worth. And yet, in such fantasies, there is a core of grandiosity which, while it serves as a compensation for feeling like nothing, may also be considered to have more than a compensatory function and a source other than the effort at restitution for the lost self-esteem. Strindge dreamed of being "important," a "leader," of having his sexual curiosities excitingly relieved, as if through his fantasies he were giving expression to the feeling, "I *am* something. I am of worth." The sense of self-worth hidden within the fantasies of heroic greatness, and so on, do reveal the core of self-esteem and healthy self-regard which must be the legacy of earlier parental relationships, and probably in particular the primary maternal relationship. Further, with firmer inner controls and a useful identification with the father or himself as a male person, these same fantasies might provide the basis for an adaptive identity, giving Strindge cues to what he wants and how to get it.

As a young boy, Strindge was painfully shy and would run from adults outside the family, even relatives. As an adolescent, and later in college, however, he was not socially withdrawn. Currently too, he has a boyish, cheerful manner, is eager to evoke a positive response, and succeeds in doing so.

The content of Strindge's fantasies are, of course, in no way remarkable. Two things about his fantasy life are of interest for us: first, the fact of withdrawal to fantasy in the face of loss, and second, the fact that incestuous fantasies remained conscious for so long. Both indicate a failure to develop inner controls and identifications with the parents which would provide a serviceable base for later identity formation. Poor inner controls over fantasy and a lot of wish-fulfilling thought unconnected with reality and realistic action are indications of an immature ego-ideal and a poorly integrated superego. Under these conditions the child may indulge a good deal in pleasurable fantasizing, but he is also prey to the anxieties that inevitably accompany incestuous fantasy. Strindge suffered such fears as a child, and more than a little remains:

> . . . somewheres between seven and eight. It was really just after World War II. Me and my mother and father were talking about these [atom] bombs and how destructive they were. And this being just terror—horror. Such a thing as that. And they talked about it being the size of a baseball. So I constructed lots of fantasies about this. I would catch it with my baseball glove or . . . I can remember, *really* scared the living hell out

of me. Just the fear of being killed. This destructive
thing destroying everything. Just terror though. Just
horrible . . . And I can identify this feeling with one
other I had. And that was that incident I remember when
my parents had that one specific argument that I
can remember them having. This same sort of feeling
like, you know, everything—nothing's certain. And I tie
this with what is my fear of the dark, which is a
pretty good fear that I have, of just being in the dark,
or being alone.

Similarly, two nightmares which Strindge remembers from
this period also reflect anxieties analogous to those he currently
experiences.

I remember we had an old barn. I used to actually
climb up on the back of it and there were some boards
across up here and you could go up and sit on those
and then climb back down. But on the way down it
was kind of hard because there's a real wide step and
it was very hard to get— . . . I can remember one night
dreaming about this. Being up there and coming down
and not being able to make this step and falling, and
continually falling and falling and falling . . . waking
up really shook. . . . Kind of scared the hell out of me
a little bit.

The classical symbolism—climbing up and down the back of an
old wooden barn—suggests an incestuous theme, and the dream,
in any event, reflects Strindge's insecurity of that time.

The other [dream] had to do with a cousin, a gal
cousin. We were out—oh I don't remember—it was a—
oh little clearing. It was like the barn was here, the house
was here, and the garage was here. It was right close to
the building. All I remember is, it was her head there
and a little long neck over to something here: I can't
remember what it was but it was something about
kind of like a monster at least . . . must have been
very bad. Anyway, the only way I could destroy that

> was to cut this thing attached to her neck, you know . . .
> her body wasn't attached. Just her head attached, which
> would kill her, and I can remember really not knowing
> what to do, and then finally chopping that off and
> she sort of saying, "Why did you do that?" and I not
> really knowing . . . waking up very frightened and
> shook up.

The setting is the same as the other dream. This dream seems to reflect an identification with the girl effected through castration, and the idea that castration is necessary to delete a monstrous part of the self.

The conservative religious belief system underlying the family culture was also integrated very early into the core of the nagging God syndrome. Religion was talked about very little in the home, and religious language was used only rarely. However, the family attended church and Strindge went to Sunday school. And while there was as much silence about religion as other emotional matters, the silence itself added to the imperative burden of the meaning of the religion.

> Not much education at home, church or religious
> education. I don't think we had any really. Matter of
> fact I don't know how much it was talked about. I'm
> not even sure it ever was. . . . I know she [Mother]
> holds these [fundamentalist] views. [Father] didn't have
> too much to do with it. He used to go to church when
> he was home. . . . It just—subtly you pick up the sense
> that, you know, this is what it is and don't challenge
> it. In a very subtle way you kind of know you don't
> question and you don't doubt and all this sort of thing
> is sin.

A subtle, frightening necessity to accept the conservative religion stayed with Strindge throughout most of his college years. He "knew" this was what his parents believed, and he took it as an assumed given, a set of beliefs that provided the basis for living but in other ways were not even consciously considered. He also recognized that his parents in their actual living were more liberal and open to others than the verbal fundamentalism they expressed at times. However, Strindge took upon himself the family's religious belief system as a heavier burden than his parents or religious instructors could have foreseen. The moralistic conservatism of the small community gave an institutional base for the primitive, unintegrated superego which had developed in Strindge in his childhood.

## 5. CASTING OFF THE BURDEN

Strindge knew as a boy that a religious vocation would please both the teachers in his community and his mother. High school was apparently his best time. He was liked by his classmates, played sports, was a leader in some ways in the school, but would never identify himself with any one group or take a girlfriend. He was everybody's friend. Anticipating college, he had dropped the idea of a religious vocation and dreamed of a fashionable position in engineering, since that was the vocation everyone was talking of at that time.

College was a crisis from the start. Academically he did poorly from the beginning, nearly flunked out, switched majors, and was faced with the fact that he really did not know what he wanted to do, and seemed ill equipped to do anything. Above all, the traditional home religion seemed to hang over his head like some kind of looming imperative which threatened destruction, but the actual meaning of which was utterly lost.

> At this point I wasn't saying, no, there wasn't any God, or anything like this. But I continued to go to church. And of course my thinking at this time was very limited and very shallow. You know, God was God. That was about it. There wasn't much more to say about it. [PH: God was God?] Yah. Just contentless, you know. Type of thing you grow up with. You just believed in God. Not very relevant in some senses, yet in other senses very relevant. Great source for guilt feelings or concern, certainly not any real force in life. More just kind of a thorn practically than anything else.

He suffered greatly from severe depressive anxiety which upset him so much that he feared going "insane."

So I really kind of zeroed in on rock bottom. I didn't
know what I wanted to go into, what I wanted to do,
and I can remember just sort of being kind of in an
agonizing way. It was during this period especially that
I kind of thought at times that I might really end up
in the nut house. I [was] very fearful almost that I
really couldn't keep control of my mind. And I remember
being pretty shook and pretty panicky through these
times and really keyed up. I remember a couple of
nights when I'd go to bed I'd think, gee if I could only
really cry this would really be great. I'd really release all
this tension inside of me. But I really couldn't.

Strindge tried to comfort himself with religious gestures, but it
did not help.

I remember I used to pray and sometimes I'd read my,
read the Bible. But it got to the point—I think every
night I used to pray, but you know, it'd be the same
thing. Almost like saying the Lord's Prayer, in a sense,
although it wasn't the Lord's Prayer. Say, sort of rambling
and my mind would be wandering off and stuff like that,
and I'd try to keep on. . . . I did that for quite
a long time. But I finally decided, ah to heck with it.
So I quit. Was almost a gamble, you know. A magical
thing perhaps.

It was during such a period that, feeling more internal pressure
to go into the ministry, he finally said, "Okay, God . . ."
Strindge at one time places this period in his first year of college,
at another time in his third year. In all likelihood, while his
memory is vague on this score, he experienced such anxiety off
and on throughout his first three years of college. He suffered
from guilt and felt the same isolation he had experienced as a
child, even though he continued to be a sociable, friendly, liked
person. He did not have resources to orient himself to the world
in some adaptive way, and he remained at the mercy of his own
superego.

It was an encounter with a minister who befriended Strindge

which allowed him to open up, cast off the burden of conservatism, and "head-on, standing firm," look at what he did or did
not believe. In this encounter, Strindge met his Staupitz, and
the friendship had the same effect in both cases. Erikson describes it this way.

> The therapist as good father gives retroactive sanction
> to the efficacy of maternal trust, and thus to the good
> which was there from the beginning. . . . He gave
> Martin his first feeling in a long, long time of a
> benevolent parental presence. This remark meant to
> Martin that he should stop doubting and start looking, use
> his senses and his judgment, grasp Christ as a male person
> like himself, and identify with the man in God's son
> instead of being terrorized by a name, an image, a halo.
> (1958, p. 168)

Strindge had met this minister his second year at the university,
but had not been able to listen to him at that time. He found
the minister's liberalism conflicted with his understanding of
what a "Christian" should be. By the end of the fourth year,
however, the bankruptcy, for him, of his traditional beliefs had
been proven, and he set them all aside.

> But finally it got to the point where I thought there just
> isn't much use going on anymore this way. I might as well
> just sort of set all of this aside. All my religious feelings
> and attitudes and beliefs and sentiments and just set them
> aside and start from scratch because this trying to
> make sense out of this from within isn't working at all.
> So that's when I sort of just set them over and didn't
> know whether I believed in God or not and perhaps did
> and perhaps didn't. . . . Sort of feeling that I kind of
> began to feel free to doubt and to look and to think,
> begin kind of from scratch looking at it again.

Strindge not only felt better, he felt more "religious":

> I felt even religious in a sense. When I could set all these
> old beliefs and stuff aside. Something about it just
> made me feel much more religious than I had ever

been before, you know. . . . I was really looking at life
a little more. I just felt a heck of a lot better. Like a
burden had been lifted and there was something positive
here to think about and to look at. . . . I remember
having remarked that I felt really more religious when I
didn't believe in God than just prior to that when I had
said, yes I did believe in God, and it didn't mean
anything. I don't even know if I had content in it, but
I felt more like I probably wished I could have felt
saying I believe in God or holding on to these beliefs
that I'd grown up with. I felt more when I said no
I don't believe. I felt more I guess then like I wished I
could have felt earlier. . . . So it was more—well, I guess
it was just me.

The contact with the minister friend freed in Strindge "the
good that was there from the beginning" (Erikson, 1958). As
Strindge puts it, "it was just me." The punitive superego was
ameliorated in the benevolent parental presence of the older
friend. Strindge was thus able to detach his sense of the religious
from the guilt with which he was confusing it and relate it to
the genetically earlier sense of the value of the self and its
existence, "maternal trust" (Erikson, 1968), where it belonged.

Strindge followed up these leads with a specific concept
which he derived from Jesus's Biblical words, "I am the way,"

. . . which sort of meant it was a path. I mean, and you
kinda started out on it and you walked and you weren't
either in or out and that was it. It's a way and this
is where I'm at now, you know. So, hell with saying
what you're supposed to say as far as people are concerned,
and here you are and say what you believe in here
and work from there. . . . Just the fact that what I am
was a way.

Strindge was able to feel at that time that what he was in himself, what he felt he could say and mean, was an acceptable version of human life; it was a way.

These developments represented major steps in liberalization
and a freeing from the burden symbolized by the traditional
religion of the family. Strindge used two other tools for this

purpose at this period. One, derived from the minister friend, was the idea that a Christian was not someone who believed this or that, but a person who responded as openly and honestly as he could at any one time. This idea met Strindge's needs also. It allowed him to look head on at his own feelings and some of what was going on around him. Strindge ended up taking a major in psychology, and he was able to use, among other things, a course in abnormal psychology as another vehicle for direct examination of his and others' emotional natures.

All these trends—feeling more religious as "just me," the idea that "I am the way," being open and honest, and the use of psychology—are in the service of the process of internalization. They allowed Strindge to attend to his own self, to see his turmoil as a function of his own emotions, and, renewing the maternal trust, to find that self basically acceptable. As it stands now, the process remains incomplete. Strindge still feels nagged, still feels the need for a justification. He also still needs to learn that, being his father's son also, he is entitled, if not to sole possession of the mother, certainly to the legacy of trust that arises in the early maternal relationship and becomes institutionalized in the relationship with God as a basic sense of the acceptableness of oneself. He did not take radically enough to the teachings of his friend to make a necessary reversal of a kind Erikson describes in Luther, namely, that his sense of being nagged at arises not from his uncertainty and worthlessness, but that he feels worthless and uncertain as a result of the nagging, which he, as it were, believes.

> Staupitz, he claimed, once said to him that one is not
> truly penitent because one anticipates God's love,
> but because one already possesses it—a simple
> configuration of a totally reversed time perspective which
> Luther later thought to be strikingly confirmed in the
> scriptures. (Erikson, 1958, p. 167)

Strindge is, as a further result, still struggling with a task necessary to him, that of reshaping his religious tradition into a vehicle that makes sense to him for his own self-expression, and doing this between conflicting desires to rebel and destroy the whole thing, or to submit totally.

## 6. SUMMARY AND COMPARISONS

Strindge's life position bears a similarity to Pale's to the degree that he is looking for love, justification, and direction from an externally defined God. However, it is just in this that Strindge is uncertain, first because he never had a relationship with God of the sort that Pale claimed, and second because, like Eyman, he had good reasons for rejecting such a relationship. Strindge felt most religious, and appropriately so, when he had thrown off the traditional conception of God. Then he felt more himself, even if still somewhat lost. However, because of the incompleteness of the internalization process, Strindge remains confused as to how to interpret the guilt and the feeling of being nagged. Perhaps the nagging is from God in some way. Holding on to this possibility, Strindge remains the victim of his own self-punitiveness, and he remains in confusion about his religious belief system because the belief system does not protect him from his own superego.

Strindge is also similar to Pale in that the psychodynamics associated with the religious confusion leave his ego prey to a good deal of primitive fantasy and affect, all of which inevitably leads to confusion about what belief is reasonable and what perception of reality is accurate. In the case of Pale, however, the mere presence of libidinous and aggressive fantasy and affect is confusing because it contradicts the purity of the self-image; and Pale struggles to reject these aspects of the self, trying to reestablish the totalistic boundaries to do so. Strindge reacts to his inner life in the converse way, and in this respect his behavior is characteristic of the liberal. Strindge both tolerates and welcomes his subjective experiences and makes an adaptive use of a tendency, which is there anyway, to immerse himself in fantasy. Strindge is trying to develop through self-knowledge, and this process, successfully carried out, would have the effect for him of both further internalization of the religious concepts and a further breaking down of the totalistic personality organization which threatens him through the medium of his passive, submissive wishes.

Strindge's struggle against the nagging God represents an effort to preserve himself from a totalistic personality organization. To give in to this God, to become the kind of minister which that God represents means, for him, a kind of total relinquishment of the self and free expression. Such a ministry would in fact entail the establishment of a rigid defensive system which would bring the personality organization into a totalistic alignment. In this struggle, Strindge bears a similarity to Eyman. Eyman, however, was successful in his battle. Strindge's continued struggle is, in part, a function of the fact that it is actually the battle itself that is cathected on an anal model, and there is therefore libidinous investment in keeping it going. There is no realistic goal which Strindge sees as possible or desirable to achieve, the lure of which would provide motivation for a resolution one way or the other. This is an indication of the immaturity of the ego-ideal structure, other concomitants of which are an infantile organization of instinct and a primitive superego, the punitive operations of which the ego must continue to suffer. The notion of "I am the way" could provide a kernel for a useful and realistic organization of the ego-ideal. But Strindge has not consistently followed through on this. If he were to, it would lead to the development of the self, another basic liberal trend in which he would bear a similarity to Eyman.

Strindge's love-battle with his religious tradition is similar to that of Joel. In both cases the religious culture of the family had become associated with an ambivalently cathected paternal imago. And in both cases the ambivalent struggle with the imperatives of culture and tradition tended to obscure the nurturing legacy of basic trust that the religion is meant to preserve.

# XIII

## Some Further Variations in the Liberal Context

For man is not equal to his own experience; he attempts
to forget it; and he knows that he *cannot* forget it.
PAUL TILLICH, THE SHAKING OF THE FOUNDATIONS

The four subjects presented in this chapter will receive a brief
presentation. The purpose of presenting them is to show some
variations, within the liberal context, of belief systems and character types. A more detailed analysis of their case studies would,
at this point, add little to the main themes or methods of
analysis so far presented. However, while the major underlying
psychodynamic themes may remain very similar to ones already
observed, it is of interest to note the variations in form and
structure of both the overt belief system and character structure.

Sal and Girth may be considered liberal non-doubters. Their
belief systems illustrate a particular use of Christian theological
language that parallels Eyman's expression, "divine dimension of
the universe." Both make use of all the traditional theological
concepts, but use these concepts in much the same way as
Eyman uses the concept of God—to refer to another dimension
or aspect of everyday events. The supernatural is rejected or re-
interpreted, so that all events are natural or interpersonal events,
and the theological concepts are expressions of human, personal

reaction to or interpretation of these events. As a result of their traditional Protestant background, Sal and Girth have at their disposal a richer and denser set of theological categories than does Eyman, and their investment in theological interpretation of daily events is greater than Eyman's.

Girth illustrates this use of theological language in a statement of his position:

> I keep putting it toward a very realistic, naturalistic revelation that is not supernaturalistic. That it comes through your ordinary processes of life, and this just happens to be how you describe it—with maybe another dimension.

The concept of "revelation," a traditional Christian theological category, is here given a nontraditional interpretation. "Revelation" is described not by describing supernatural events but by describing natural ones. "Another dimension" is added, but the characteristically liberal rejection of supernaturalism is indicated.

Girth gives a similar interpretation of the notion of God's activity as "creator and sustainer" of the universe. For example, he is a member of a group which helps organize and give structure to a slum community, and he says these efforts *are* God's activity.

> Now—we interpret this as God being active in the community. This *is* God's activity—but it's not God's activity. God is the creator and sustainer of the universe such that—normally [sic] social structure is His means of maintaining the world.

While the precise nature of the "other dimension" described by the theological language is problematic, it may consist in serious response to the human situation:

> God's act in Christ—the center of the history of the world . . . saying that we are coming to grips with in our lives the thing which really demands complete seriousness. (Girth)

The purpose of life in the religious belief systems of both Sal and Girth is meaningful engagement with the here and now.

> The purpose of this world is not to be a good guy
> and you have eternal life. But it is much rather to engage
> in meaningful activity, which for me now more and
> more becomes participating in the working out of the
> Kingdom of God, to put it theologically. (Girth)

> I think perhaps the idea of God's will kind of stands
> central—for me at least—in all of life. The sovereignty
> of God in creation—in the world and life today—as I
> understand it—is one that is incontrovertible. Life is
> directed—is drawn internally by this—well, by God's will.
> God's will is the direction by which life—as hopefully
> it seeks to be as full and complete and authentic as it
> can be. This is what I understand as God's will. The
> power, the force, the authority of the authentic life in
> relationship to others. . . . It is one's relationship to
> life—not just a private relationship to others—relationship
> to society, to all mankind. The reality is life in relation
> —not life divorced—not life isolated—so that God's
> will I would express as a—well, being fully human. (Sal)

A particular kind of very deep ambiguity is present in the belief systems of Sal and Girth, and the ambiguity is obscured or perhaps it is one that is expressed and made possible by the use of theological language just described. As the excerpts from Sal and Girth indicate, their theological positions can *sound* as orthodox as the most conservative Barthian. Indeed, Girth says that his position is orthodox, not liberal, and theologically he is quite justified in saying so. The question is, of course, to what, precisely, in daily events do the theological categories refer? What is the "other dimension," the theological one? It would be possible to use consistently the theological categories to refer to various aspects of response to the human condition. Sometimes Sal and Girth do use the theological categories in this manner, but they are not consistent. For example, Girth says:

> Now—we interpret this as God being active in the
> community. Now at the same time I say that I don't

really believe it, you know, with all my heart and all my soul. And all this stuff.

What is it that he does not believe? Girth says that, as he understands the theological categories, there is not really a question of God existing or not. However, this seems to be the kind of question which he raises here. Theological language as it is used by both Sal and Girth seems to contain and express doubts about God, Jesus, immortality, and so on, that would have to be expressed in traditional, supernaturalistic language. For example, consider Sal's speculation about what follows death:

> Life is too precious to just think it's just a matter of circumstance—that it's born at a certain time—pops into being at a certain time and then disappears completely. This kind of rubs me the wrong way—to think that life is that expendable. . . . I think the idea of eternal life— as a phrase—life that's open-ended—lived ever in progress. One just keeps growing and keeps living. The time of death just comes when it comes and there may well—I see no reason why there couldn't be a continuation. . . . But I think life now should be lived in this kind of confidence of death being no different than birth—except that it's the end rather than the beginning.

Further, the extreme open-endedness which often characterizes the use of theological language by both Sal and Girth also reveals the ambiguity of their attitude to the theological dimension.

> We really can't understand all the dimensions of life— all the dimensions of our own beings, our own personalities, our own minds. There are many, there are levels, I think, of thought, of feeling which are not accessible to our conscious. Not that there are places in the universe from which supernatural beings penetrate our lives, penetrate history. But that there are dimensions of life beyond those of which we are conscious. So if by this we refer to the supernatural, which is to our minds above or beyond the nature of things, fine. I think there is a supernatural. But in the sense of magic, stirring the water

with one's staff, turning it to blood; this kind of thing
I think is completely foreign to reality. (Sal)

The ambiguity being examined in these uses of theological
language is a version of one discussed in the case of Strindge.
The ambiguity comes down to the question of whether the
theological language is being used from an internalizing or an
externalizing, projective point of view. In Strindge's case, it was
seen that his state of doubt and confusion was, in part, a consequence of the fact that an externalizing system was in sharp
competition with an internalizing one, and, as a result, there was
a deep confusion about how to interpret very básic experiences.
Generally, we noted, that doubt in the context of a liberal belief
system is related to, an expression of, just such a conflict between
an internalizing and externalizing process. In the cases of Sal
and Girth, the internalizing point of view clearly predominates.
The process which results in deep doubt and confusion in
Strindge's case, results in ambiguity in theirs.

It is likely that additional analysis of the ambiguities in the
use of theological language by Sal and Girth would reveal por-
tions of the developmentally earlier and dynamically unconscious sources of their belief systems. In any event, these points
of ambiguity are points at which further analysis of their belief
systems as aspects of their personalities might be initiated.

The intellectual sophistication and particular use of religious
language which characterize the belief systems of Sal and Girth
can be used in the service of expressing theological ideologies
that differ widely. At one extreme may be a kind of *Weltan-
schauung* implying only a very general philosophical orientation
to the world based on the Judeo-Christian tradition. At another
extreme may be a form of mysticism in which the notion of
God's will really plays a role similar to the one it plays in a
belief system such as Pale's or Joel's—where every act may be
considered in light of the question whether it is or is not in
God's will.

The families of both Sal and Girth were involved in fundamentalist communities. While Sal's family took fundamentalism
into itself, in the parental beliefs, Girth's family did not. In any
event, both Sal and Girth separated out, with relative ease, what
they felt to be the dogmatic, narrow, rigid moralistic background
of the Protestantism with which they grew up from the religious

core which they find meaningful in their adult lives. In this respect, they contrast with Strindge, and also with Cliff, another liberal doubter.

Cliff's effort to find and maintain a faith that will sustain him is very similar to Strindge's, both phenomenologically and psychodynamically. Like Strindge, Cliff has struggled for years to separate the inhibiting, burdensome yoke of moral law from his belief in a personal, caring God. Cliff has also been caught up for years in a repelling attraction to a ministerial role which, again like Strindge, he sees as inordinately constricting and destructive to being a real man. Further, Cliff is quite depressed. The source of his depression is a kind of oral emptiness which is expressed in his finding the world almost empty of meaning or offering such a tenuous source of meaning that it could evaporate at any instant. In addition, he is self-critical to the greatest degree, and, beyond being simply self-critical, he experiences an externalized, generalized threat that something will destroy or take away his tenuous grasp on an inner source of meaning. The formulation which applied to Strindge therefore also applies to Cliff: Cliff is in doubt about his faith because his belief system does not protect him from his own superego.

A great deal of the emotional syndrome which underlies and makes problematic the belief system is condensed in a dream or nightmare which Cliff had during the course of our interviews.

> It just so happens that a couple of days ago I had what I would consider a nightmare and is the third nightmare that I ever recall in my whole life. . . . I dreamt that I had been convicted to die twice. I don't know why twice. I know in the dream, at least, this was an indication that I was certainly going to die. I was waiting for this death sentence to come about, and there were people watching. How many I haven't the slightest idea. I couldn't see anybody. As I waited I became more and more frightened until at last I could no longer control it and I screamed; and at this time I woke up.

Some of Cliff's associations with this dream related to a period in college when he contemplated suicide. "I didn't feel that life had any meaning for me—any reason to go on living. . . . If life is without meaning there's no sense in living." This comment also reflects the emptiness he experiences. Currently Cliff speaks of a threat he feels to his inner sources of meaning:

> I feel that I have to believe in a personal God. This is the one thing that is a little disturbing to me. No one could ever prove to me that there were not a personal God. Because I have to believe it. And, well, that disturbs me a little bit, because I would basically like to really know that He does exist, I guess. But it can't be proved one way or the other. I just have to believe it. And I couldn't —life would have no meaning to me whatsoever without it. And I suppose this is the part that causes the doubt. Am I just building a big illusion for myself? Is this real or is it something I am making up? I feel it's real, but if I try to look at it as other people would look at it or could look at it, I can see an awful lot of validity in saying it's pie in the sky. It's something you just want to believe in and so you're going to believe in it. . . . [This latter position is] very threatening to me, because it is a viable position, and it is conceivable that I could one day take such a position, but if I did this would completely shatter everything I have. And I don't know what would replace it, because I can see no sense of meaning with such a position. And I'm struggling so hard for meaning now, that to take away what little I have would really, really threaten me.

The unconscious referent in this statement seems to be the threat of a loss of oral supplies or the repetition of such a loss. The oldest child in a family of three, Cliff was succeeded very soon by the birth of a sister when he was one year old, and the third sibling was not born until Cliff was ten.

Cliff says that if "other people" looked at his belief in a personal God "rationally" and "from the outside," they might find it "a lot of foolishness" or "pie in the sky." When asked who these "other people" might be, Cliff's thoughts soon led him to his father, whose life he found disturbingly meaningless. In Cliff's development, the paternal relationship holds a place similar to the one it holds in Strindge's development. Cliff experienced a great deal of criticism from Father, longed for approval and affection from him, but found little. Apart from

Father's irritability and temper, Cliff describes his family, including Mother, as emotionally inexpressive. As he approached adolescence, Cliff began to see his father's way of life as meaningless, felt Father encouraged him to participate in activities of a sort that he, the father, would not participate in, such as the church, and generally took his father as a negative model of what he himself would wish to be. These factors make a masculine identification problematic, at best, and leave the son subject to the punitive effects of early, more primitive introjects of the paternal imago. The problematic, negative identification with the father also leaves Cliff more vulnerable to the unresolved ambivalences remaining from the early maternal relationship. Thus Cliff experiences a struggle to maintain a tenuous grasp on a threatened and seemingly insubstantial source of meaning.

Jameson, the third subject in the liberal doubter category, provides a contrast with Cliff and Strindge. His selection as a doubter was appropriately based on the attitude, expressed in his questionnaire, of searching, doubt, and uncertainty about God and other basic theological categories. He sees his religious quest as a process of searching for answers or "better, ways of thinking." However, his doubt and his search are of a different order from those of the other doubters. The difference can be put very simply. Jameson is seeking theological *truth*, not religious *meaning*. "Truth" and "meaning"—certainly the words are closely related, but the psychology of the search for truth is different in an important way from the psychology of the quest for meaning, although we can only hint at that difference here.

Of our liberal subjects, Jameson is the only one who is planning on becoming a professional theologian. He is making "religious thinking" his "business." He *is* a thinker. Unusually clearheaded about philosophical matters, his recounting of his first years in seminary consists of his encounters with a series of philosophers and theologians and his effort to find an epistemologically satisfactory theological definition of God and Christianity. His emotional stake in that definition consisted less in finding a content for the concept of God which would support his sense of meaning or self than in finding a content which he felt to be true. This observation is supported by the fact that the definitions of religion and God which Jameson found most satisfactory were the peculiarly empty definitions formulated by Schleiermacher, the nineteenth-century German philosopher.

Schleiermacher, very roughly, defines religion as man's awareness that he is dependent, and he says that God is the name men give to the feelings expressed in questions about the ultimate origins of their existence. The very spareness of these definitions was satisfying to Jameson, who felt that more conservative Christians put too much into their definitions. He also found it satisfying that Schleiermacher put religion into the realm of feeling, because Jameson, like Descartes, had come to the conclusion that the only thing he could not doubt were certain of his own feelings.

Jameson comes from an unusual family in which the Protestant tradition provided a firm, unquestioned base for the family culture. He felt his parents were the kind of people they wanted their son to become, and he felt that his father's gentle and reasonable but sure authority was itself subject to a similar but higher authority. Father's story is an American one—a sixth-grade rural education, a job for several years as a postal clerk, the feeling of a religious calling as he matured, the interruption of World War I, the struggle for an education when he was already a grown man, and eventually the presidency and development of the junior college which had in the first place taken a chance on a local youth with little formal education. Jameson says his father is a very wise man, and the listener agrees upon hearing the story of Father's development or the story of how Father achieved the racial integration of his college. Of his mother, Jameson says, she has lived "a strong, placid, calm life."

Jameson's early years were a firm foundation for his later development. The identification with the minister father is clear and unquestioned. His religious seeking takes the form of theological investigation and does not leave him personally undermined. The clinician examining his projective test protocols (Rorschach and TAT) will quickly notice the heavy control, almost to the point of impoverishment, of affective and impulse expression. However, this is also the basis for a strong moral point of view, including a kind of austerity and even a sense of aristocracy that Jameson conveys.

It would be inaccurate to imply that Jameson's theological inquiries are without personal meaning and emotional upset. Like Cliff and Strindge, he has been in the process of separating himself from his upbringing—sorting out from his tradition what he can really believe. One issue in particular has touched him very closely. He has found himself casting off a good deal of what he has always understood as being part of Christianity. If he casts off so much, will anything be left? Will he still be able to consider himself a Christian? He worried for some time about being "robbed" of what he calls his "history." In particular, the underlying meaning of his history seems to refer to his ties to his own personal past, his familial roots. To cast off the traditional conceptions of Protestant Christianity is to sever symbolic representations of deep ties to his parents, requiring radical reorganization of his identity.

Jameson's ambivalent concern about his history and his identity as a Christian represents a conflict similar to one observed in Strindge and Cliff. In challenging and reworking his father's tradition, Jameson finds himself feeling a threat to the core of his identity. In Jameson's case, however, he is able to stick with the battle without being undermined, and he is able to come out on top. Since the early foundation is firm, his dissent can take the form of a meaningful and potentially fruitful reexamination of the concept of God and what it means to be a Christian.

Jameson's doubt might appear to be potentially productive in one way that Cliff's and Strindge's, at this point in their lives at least, are not. Reexaminations of the basic theological categories of the sort Jameson is involved in, may eventually lead to new versions of religious identity more nearly in tune with contemporary forms of personal identity and contemporary society. Doubt and dissent from tradition are the prime movers for such reexamination. The sheer degree to which Cliff and Strindge are personally threatened by their doubts and dissents might lead the observer to question the likelihood of their finding new forms of faith for others. On the other hand, it is only by experiencing the depths, "by living, nay dying" (Luther, quoted in Erikson, 1958, p. 251), that a new vision is arrived at, and it is perhaps Jameson's very austerity, stability, and philosophical placidity that may limit *his* particular quest. In any case, it is the power of the liberal position that, more accepting of doubt and ambivalence, it institutionalizes the process of dissent and change by allowing for a more individual, personal use of the religious symbols. Fruitful doubt might, of course, arise within a conservative context. However, doubt for the conservative is, to a large degree, a contradiction in terms. For doubt to be productive in this context must require a heroic upheaval and reintegration.

# XIV

## Conclusion: Doubt and Ego Synthesis in Religious Belief Systems

It is the divine side of man, his inward action which means everything, not a mass of information; for that will certainly follow and then all that knowledge will not be a chance assemblage, or a succession of details, without system and without a focussing point. I too have certainly looked for such a center.　　SÖREN KIERKEGAARD, JOURNALS

## 1. THE MEANING OF RELIGIOUS DOUBT

(a) *Religion as a response to life*
The idea of looking at religion as a "response to life" is not original, but it came to me as an insight in a way that I wish to describe briefly, largely as a way of honoring the man from whose life I took an inspiration. In the spring of 1968, following the murder of Martin Luther King, Jr., one had the opportunity to see a number of films on television that documented various periods and episodes in this great man's life. While King's life and death are perhaps still too close to us for many reasons, including the dreadful urgency of his civil rights causes, the student of religion cannot but be interested in King as well as moved

because he is a great religious figure. It is King's life—not simply his ideological verbalizations—which provide us with a paradigm of religious faith as a deep expression of and response to life. Again and again in the films of him one saw a man with the deep, ever-present sense of the ultimate and the charisma and eloquence of an Old Testament prophet. At the same time, he was responding to the social realities of his time which stood in contradiction to his beliefs and the best in the beliefs of his wider society. He lived out his faith in intense engagement with society, and thereby the meaning of his faith transcended the meanings it held simply in the context of the workings of his own personality. Traditional Protestantism speaks of a man—a preacher or minister or prophet—"standing aside" as a person and becoming a medium, a channel for God's message. This description fits the picture of King conveyed through the documentaries. He seemed to have become a medium, a channel for the causes he represented, transcending egocentric involvement and the personal meanings his activities might have had for him. This transcendence appeared, to me, in a striking way in the films. King was always impressive delivering a speech or sermon before crowd or congregation, but I found him even more impressive at a midnight planning session with colleagues and lieutenants. Even in these undramatic, often humble, circumstances, he displayed the same remarkable simple eloquence and vision, and the sense of ultimate purpose he conveyed showed as strongly and clearly. There seemed to be no lapse from a public image to private man—the living of his faith went on as always.

We cannot, of course, report certainties or doubts this man held at the heart of his belief system. It is easy enough, however, to see that whatever these might have been, they can be understood only in the overall context of his life—which itself was a great response to life. In theoretical terms, this is a statement of the holistic view of personality.[1] The religious belief system is a response of the total organism to its life. Subsequent discussion will show that this principle has more explanatory power than might be expected from so abstract a proposition.

One of our subjects, Girth, helps sustain his own belief system with a similar understanding:

> I'm caught up in doing something for which the faith and the meaning are going to become the rationalization

or the understanding of what's going on—and so I'm not
thrown only on the intellectual process going on in my
head. So that if I weren't involved in something, then this
might become oppressive and might become disintegrative.

The beliefs "in my head," Girth is saying, alone do not make up
his faith. The beliefs take their meaning from his life, his life-
style, and actions, and vice versa.

(b) *How should religious doubt be defined?*
In chapter I, religious doubt was defined in phenomenological
terms. That is, if a subject stated, in one way or another, that
he had such and such doubts about his religious beliefs, that was
a sufficient criterion for considering him a "doubter." The doubt
itself was defined in terms of the subject's verbal description
of it. The criteria for defining religious doubt may be expanded
through an application of the holistic principle.

Chelly, for example, was considered a non-doubter. He does
not profess any doubt; indeed he makes it clear that he has little
real notion of what meaningful doubt is. Within his personality,
barriers have been erected that not only exclude doubt but almost any awareness of fresh experience which might give rise
to doubt. In what sense can we say that his religious belief
system is "a response to life"? The belief system functions in
many respects to protect him from life and to preserve those
ways of responding to life he learned as a child. This itself is a
kind of doubt.

To what is Chelly's belief system a response? This question
and the previous observations about Chelly suggest that the
holistic principle gives a meaning to the question, What is the psychological makeup of a person's "world"?[2] To assess an individual's personality or belief system from a holistic point of view,
then, involves some kind of description of the world to which
he is responding.

Chelly's belief system is a response to the limited, familial
world of his childhood. He defines his current and future social
roles in such a way as not only to maintain himself within the
homogeneous subculture in which he was raised but also to do so
according to his childhood model. All subsequent theological
elaborations of the belief system may then be carried out without
meaningfully encountering any new personal or social realities.

The belief system then continues to be a response primarily to the childhood conflicts. These continue to be the primary contents of life, of the world to which the belief system is a response. The inability to reevaluate the world view of childhood and the childhood premises upon which conflicts were resolved and the sense of self established may be considered a form of doubt, or to be based upon a form of doubt. It is as if there is such a deep-seated doubt as to the viability of solutions—of the response to life—and the integrity of the personality that the personality protects itself against any encroachments upon its structures and against new adult experience. The real doubts, despair, and hopelessness are hidden, but reveal themselves in the form of the response of the individual to his life. Thus Chelly plans to prolong his academic studenthood almost indefinitely. In these roles, there can only be further elaborations of relatively superficial theologizings.

### (c) *Further cases in the light of the holistic definition of doubt*

The holistic principle also sheds further light on those cases already defined as doubters. Pale's pervasive doubt has been described primarily in terms of his intrapsychic conflicts. A fuller delineation of his doubt was achieved when we recognized that Pale stands in profound bafflement toward his world—that his religious doubt represents this bafflement. He literally does not know how to respond to the world, because for him it contains qualities that evoke contradictory responses. Pale's world contains a welcoming, protecting aspect, forever "wooing" him "into life." But it also contains a deep evil that is inimical to his very being. He has not been able to combine these two images.

Pale's world, like Chelly's, is quite constricted. Pale tries to deal with his doubt—with the dual image of the world—by making the dichotomy between good and evil sharp and by trying to reduce the contents of his world to that which is good. Pale is actually trying to eject from his world perceptions and experiences which have already entered it and which are contrary to the principles whereby he orders his world. All that is evil and inimical to him is to be contained in a variety of ways such that evil does not impinge on his world. This is the strategy implied by the conservative belief system. Another dimension, then, can be added to our description of the conservative belief system and the totalistic personality. In totalism, the individual's world will be constricted and dichotomized. Where a precocious identity formation is involved, the world will be essentially that of the early familial environment and the closed homogeneous conservative subculture. The good and evil aspects of the world will be categorized, conceptualized, and perceived in such a way that evil does not impinge in certain ways directly on the individual. It is not a part of *him*, of *his* world. The world will be perceived totally in terms of the traditional categories of the belief system, and there will be a tendency to minimize fresh interchange or feedback between the individual and his world.

It is interesting to consider Electon in the light of the conception we are suggesting. Electon's conversion may be regarded in the light of an individual constructing his world. In establishing his own identity as a Christian, as one who stands over against others, is called out by God, who is looking for a cause through which he can strike out at large numbers of people whom he can consider wrong, he is, *as he said, defining* reality. He is creating the world. In Electon's case, too, it is striking the degree to which the world has few contents other than those from his personal past and his current fantasies. The events surrounding his Peace Corps experience and his summer clinical work were created largely by himself. We may in fact define Electon's current relationship with reality by saying that it consists in a search for some social reality to which he can attach his own conception of the world—a social reality which will allow an interpretation in the light of his own conception of the world. Even in participating in this research, for example, he was looking for another vindication of his battle with "psychology."

Electon's belief system is a response to identity diffusion, a disturbing lack of closure, and lack of definition of the personality. It is a response to the global, pervasive doubts and uncertainties arising out of such diffusion. The belief system—with its arbitrary dichotomizing of good and evil, and with its constricted construction of the world—still represents profound doubts. Electon's belief system, like Chelly's, may also be seen to contain an expression of doubt. As a response to life, the belief system implicitly conveys a very basic doubt which can be expressed in Electon's own words: "Either this is really true or, man, I am just a goner." When the individual doubts the integrity of his own personality without the support of the belief system, doubt is necessarily cast back upon the belief system.

In the case of Briting, who was presented as a non-doubter, we noticed that Briting describes his belief system as a response to "life as it is." In his case we were able to analyze and describe his conception of the world, of "life as it is." Here too the qualities of life were circumscribed and determined primarily by the oral fantasies derived from familial experience.

If we consider the doubts of two liberal doubters, Strindge and Cliff, in the light of the principle that religion is a response to life, two qualities of their doubt become clearer. The case of Strindge may serve as the example. Strindge's intellectual assertions about God contain, in themselves, little expression of doubt. It seems difficult, at times, to pinpoint just what it is, in terms of the religious belief system, that is troubling Strindge—whether he is really a "religious doubter" in some sense. Yet, when we consider Strindge's current response to life, it is clear that he is a doubter and that he is a religious doubter. He is deeply baffled in his response to life. He feels unable to find a meaning in life and a path to take in life. His feelings confuse him, he feels uncomfortable with others, yet wanting to make contact, and he suffers unexplained anxiety and guilt—in short he is suffering. Furthermore, he makes it perfectly clear that he seeks a religious solution to these uncertainties and sufferings. He does not feel the way he thinks he should feel and the way he would like to feel as one who believes in God. To understand Strindge as a religious doubter, we simply need recognize the extent of his bafflement in the face of life and the fact that he seeks a religious solution. The religious doubt is defined by the confusion, doubt, uncertainty, and so on regarding life that the religious doubt expresses and which the individual is trying to resolve through the religious belief system.

Strindge's recent history, in fact, reveals two quite different responses to life. One is manifested in the period during which he cast off his burden of traditional religiosity and for the first time felt religious in the way in which he wished to. The other response to life is manifested in the agonizing suffering, the feelings of being nagged, and so on. What makes it difficult at times to understand Strindge's doubt is that he does not have separate conceptions of God for these two different ways of responding to life; the same theology holds for both. This fact adds to Strindge's confusion.

The nature of Strindge's doubt becomes clearer, then, when we relate the doubt to the most general and overall ways in which he stands baffled in his response to life.

The other quality of Strindge's doubt that reveals itself when we reconsider it is that his doubt is itself an effort to respond to life. In contrast with Pale, Electon, and Chelly, Strindge is trying to open up his world—to other people and to a broader sector of society. Strindge, and Cliff also, as well as Jameson in certain respects, are trying to break out of a world defined too narrowly by an earlier belief system. Possibly one reason why Tillich asserted that doubt is an element of faith is that doubt of this sort does represent an openness to the world, an effort to expand one's conception of the world and respond to the full range of personal experience. In any event, within liberal theology, the type of doubt represented by Strindge and Cliff is an aspect of faith.

Liberal theology in general recognizes religion as a response to life. It institutionalizes and values an open-ended interchange between the individual and his world, and the continued development of a world that contains as great a range as possible of personal and social reality. This aspect of liberalism is exemplified in the cases of Eyman, Sal, and Girth by the broad range of activities and experiences subsumed under their religious interests. Conservative theology, in contrast, tends to institutionalize a conception of the world which, at least in its religious aspects, is highly circumscribed and in which there seems to be a more limited range of conventionalized human expression.

Conservative theology rejects doubt partly for the very reason that doubt represents open interchange between the individual and his world and a change in conception of the world in the direction of expanding its contents and meanings in the light of experience.

The holistic notion that religion is a response to life adds a further dimension to our understanding of religious doubt. A belief system which contains no explicit expression of doubt may in some ways be seen to be an essentially doubting response to life. Conversely some forms of religious doubt may be seen as an effort to respond more openly and fully to life, thereby becoming, in the context of liberal theology, an act of faith.

### (d) *Doubt and identity*

The picture of a religionist in conflict and doubt about his belief system strikes an immediate and powerful impression. Here is a man at odds with himself and his life in a particularly pointed way. This intuitive picture of the religious doubter gives an image of the human condition with all the ambiguity of life stretched to the limit, where man stands in utter bafflement before life.

This intuitive picture of the religious doubter—one which I think would be called up for any observer—contains a message. One's first response to it, I believe, is the temptation to find a more precise description or explanation of what it is that is so poignant about the condition of the religious doubter. The next temptation is to try to explain or describe the poignancy of that emotional state by discussing the underlying psychodynamics. Both these temptations lead one away from an essential observation.

The most accurate picture of the religious doubter and the one that conveys the primary meaning of religious doubt *is* the intuitive picture of the man baffled in his response to life in a very deep way. Religious doubt is one of man's fates—a human condition—one of the ways in which a foundering quest for identity is expressed. Further, there is no more direct, precise, or specific way to describe this condition than in the language of the doubter himself: "I don't know where I stand in relation to God." This is the simplest symbolic formulation of the religious doubter's emotional state. It condenses and symbolizes everything else. It is the sign, as it were, the mark, of his identity. The essential observation here, the message, is that the symbols of identity, in certain of their primary functions, are irreducible. This is to say that spelling out the psychological processes underlying them does not in fact account for all of their meaning; nor therefore do the psychological processes underlying or producing religious doubt state the primary meaning of religious doubt.

## 2. *EGO SYNTHESIS IN THE RELIGIOUS BELIEF SYSTEM*

The case studies repeatedly demonstrate the operations of the processes and functions of ego synthesis in the religious belief system. A few central considerations will be taken up in this section.

The synthetic functions of the ego may be seen to have an evolutionary significance, that is, they are an adaptational response to the biological and social conditions of human living. The needs of any animal are met by the channeling of motivational or drive energies through patterns of behavior, the consistencies and cycles of which integrate its life with its environment. A consistent feedback process occurs between the organism and its environment with the consequential meeting of the organism's needs for survival. In the case of man social reality is a part of the environment to which he must adapt. In his case, it is the ego-identity which consists, in part, in an integrated set of functions whereby a consistent feedback is established between the individual and his sociocultural matrix. In this regard, we may point out that consciousness itself also has an evolutionary, adaptational function. It is through consciousness, that is, the sense of self and the awareness of the self-in-the-social-group, that the individual monitors the feedback between himself and his social environment.

It has been said a number of times that the religious belief system is "a vehicle for and an outcome of" ego synthesis. This implies that ego synthesis operates through a complex kind of double feedback process. On the one hand, the individual's religious belief system is an outcome of ego synthesis, an expression in symbols, rituals and other actions, and conscious beliefs of an integrated coherence of the ego achieved through successive mastery of emerging developmental crises. In this sense, the religious belief system is an achievement, a creative product of the individual. On the other hand, the synthetic functions clearly make use of religious symbolisms in the process of establishing an integrated coherence within the ego. In this phase the individual borrows the available religious symbols from his familial and cultural environment, adding to the consensual meanings of these symbols his own idiosyncratic meanings. The fusion of the deepest personal meanings to the religious symbolisms is permitted and facilitated by the global, ambiguous quality of those symbols. More than that, however, the integration of personal meanings with the cultural symbols of religion is actively fostered by the ambience, traditions, and rituals of religious practices. Because the religious belief system is both a vehicle for ego synthesis, makes use of consensually shared symbols, and is an outcome of ego synthesis, containing deeply personal meanings, it is a primary symbolic vehicle through which the individual may establish a coherent, consistent relationship with social reality. It is through such symbolic vehicles that the individual's deeper, personal nature receives a social meaning and a public voice.

The case studies reveal the variety, richness, and genetic depth of the personal meanings which may accrue to a religious symbolism or some feature of the belief system. Earliest emotional states arising within the maternal relationship, partial and fragmented identifications with the parents, as well as later forms of identity, become integrated into the religious belief system. The concept of God, in particular, receives its emotional meanings from a variety of sources within the personality, from a wide range of the individual's important earlier emotional experiences and relationships. The core source of these meanings, however, is always the primary maternal relationship. The concept of God, for the individual, preserves and expresses the sense of wholeness, nurturance, and goodness first experienced in the fusion with the primary mother. It protects the individual against the effects of this earliest separation while it keeps alive the hopeful legacy of the fusion that the child experiences in its earliest months.

The religious symbol as well as other features of the belief system, including the religious role, are tools of consciousness. Once the individual has made a religious concept his own he stands in a different relationship to the personal psychic contents which have become associated with the religious symbol. The conscious awareness and manipulation of the religious symbolisms provide a kind of cybernetic monitoring of the unconscious meanings attached to them. Thus while the religious symbolism may function in the service of defense—protecting the individual from awareness of certain emotions—it also provides a kind of access to and control over preconscious and unconscious processes which would be unavailable without the symbolisms of the belief system. This "monitoring" proceeds, in part, through the individual's development of his belief system as an aspect of his identity, that is, as the development of the belief system becomes integrated with the feedback between the individual and his social environment. Through some such processes as these, perhaps, religion functions in "the problem of dealing with inputs of motivation from within the system that are not under immediate control of conscious decision processes" (Bellah, 1968, p. 11; see chapter I). Such processes would also establish connections between unconscious processes and identity and explain why "the problem of identity and of unconscious motivation are closely related" (Bellah, 1968, p. 11). In general, the series of considerations presented in this section support and give some explanations for Bellah's contention that religion emerges in action systems in response to the problems of unconscious motivation and of identity.

Some of the foregoing considerations may be clarified by reviewing the multiplicity of meanings synthesized within the belief system of one of our subjects. Eyman serves as a good example for this purpose because of his maturity and high degree of professional development. For present purposes we may consider five categories of psychic contents which in different ways contribute to the meanings of the belief system.

(a) *Part-identities or part-roles.* Most individuals of any complexity will reveal a small number of what we may call part-identities which become subsumed under and integrated into a superordinate primary identity.[3] Within Eyman's conception of himself as a minister, we found these part-identities: the prophet, the Southerner, the creative one, his brother's keeper (the one who serves others, is the mediator, relates to and stands up for others in an impersonal world, and who expiates others' sin). The role of mediator and expiator is frequent among our subjects (Chelly, Pale, Electon, Briting, Mudge, Sal, and Girth) and of course establishes a basis for identifying with the role of Jesus. In Eyman's case, all these part-identities are synthesized in the ministerial role and become parts of its meaning.

(b) *Ego structures.* Various ego structures or qualities of character become integrated into and are expressed through the religious belief system. The ego-ideal and superego, of course, make central contributions to the belief system, each in more than one way. The self-control and guilt, for example, which enter into the belief system are superego functions. Centering life around service to others and such social concerns as the civil rights movement may be considered ego-ideal derivatives. In addition,

Eyman's particular complex style of cognitive defenses gives a certain quality to the belief system. We noted his long-time perspective and use of global, intellectually integrating concepts—both of which become a part of his philosophical perspective. Similarly, his style of object relations—sensitive, intraceptive, empathic—also provides a central quality of the belief system. Finally, the self concept is integrated into a central place in the belief system: the self as one's major creative contribution to society, and so on.

(c) *Introjects and identification fragments.* Evidence of early introjects and identification fragments appears throughout the belief system, and their influence is centrally determinative. In Eyman's case, as in the other subjects, ambivalence in the early relationships is responded to by the creation of two separate images—a positive one and a negative one. The positive and negative introjects appear as distinguishable influences in the belief system. In Eyman's belief system the positive maternal introject appears as the "divine" or "creative dimension of the universe." A negative maternal introject appears as the diabolical underlying the placid surface of the world, subsequently elaborated into the forces of supernaturalism which still bind men and which Eyman feels committed to fight. Similarly, a negative introject of the father appears in the dreary picture of the business world, and a controlling, superego introject of the father appears in Eyman's sense of being bound up and unable to move. A positive identification with the father appears in Eyman's social concerns.

(d) *Universal threats to ego boundaries: the unconscious, sex, and death.* The ego is constantly beset with anxiety and stimuli, some closely connected with the autonomic processes underlying affective states (Kubie, 1961, p. 45), of such a nature as to threaten its boundaries (Tarachow, 1964, p. 10). Three main sources of anxiety and stimuli which threaten ego boundaries are: sexual instincts and sexual identity, infantile fantasies concerning death and the reality of death, and the general, continual press on the ego of unconscious mental contents. For example, at the heart of every identity formation or belief system there will lie close connections with the early fantasies and real experiences with death and the defensive reactions to those. In Eyman's case, we see him consciously dealing with the problem of death as a part of his involvement with the civil rights movement. Indications of much earlier fantasy concerns about death appear in the Killer-Man fantasy which holds a central role in the development of the belief system. Although we touched on the issue of sexual identity only peripherally in the case studies, this issue too has connections with the central features of the belief system in every case. In Eyman's case, we noted the problematic quality of action, its association with castration anxiety and therefore with sexual identity. As to the connection between the religious belief system and the problem of the ego in coping with its own unconscious, this was discussed earlier in this section. In its close associations with the archetypal human problems, the religious symbol is similar to the dream symbol, and it arrives at these associations through similar psychic functions. The religious symbol is highly ambiguous, easily becomes associated with personal idiosyncratic meanings, and these associated meanings are not subjected to reality-testing. The religious symbol through the network of preconscious associations can therefore easily become associated with the deepest sources of anxiety within the personality. Institutionalized religion fosters the development of these associations. The ego is aided in dealing with these primary sources of anxiety when they become symbolically linked to the belief system and its integrative functions.

(e) *Sense of fusion with the maternal imago.* At the heart of each belief system studied is the preservation and symbolization through the concept of God of the sense of wholeness, nurturance, and goodness that is first experienced in the primary maternal relationship. The "divine dimension of the universe" is one such symbolization in Eyman's case. Other expressions of the wish for fusion suffuse Eyman's belief system and are revealed clearly in the analysis of his fantasy productions on the TAT.

## 3. THE MECHANISMS OF DOUBT

(a) *Doubt represents a problem of ego synthesis*
The religious doubter, lacking a unified, coherent orientation to life, is in conflict about how to respond to his world and life. This bafflement before life, in our view, represents a problematic

disruption of the processes of ego synthesis in which the ego is either unable to integrate around one superordinate life orientation or, having relinquished an older orientation, is in the process of renewed conflict resolution in the service of establishing a new one.

(b) *The wish for and dread of fusion*
The basic *source* of doubt is the wish for and the dread of fusion with the primary mother. The wish for fusion is stirred by the longing for a renewed sense of hope, wholeness, and meaning. But the wish for fusion itself also arouses the dread of engulfment and annihilation and a sense of pervasive evil.

The worlds of our twelve subjects contain, in each case, a domain of evil and a domain of good. This phenomenon is closely related to the wish for and dread of fusion. It represents the effort to deal with the ambivalently experienced maternal imago by "splitting" it and creating a separate good imago and a separate evil one. In the case of a few subjects, the evil and good are sharply demarcated and institutionalized. In Electon's case, for example, Christian doctrine is the good realm and "psychology" the evil realm, the threat to his being. In Briting's case also, the good and evil are clearly separated and institutionalized. "Life as it is" is empty and meaningless, while the Gospel, the Christ event, provide meaning. This kind of demarcation is not limited entirely to the conservative subjects. Eyman makes a somewhat similar dichotomy: liberal naturalism *versus* supernaturalism. His tendency to make such a dichotomy is another indication of his underlying conservatism.

Good and evil are not as clearly separated and institutionalized in the case of the subject disrupted by doubt and whose belief system is less developed and coherent. Pale, for example, suffers from alternating, conflicting views of the world as good or evil, and these alternative outlooks represent very basic, general orientations that have not been differentiated and separated or integrated together. A similar observation holds for both Cliff and Strindge. A dual, unintegrated orientation toward the world exists and accounts for the basic confusion about the self and life. In their case, the dual orientation comes out most clearly in the contrast between the times when Strindge, for example, was able to feel good about himself, feel comfortably religious, as compared to the times he is most agonizingly suffering. The self and world are regarded from a different perspective in these two states.

What is suggested by these phenomena is the introjection of an intensely ambivalent maternal object and the effort to resolve the intolerable tension of that ambivalence by the creation of two separate maternal images, a good one and an evil one. In this way the positive promises inherent in the wish for fusion may be separated from the dread of fusion with the evil object. These two contrasting images, however, may become the basis for establishing two conflicting and contradictory views of the self and the world. The confusional state produced by two globally opposing views of self and world may then find expression through the religious symbolisms as religious doubt.

A secondary source of doubt has also been illustrated in the case studies. The immediate source of doubt in some instances is not simply the dread of fusion. It is the experience that arises when the individual is emotionally unable to experience with any fullness contact with his own internal legacies of early maternal goodness and nurturance. In Strindge's case, for example, his contact with the brotherly, nonmoralistic minister relieved blocks to self-acceptance, and for the first time he felt "religious" in the way in which he had always wanted to. He could feel that he too was "a way," that he was a man and acceptable. The basic sources of the sense of goodness of the self once more had a predominating influence in his personality. When the individual, as in Strindge's case, becomes the victim of his own punitive conscience, and when inner and outer circumstances contrive drastically to undermine self-esteem and the sense of self, then the individual is subject to the powerful feelings of abandonment, worthlessness, and confusion that give rise to religious doubts. All of these feelings are a block to experiencing the effects of "the good which was there from the beginning" (Erikson, 1958, p. 168). In this condition, it is, in a sense, not being able to experience the effects of a positive sense of fusion that is the source of doubt. This dynamic is closely related to the mechanisms whereby doubt arises, summarized in the following section.

The discussion of the basic source of doubt in the dread of fusion must be qualified in light of the above remarks. I will take the presentation of this qualification as the opportunity to set forth qualifying remarks of a more general sort. I have focused in these studies primarily on mechanisms of faith and doubt relating to the early maternal relationship. There are certainly other sources of the sense of hope, meaning, and wholeness and their opposites. Some of these have received direct or indirect attention in the case studies, but they have not been given as much explicit theoretical attention. "Faith"—in God, life, a political ideology, or oneself—depends on a healthy sense of the self and a strong sense of connection with life energies whether in the form of an ideological object or in some way not mediated by an ideological object. Similarly, hope and wholeness depend on the continued successful synthesis of the crises and conflicts arising out of a lifelong series of "emergent maturational and convergent environmental forces" (Jones, 1962, p. 55). Blocks occurring at any point in this series can bring into question the sense of hope, meaning, and wholeness. It is at such points, however, that the individual may seek restoration through the processes that have been emphasized throughout these studies. We have in fact had the opportunity to learn about a number of men who, by virtue of their own unique experiences, have had to struggle repeatedly in the course of their lives with the original sources of faith and doubt, hope and despair.

### (c) How doubt arises

Two general formulations purporting to explain how doubt *arises* have been presented. In the case of the more conservative subject, doubt arises when the religious belief system does not protect the individual in his life. In this instance, undue anxiety and stress initiate the question, "Am I in the Lord's will?" A process of disintegrative doubt may follow if this condition continues and the feelings of despair, abandonment, and hopelessness increase. A corollary to this formulation is that when the belief system does aid and abet the believer, the beliefs are "reinforced"; that is, the positive experience facilitates the use of the beliefs in ego synthesis. (These formulations are consistent with the holistic formulation of religion as a response to life.)

In the case of the liberal, doubt arises when the belief system does not protect the individual from his own superego. In this case the individual suffers from guilt, anxiety, and confusion about how to interpret his own feelings, and, in general, he suffers in his life. This formulation is really a special case of the formulation applied to the conservative.

The liberal tends not to externalize as broad a range of

psychic functions and contents as does the conservative. He therefore does not experience his suffering as arising simply from an external source or solely as the result of a relationship with an external object. He tends to see his suffering as a misarrangement of his own beliefs and attitudes. He also gets caught up in two kinds of processes which make it difficult for him to resolve his doubts. First, as pointed out in the case of Strindge, he experiences conflict between an externalizing belief system and an internalizing one, a conflict which may be particularly confusing because it leaves ambiguous the significance of basic emotional experiences. Second, he takes an inordinately punitive attitude toward himself, and he misjudges the kinds of rearrangements in his attitudes toward himself (always choosing the more punitive) that would actually alleviate his suffering.

When doubt does arise, we also must presuppose underlying conditions which make it possible and account for its destructive or constructive effects, as the case may be.

(d) *The maternal identification as a primary underlying condition of doubt*

A prolonged special relationship with the mother resulting in an identification with her which is more influential in the structure and development of the ego than the identification with the father has a number of possible consequences which leave the individual vulnerable to irruption of a disruptive doubt. A problematic masculine identification leaves the individual with weaker and less flexible coping mechanisms as well as with problematic qualities of the self-image and a heavier burden on the defensive structure. Inevitably finding considerable difficulty in coping, the individual is vulnerable to all sorts of stresses and anxieties which he tries to understand religiously and to relate to his religious belief system, putting a heavier emotional burden on it. A sequence of this sort inevitably leads to doubts about the religious beliefs. Furthermore, the problematic masculine identification, while it may itself involve an ambivalence which is reflected in the belief system, more importantly leaves the individual vulnerable to the more profound ambivalences and problems of the early maternal relationship. It is out of these earlier ambivalences that arise the archetypal, cosmic, and primitive kinds of wishes, expectations, and fears for which religious ideas and symbols provide a ready vehicle of expression. A profound ambivalence arising in an intense maternal relationship which is not neutralized by a later identification with the father, also leaves the individual more susceptible to the influence of the two powerful images discussed earlier, each of which provides a kernel around which a life orientation could be organized. The contradiction between such implicit life orientations is the basis for a deep rift and doubt which is very difficult to overcome. Finally, the prolonged special relationship with the mother may result in the development of an ego-ideal which is essentially grandiose and unrealistic, leading the individual to expect things of himself and life that are beyond the realm of possibility—absolute purity for example; and falling from this ideal, the individual doubts his belief system as a whole.

## 4. CAN THE CONCLUSIONS BE GENERALIZED?

To what extent can the conclusions we have discussed be generalized? The small number of subjects, the fact that all are traditional American Protestants (with the partial exception of Eyman), and the fact that the studies were done during a particular transitional period in the recent history of Protestantism, all these factors may be considered to limit the extent to which we can generalize the observations and conclusions here presented. In addition, not only are there no Catholic or Jewish cases considered, but, far more important, forms of religious experience that do not fit into one of the conventional religious molds found in America were not considered. Devout dedication to a way of life, a meditative practice, a form of self-development, or a new form of social living may all have a religious component. Further, there arises the even more general question as to whether any of the conclusions would apply to ideologies other than religious—political or scientific, say.

Not only can none of these limitations be dismissed, but together they can only impose the greatest modesty on any effort to generalize. Even in the face of such severe restrictions, however, certain phases of this work would seem to have universality. First, a particular *style of inquiry* has been set forth, a method of investigating a particular kind of question, a particular way of gathering information, and a way of thinking about and looking at the information gathered. The method could be applied to the instances not taken into consideration in this work. Beyond considerations of method, I believe there is some basis for generalizing what the method has revealed. First, any ideology—religious, scientific, or political—can serve as a vehicle for and expression of identity formation, and certain processes involved in identity formation are what have been described. Second, any ideology or way of life can take on the character, for the individual, of an ideological object. An ideological object is experienced as a source of hope, meaning, and wholeness, and when this occurs the processes of faith and doubt herein described are brought into play. There are no doubt exceptions to this generalization too, as in the case of object-less religious practices such as Zen Buddhism or in the case of individuals who are ideology-free in some sense even while experiencing a certain religious sense of life. But even these exceptions are not simple ones.

It is only an awareness of these questions that can be indicated at this point. Their actual examination would require several more volumes.

## 5. A CONCLUDING SPECULATION

The English psychoanalyst, Winnicott, speaks of the "I am" feeling (Holbrook, 1969, p. 19) as a basic component of the self arising in the early mother-child relationship. We might say that the quest for the God relationship, for the religious in any form, is the quest for continued reestablishment and reaffirmation of the "I am" feeling. It is the search for the ideological object in relationship to which that experience may always be guaranteed, making restitution thereby for the loss of the first object, the mother.

I will allow myself a final imaginative elaboration. Perhaps this intuition of Winnicott's was felt in another form by the Old Testament prophet who wrote for Jehovah the words, "I AM WHO AM." And in the New Testament the first great commandment, Love God, seems an appropriate directive to put first in human priorities the continued reestablishment of a dyadic relationship in which a basic sense of the existence, uniqueness, continuity, and goodness of the self may forever be regained.

# Appendix A

## QUESTIONNAIRE

---

### A *Study of Orientations of Theology Students*[1]

NAME _____ SCHOOL _____ YEAR _____

ADDRESS _____ PHONE _____

## I. Introduction

This questionnaire is a request for your help in gathering preliminary information about the life experiences and variations in world outlooks of students in theology schools. It is the initial phase of a study in the psychology of religion undertaken as doctoral research in the Department of Social Relations, Harvard University. The goal is to gain a better understanding of the individual and the nature and sources of his deepest concerns. The working assumption is that there are numerous, complex relationships between the individual's personality and his orientation in theology and religion. This assumption gives rise to many questions for which there are as yet no satisfying answers. Easy reductions of religion or religious experience to simple psychological formulae are not valid. To begin to approach partial, humanly relevant answers, I am asking for your help in the form of information about yourself. Certainly this area of research is too complex to arrive at final answers. However, this seems to be a time in which many of us, in this country and elsewhere, have difficulty in finding deep meaning in our lives and in which to seek and ask is considered unsophisticated. This is reason enough, I think, to try to gain some further understanding of the personality functioning that accompanies, perhaps provides a natural base for, faith, commitment, or a sense of meaning. To this end, please answer the questions that follow in whatever way that seems to best represent *your own* experience, thought, and feeling. The scientific and human value which may derive from this work depends on your participation in this spirit.

This questionnaire is not intended to be constructed from the point of view of any specific denomination or theological orientation, nor is the intention to evaluate in any way the beliefs of those who respond. The purpose is to gather factual information about the individual, his experience, and his beliefs.

## II. *Background*

age:                              sex:                    marital status:

undergraduate college:                        undergraduate major:

other graduate work, professional training, or non-academic experience:

where were you born?                    where did you live during your
                                                        early years?

Father's occupation:                      Father's education:

Father's religion:

How would you characterize your father's religious views, involvement, and behavior?

Mother's religion:                    education:                    occupation:

How would you characterize your mother's religious views, involvement, and behavior?

How would you characterize your own religious views, involvement, and behavior?

What religious education and training did you receive as a child and later when you were in secondary school?

What are you planning to do when you leave school?

## III.

1. How did you happen to come to theology school? (E.g., what went into the decision to prepare for the ministry, study theology, or etc.?)

2. In *The Advancement of Theological Education*, H. R. Niebuhr, D. D. Williams and J. M. Gustafson distinguish "ten kinds of persons" who "seek theological education," giving different sorts of goals and motivations for each. Below are brief summaries of their descriptions. Please rate the three most relevant to yourself and the three least relevant to yourself by assigning 1, 2, and 3 respectively to the three relevant ones and 8, 9, and 10 to the

three irrelevant ones. Underline any part of the description which is particularly pertinent.

_____someone who received encouragement from family, pastor, and home congregation who believe he would make a good minister

_____someone who finds the searching, contemplative atmosphere of the seminary an environment in which he can seek a comprehension of life leading to inner peace and quiet

_____someone who finds the ministry a necessary and satisfying role in society; interested in interperson relations, concerned about taking care of the social and institutional aspects of the ministry

_____someone who had early satisfying experience in church work, as leader or active participant in a church student or youth movement, or etc.; may come to the seminary already with a sense of accomplishment in the ministry

_____someone who decided quite early to be a minister; a moral, conscientious person who grew up in a moral, religious environment

_____someone who "found a saving truth and out of the abundance of its meaning for him, he wishes to share it with the world," perhaps a belief in "social salvation of the world through Christian pacifism"

_____someone with "objective intellectual interest in theological problems," logical analysis of theological statements, and who views religion as "a phenomenon to be understood objectively and scientifically and logically"

_____someone with humanitarian concerns; the Church or religion as a healing force in society; application of the law of love in healing individual ills, counseling or in social reform

_____someone seeking a faith that will bring order into the intellectual and moral confusion that he sees; may be uncertain about a vocation in religion; asking questions about the meaning of human existence; a religious seeker

_____those "of mature faith who have come to a genuine acceptance of their environment and themselves" perhaps through "a lived experience of the justifying graciousness of God"; not without questions and doubts

Please comment on the particular autobiographical form in which one or two of the more relevant generalized descriptions are expressed in your own life.

IV.

Following are several questions pertaining to your religious beliefs and faith, to doubt, and to seeking. You are probably aware that theologians as different as Karl Barth and Paul Tillich have recognized the inevitable, persisting existence of doubt in theology and faith. Doubt, uncertainty, and seeking and their role in the religious life are of special interest to me, experiences which I would like to try to understand with you.

1. How would you describe your faith and your religious beliefs, including your conception of God, if you hold such a conception? (Say you wanted to convey these things broadly and briefly to someone you had just met, trying to give him some idea of your position.)

2. Two questions which may or may not be related: Is this a time for you of fairly intense seeking for needed answers? Is this a time for you in which you have quite strong doubt or are quite uncertain of your faith and/or commitment? (Explain, if you will.)

3. Are you uncertain about your vocational calling at this point? (Or do you feel relatively certain about the course you have set for yourself?)

4. If it is not now, at what period in your life did you doubt most intensely, or experience most uncertainty, or most urgently need answers? (At what age? Where were you and what were you doing? What was the experience for you?)

5. In addition to what you have already written, is there anything else you could say about the role of doubt, uncertainty, or seeking in your life at this time?

6a. In contrast, are there aspects of your beliefs or faith that you have never questioned, that have remained constant with you, perhaps been a source of guidance, comfort?

b. What were the circumstances under which you became convinced of the meaning of your religion? Have there been moments of comfort, joy, exaltation? Under what circumstances?

7. What particular theological or religious issue or question is currently most absorbing to you, that you are trying to settle in your own mind?

8. Try to imagine the following: After much study, thought, and further experience in life, you become convinced that your faith and religious beliefs are no longer tenable—that, as a result of your own thinking and the demands of intellectual honesty, integrity, and truth, you must give them all up (for whatever

reasons). What thoughts and feelings occur to you when you put yourself in this frame of mind?

9. Is this a time in which you are experiencing a good deal of depression, *or* feelings of being unworthy, *or* anxiety about your life and doing something worthwhile with it?

10. Was there a period in your life of change or development in your faith or beliefs? (At what age? What was the experience?)

11. Try to recall learning about death as a child. At what age did you come to understand death? How did this come about? What were your feelings? What are your feelings about it now?

## V. *Theological Positions*

The propositions listed below have been taken from a variety of theological writings. Most are direct quotations. Some have been modified slightly, but never in such a way as to change their original sense. In some instances you may know the source. I would like to get some idea of the type of theological statement with which you would express agreement or disagreement. Therefore, for each proposition, ask yourself whether you would agree or disagree with it, whether you believe it to be true or false.

Each proposition is followed by six response alternatives:[2]

| | |
|---|---|
| SD = Strongly Disagree | SA = Strongly Agree |
| D = Disagree | A = Agree |
| MD = Mildly Disagree | MA = Mildly Agree |

Circle the alternative that comes closest to your own attitude toward the proposition. Please rate every one.

1. The New Testament presentation of the incarnation, the redemption in Christ does not, properly speaking, describe a supranatural transaction of any kind, but it is an attempt to express the real depth, dimension, and significance of the *historical* event of Jesus Christ.

2. Death is not the end of all—the body dies and disintegrates, but the soul lives on.

3. Theological statements are not a description of "the highest Being" but an analysis of the depths of personal relationships— or, rather, an analysis of the depths of all experience "interpreted by love."

4. Uncertainty and doubt belong to man's essential finitude, to the goodness of the creative in so far as it is created.

5. God can be considered only as "wholly other."

6. For the movement of faith must always be performed by virtue of the absurd.

7. The decisive expression of religion is guilt.

8. There is no way from man to God—man brings nothing to what happens, God all.

9. A right relationship to God depends on nothing religious; in fact religion could be the greatest barrier to it.

10. God is the transcendent Intelligence in a world of intelligent beings.

11. In the long run, it will be found that to deny the Virgin Birth is to call in question the divinity of Christ: What God has joined in his revelation, let no man therefore put asunder.

12. Faith begins where thought leaves off.

13. Christianity, truthfully presented, means suffering, ever greater as one advances further in it.

14. The name of this infinite and inexhaustible depth and ground of all being is God. That depth is what the word God means. And if that word has not much meaning for you, translate it, and speak of the depths of your life, of the sources of your being, of your ultimate concern, of what you take seriously without any reservation.

15. A man's knowledge of the Word of God is, in the last analysis, based on his own awareness and interpretation of his own experience.

16. In the relation between man and God, man's initiative, will, and affection are all involved, in addition to God's active grace and response.

17. The reality of God, the divinity of Christ, and the authority of Scripture—are not propositions to be argued for, but basic facts, the presuppositions of any sound thinking.

18. Of ourselves we do not know what we say when we say "God," i.e. that all that we think we know when we say "God" does not reach and comprehend Him Who is called "God," but always one of our self-conceived and self-made symbols, whether it is "spirit" or "nature," "fate" or "idea" that we really have in view.

19. Theological statements can be translated into statements about human life and therefore we do not need the category of God.

20. We must begin, each of us, by seeing ourselves as a man who has sinned, is sinning, and will sin, and who can recognize himself as nothing else than lost.

21. Those men who have been claimed by God's mercy are called to bear witness on the one hand against the form of this world, and on the other in favor of the form of the coming world.

22. If doubt appears, it should not be considered as the negation of faith, but as an intrinsic element which was always and will always be present in the act of faith.

23. It is a widely prevalent error of the present day that Satan plays no role in the affairs of government or in the lives of individual men.

24. Doubt about the existence of God should, at some point, be seen through and despised as the act of an *insipiens*, the "fool" of Psalm 53.

25. There are no proofs for Christian belief—one only can and must make his choice and stake his whole life on the risk.

26. The depth of suffering is the door, the only door, to the depth of truth.

27. Belief in God does not, indeed cannot mean being persuaded of the existence of some entity, even a supreme entity.

28. In doubt, human thought is unnatural—diseased by man's original estrangement, and consistently exposed to the corruption and error which arise and follow from a primal error, that is, the presumption to ask, "Did God say . . .", or to boldly affirm, "There is no God," or, "I am a God."

29. When he too, who abhors the name, and believes himself to be godless, gives his whole being to addressing the *Thou* of his life, as a *Thou* that cannot be limited by another, then he addresses God.

30. Historical doubt concerning the existence and the life of someone with the name Jesus of Nazareth cannot be overruled.

31. Our fundamental attitude to God is one of gratitude: He has given his all to and for us, and we have made so poor a return, yet he receives us still as his children.

32. The fact that man *does* evil indicates that he is evil—evil *is* lodged in the very center of his will.

33. God is teaching us that we must live as men who can get along very well without him.

34. It has only been in terms of the structure of the human situation—of a centered self trying to make sense out of an encompassing world—that theology has made any sense.

35. To believe in God as love means to believe that in pure personal relationship we encounter, not merely what ought to be, but what is, the deepest, veriest truth about the structure of reality.

36. Jesus Christ is the "moment," the point of crisis at which eternity impinges upon time; he is actually God breaking into our world of time and space.

37. Christian belief and practice require a new mold and we have to be prepared for everything to go into the melting—even our most cherished religious categories and moral absolutes; and the first thing we must be ready to let go is our image of God himself.

38. The distinguishing mark of religious action is suffering, for suffering is precisely the expression of the God relationship.

39. It is questionable whether the whole theological enterprise, in general or in particulars, should even be ventured, much less carried out.

40. No one should flirt with his unbelief or with his doubt—the theologian should only be sincerely ashamed of it.

41. Theology cannot demonstrate why or how human beings know the word of God, it can only investigate and make intelligible the fact man has heard the Word.

42. To be a Christian does not mean to be religious in a particular way, to cultivate some particular form of asceticism (as a sinner, a penitent, or a saint), but to be a man.

43. Revelation has come about by the irruption into this world of another and wholly different one.

44. Doubt is essentially connected with the quest for truth; there is no truth without doubt, and no doubt without truth.

45. Faith cannot bridge the gulf between man and God for faith renders necessary and unavoidable the perception of the con-

tradiction between God and the world of time and things and man.

46. Today, the last secret place from which God has not been elbowed out of the world is the need of unhappy and ignorant individuals.

## VI.

The following several statements are expressions of feelings and self-evaluations drawn from various writings and from interviews. They are not meant to be theological propositions or propositions about the nature of reality and are therefore neither true nor false. Please rate these statements according to the degree to which they apply to you. In each case ask yourself if the statement corresponds with your own feelings regardless of whether you consider the attitude expressed to be desirable or undesirable.

1. I am having to seriously consider the limitations and relativities of the denomination in which I was raised.

2. It sometimes occurs to me that it is only by the belief in God that a man is restrained from using people for his own selfish needs.

3. Questions and doubts are dogging me which spiritual necessity and honesty require me to try to answer.

4. I pray well.

5. I am concerned, now, about the authority and relevance of the Bible for modern life.

6. It is, after all, possible that in spite of my insignificance before God, in personal humiliation at what I personally have committed, I may be "the gift of God" to my people.

7. My doubt is terrible—nothing can withstand it—it is a cursed hunger and I can swallow up every argument, every consolation and sedative.

8. I never knew what it meant to be young.

9. Periods of deep uncertainty sometimes settle on me, and then life seems empty and meaningless.

## VII.

Please rate the following statements according to the degree to which you agree or disagree with them.

1. Every explanation of man and the world is incomplete unless it takes account of God's will.

2. Life would hardly be worth living without the promise of immortality and life after death.

3. Christianity and all other religions are, at best, only partly true.

4. In times of personal grief, such as the death of a loved one, prayer is the greatest source of comfort.

5. Man can solve all his important problems without help from a Supreme Being.

6. Many events in human history took place only because a Supreme Being stepped in to make them happen.

7. Every person needs the church—a place where he can go for prayer, moral uplifting, and a feeling of security.

8. The Bible contains many magical and superstitious beliefs.

9. The fate of civilization depends on the strength and ability of the church.

10. Every person should have complete faith in a Supreme Being whose rules he obeys without question.

11. In addition to faith we need help from God in order to resist temptation.

12. Heaven and Hell are products of man's imagination, and do not actually exist.

To pursue this work further, I hope to have the opportunity to meet with theology students individually, perhaps at some length. As I indicated in the Introduction, this research lives only by the participation and collaboration of those people who, by sharing their experience, can provide information that will begin to suggest humanly relevant answers. The work proceeds between people who have complementary goals. The process is the effort—on both sides—to understand, clarify, and gain deeper insight into experience. In the past most of my collaborators have found this process to be of some interest and use to themselves as a way of increasing awareness and understanding of some aspects of their thinking and experience.

Thank you for your time, interest, and what you have given.

# Appendix B

*Description of Thematic Apperception Test (TAT) Cards*

Pictures from the standard series, with descriptions from Murray (1943).

1. A young boy is contemplating a violin which rests on a table in front of him.

6BM. A short elderly woman stands with her back turned to a tall young man. The latter is looking downward with a perplexed expression.

7BM. A gray-haired man is looking at a younger man who is sullenly staring into space.

11. A road skirting a deep chasm between high cliffs. On the road in the distance are obscure figures. Protruding from the rocky wall on one side is the long head and neck of a dragon.

12M. A young man is lying on a couch with his eyes closed. Leaning over him is the gaunt form of an elderly man, his hand stretched out above the face of the reclining figure.

13MF. A young man is standing with downcast head buried in his arm. Behind him is the figure of a woman lying in bed.

16. Blank card.

Symbolic TAT pictures.

    I. A bleak barn, surrounded by snow, rises behind the head of an old, bearded man which is right foreground. In the background above the barn is the outline of a winged horse. A small woman's head vaguely outlined appears left foreground.

   II. A collection of figures and symbols with a vaguely religious tone. In foreground right center a large snake faces the viewer. Behind and above him is the praying figure of a bearded, prophetic-looking man. To his left and further back is a mosque. In the left foreground is the bust of a young, turbaned man.

III. In the left foreground are the head and shoulders of a young man. Behind him the picture is filled with a large ecclesiastical-looking building, one side of which is in dark shadow, and a flower is superimposed on the shadowed wall. A long flight of steps leads up to an arched doorway and to the left of that is a tree with no leaves.

IV. In right foreground a naked man clings to a pole. Behind him is an infinite expanse of land, sea, and sky. A flaming arrow rises out of the sea. A very small figure in the distance stands on the shore.

V. A kneeling man, bare to the waist, is center foreground, and three men to his left point accusingly. To the man's right and to the rear, a woman crouches, holding an infant.

VI. In right foreground is a young boy's head and shoulders with the branches from a tree hanging over him. Behind him is the silhouetted skyline of a city. A skeleton waves from behind a church spire.

# Bibliography

Abbreviation: SE = *Standard Edition of the Complete Psychological Works of Sigmund Freud*, edited by James Strachey. 24 vols. London: Hogarth Press and Institute of Psycho-Analysis, 1964.

Adorno, T. W., Else Frenkel-Brunswick, Daniel J. Levinson, and R. Nevitt Sanford. 1950. *The Authoritarian Personality.* New York: Harper and Row.

Allen, E. L. n.d. *The Sovereignty of God and the Word of God.* London: Hodder and Stoughton.

Angyal, A. 1965. *Neurosis and Treatment: A Holistic Theory.* New York: Wiley.

Baranger, W. 1958. "The Ego and the Functions of Ideology." *International Journal of Psychoanalysis,* vol. 39, pp. 191 ff.

Barth, Karl. 1962. *Credo.* New York: Scribner.

———. 1963. *Evangelical Theology.* New York: Holt, Rinehart and Winston.

Bellah, Robert N. 1963. "It Doesn't Go Far Enough." Review of Robinson's *Honest to God.* In Robert N. Bellah, *Beyond Belief: Essays on Religion in a Post-Traditional World.* New York: Harper and Row, 1970.

———. 1964. "Religious Evolution." In Robert N. Bellah, *Beyond Belief.* New York: Harper and Row, 1970.

———. 1965. "Father and Son in Christianity and Confucianism." In Robert N. Bellah, *Beyond Belief.* New York: Harper and Row, 1970.

———. 1968. "Sociology of Religion." In Robert N. Bellah, *Beyond Belief.* New York: Harper and Row, 1970.

Bonhoeffer, Dietrich. 1953. *Letters and Papers from Prison.* New York: Macmillan Co.

Buber, Martin. 1923. *I and Thou.* New York: Scribner, reissued 1955.

Erikson, E. H. 1953. "Wholeness and Totality." In *Totalitarianism,* edited by C. J. Friedrich. Cambridge, Mass.: Harvard University Press, 1954.

————. 1958. *Young Man Luther*. New York: Norton, paperback edition 1962.

————. 1959. "Identity and the Life Cycle." *Psychological Issues*, vol. 1, no. 1, monograph 1. New York: International Universities Press.

————. 1965. "The Development of Ritualization." In *The Religious Situation: 1968*, edited by Donald R. Cutler. Boston: Beacon Press, 1968.

Fenichel, O. 1945. *The Psychoanalytic Theory of Neurosis*. New York: Norton.

Flugel, J. C. 1921. *The Psycho-Analytic Study of the Family*. London: Hogarth Press, reissued 1960.

Freud, Anna. 1946. *The Ego and the Mechanisms of Defense*. New York: International Universities Press.

Freud, Sigmund. 1899. "Screen Memories." In *SE*, vol. 3, pp. 303–322.

————. 1909. "Analysis of a Phobia in a Five Year Old Boy." In *SE*, vol. 10, pp. 5–149.

————. 1914. "On Narcissism." In *SE*, vol. 14, pp. 73–102.

————. 1917. "Mourning and Melancholia." In *SE*, vol. 14, pp. 243–258.

————. 1921. "Group Psychology and the Analysis of the Ego." In *SE*, vol. 18, pp. 69–143.

————. 1923. "The Ego and the Id." In *SE*, vol. 19, pp. 13–66.

————. 1926. "Inhibitions, Symptoms and Anxiety." In *SE*, vol. 20, pp. 87–102.

————. 1927. *The Future of an Illusion*. In *SE*, vol. 21, pp. 5–56.

————. 1930. *Civilization and Its Discontents*. In *SE*, vol. 21, pp. 64–145.

————. 1939. *Moses and Monotheism*. In *SE*, vol. 23, pp. 7–137.

Gustafson, J. M. 1963. "The Clergy in the United States." *Daedalus*, Fall 1963, no. 4.

Harris, T. G. 1965. "The Battle of the Bible." *Look* magazine, July 27, 1965.

Hartmann, H. 1939. *Ego Psychology and the Problem of Adaptation*. New York: International Universities Press, 1958.

Heath, C. n.d. *The Challenge of Karl Barth*. London: H. R. Allenson.

Helfaer, Philip M. 1968. "The Psychology of Religious Doubt: Clinical Studies of Protestant Theological Students." Ph.D. dissertation, Department of Social Relations, Harvard University.

Holbrook, David. 1969. "R. D. Laing and the Death Circuit." *Psychiatry and Social Science Review*, vol. 3, no. 4.

James, William. 1902. *The Varieties of Religious Experience.* New York: New American Library, Mentor Books, 1958.

Jones, R. M. 1962. *Ego Synthesis in Dreams.* Cambridge, Mass.: Schenkman.

Jung, Carl. 1951. *Aion.* Princeton, N.J.: Princeton University Press, Bollingen Series, 1959.

Kierkegaard, Soren. 1959. *The Journals of Kierkegaard.* New York: Harper and Row.

———. 1960. *The Witness of Kierkegaard,* edited by C. Michalson. New York: Association Press.

Kubie, Lawrence. 1961. *Neurotic Distortion in the Creative Process.* New York: Noonday Press.

Leibrecht, W. 1959. *Religion and Culture: Essays in Honor of Paul Tillich.* New York: Harper and Row.

Levinson, Daniel J. 1963. "Personality, Sociocultural System, and the Process of Role-Definition." Unpublished paper presented at the meetings of the American Sociological Association.

———. 1964. "Idea Systems in the Individual and in Society." In *Explorations in Social Change,* edited by G. K. Zollschan and W. Hirsch. Boston: Houghton Mifflin Co.

Mann, Thomas. 1936. "Freud and the Future." In *Essays of Three Decades.* New York: Knopf, 1948.

Moore, Burness E. 1962. "A Review of Narcissism from the Meta-psychological Point of View." Unpublished paper presented at the Boston Psychoanalytic Society and Institute.

Murray, Henry A. 1938. *Explorations in Personality.* New York: Oxford University Press.

———. 1943. *Thematic Apperception Test Manual.* Cambridge, Mass.: Harvard University Press.

Murray, John M. 1964. "Narcissism and the Ego-Ideal." *Journal of the American Psychoanalytic Association,* vol. 12, pp. 477–516.

Niebuhr, H. R., D. D. Williams, and J. M. Gustafson. 1957. *The Advancement of Theological Education.* New York: Harper.

Piers, G., and M. B. Singer. 1953. *Shame and Guilt.* Springfield, Ill.: Charles Thomas.

Pruyser, Paul. 1960. "Some Trends in the Psychology of Religion." *Journal of Religion,* vol. 40.

Rapaport, D. 1959. "A Historical Survey of Psychoanalytic Ego Psychology." In *Psychological Issues,* vol. 1, no. 1.

Reich, Annie. 1954. "Early Identifications as Archaic Elements in the Superego." *Journal of the American Psychoanalytic Association,* vol. 2, pp. 218 ff.

Robinson, J. A. T. 1963. *Honest to God.* Philadelphia: Westminster Press.

Rorschach, Hermann. *Psychodiagnostics, Plates*. Switzerland: Hans Huber.

Rosen, J. N. 1964. "Psychotic Creativity." In *Annals of Psychotherapy*, vol. 5, no. 1, monograph no. 8, pp. 57–61.

Sharaf, Myron R. 1962. "An Approach to the Theory and Measurement of Intraception." Ph.D. dissertation, Harvard University.

Tarachow, Sidney. 1964. "Introductory Remarks." In *The Psychoanalytic Study of Society*, edited by W. Muensterberger and S. Axelrad. Vol. 3. New York: International Universities Press.

Tillich, Paul. 1948. *The Shaking of the Foundations*. New York: Scribner.

————. 1957a. *Systematic Theology*, vol. 2. Chicago: University of Chicago Press.

————. 1957b. *The Dynamics of Faith*. New York: Harper and Brothers.

Wagoner, W. D. 1963. *Bachelor of Divinity: Uncertain Servants in Seminary and Ministry*. New York: Association Press.

Wittgenstein, Ludwig. 1918. *Tractatus Logico-Philosophicus*. London: Routledge and Kegan Paul, 1955.

————. 1953. *Philosophical Investigations*, translated by G. E. M. Anscombe. New York: Macmillan Co.

# Notes

## I. INTRODUCTION: RELIGIOUS DOUBT AS A PHENOME-NON FOR PSYCHOLOGICAL STUDY

1. The major ones are "On Narcissism" (1914), "Mourning and Melancholia" (1917), "Group Psychology and the Analysis of the Ego" (1921), "The Ego and the Id" (1923), and "Inhibitions, Symptoms and Anxiety" (1926).

## II. ON THE SOCIAL PSYCHOLOGY OF THE PROTESTANT THEOLOGICAL STUDENT

1. See Appendix A. Partial analysis of questionnaire data may be found in Helfaer (1968).

2. This and subsequent theological quotations in this and the following sections have been used as items in the questionnaire, Appendix A, part V.

3. An autobiographical account of a man living according to this practice that has become well known and has been made into a movie is *The Cross and the Switchblade*, by David Wilkerson.

4. Henry A. Murray, personal communication.

## III. THE RELIGIOUS BELIEF SYSTEM AS AN ASPECT OF PERSONALITY

1. A number of authors express general agreement with the distinctions between superego and ego-ideal that are followed here: W. Baranger, 1958; Erikson, 1959, pp. 148–149; B. E. Moore, 1962; J. Murray, 1964; G. Piers and M. B. Singer, 1953. The distinction is based upon developmental, functional, and psychopathological considerations. John Murray's (1964) discussion of the ego-ideal is particularly useful and influences what follows.

2. 63 out of 107, or nearly 59 percent of questionnaire respondents expressed some form of agreement with the following statement: "It is, after all, possible that in spite of my insignificance before God, in personal humiliation at what I personally have committed, I may be 'the gift of God' to my people." See part VI, item 6, of Appendix A.

## IV. CHELLY: A TEXAS IDYLL

1. There are a number of difficulties with this interpretation of Chelly's childhood dreams of which I am aware. A dream interpretation, in the clinical setting, is based upon and supported by the dreamer's associations. These, of course, are not available in the same way in the case of a dream

remembered from childhood. In fact, the dream itself is remembered as an association in the context of discussing with the interviewer a certain phase of life. The historical context, then, becomes part of the evidence for the interpretation, in addition to the reliance on the repetition of a theme (in this case passivity, death, in relation to the active mother) and certain regularities in primary process symbolization. Further, the present interpretation is simplified in more than one way. The meaning of Chelly's passivity for his relationship with his father (perhaps suggested in the "Red Shirt" dream) has been neglected, as has, in turn, the possibility that the wish for fusion may be partly reinforced because it offered a solution to conflicts with the father. Hopefully, this simplification is justified for the purpose of developing clarity in the major hypothesis presented above.

2. For example, see Flugel, 1921, pp. 133 ff.

3. Rorschach cards will be indicated by a Roman numeral preceded by "R" parenthesized, as (RII). The standard set of ten Rorschach cards was used. Thematic Apperception Test (TAT) cards will be indicated by "T" followed by a number, either Arabic or Roman, as (T6BM) or (TIV). See Appendix B for description of TAT cards used.

4. Webster's Collegiate Dictionary. 5th edition.

5. During periods of identity formation, the person needs to and should *feel* free to find and become who he is, and that this is a *free* choice, and *his* choice. In later years, there is a converse sort of wisdom. That is the sense that life is being lived *through* one, that one's life is no more than the vehicle for the concrete articulation of an age-old archetypal, mythological pattern. Thomas Mann expresses this beautifully in his essay "Freud and the Future" (Mann, 1936).

6. Freud mentions this idea in "The Ego and the Id" (1923, p. 48): "It would seem that the mechanism of the fear of death can only be that the ego relinquishes its narcissitic libidinal cathexis in a very large measure— that is, that it gives up itself, just as it gives up some *external* object in other cases in which it feels anxiety." His ideas on the subject, however, were apparently not at all clear. He introduces this idea in among others and did not follow it up.

## V. PERVASIVE DOUBT AND THE PRECOCIOUS IDENTITY: THE CASE OF PALE

1. This bears on Freud's discussion in "The Ego and the Id" on how something becomes conscious. ". . . The answer would be: 'through becoming connected with the word-presentations corresponding to it' " (1923, p. 10). As to what "corresponds" to religious words, cf. the rest of the above discussion.

2. I am very grateful to Professor Henry A. Murray for the use of a set of symbolic TAT cards. These cards are described in Appendix B. They are indicated in the text and in the Appendix by a Roman numeral. The standard numbering is used for the cards of the standard set.

3. See Appendix B.

## VI. PRECOCIOUS IDENTITY FORMATION IN CONSERVATIVE PROTESTANTISM

1. This subject was interviewed only once. He will not be discussed in

subsequent chapters. However this material exemplifies particularly well the orientation to God's will we are discussing.

### VII. ELECTON: RESOLUTION THROUGH CONVERSION

1. See Flugel, 1921, pp. 160–161, for a discussion of the identification of a child with his grandparent.

2. "For we are not contending against flesh and blood, but against the principalities, against the powers, against the world rulers of this present darkness, against the spiritual hosts of wickedness in the heavenly places." Ephesians 6:12. See also Ephesians 1:21; Colossians 1:6, 16; 2:10, 15.

3. This is another instance in which theology has institutionalized a universal psychological tendency: the tendency to accept uncritically an interpretation of reality on the basis of the criterion that it carries a feeling of truth. This tendency has played a role in philosophy in a somewhat different form. In the *Meditations*, for example, Descartes argues from the existence in his mind of the idea of God to God's existence. The psychological mechanism is the same. An inner experience is accepted as carrying its own criterion of an externally existing reality.

### VIII. MUDGE: RESOLUTION THROUGH LIBERALIZATION

1. 1 Samuel 1:11–28: "And she vowed a vow and said, 'O Lord of hosts, if thou wilt indeed look on the affliction of thy maidservant, and remember me, and not forget thy maidservant, but wilt give to thy maidservant a son, then I will give him to the Lord all the days of his life, and no razor shall touch his head.' . . . And in due time Hannah conceived and bore a son, and she called his name Samuel, for she said, 'I have asked him of the Lord. . . . Therefore I have lent him to the Lord; as long as he lives, he is lent to the Lord.'"

2. This observation is presented by Annie Reich (1954) as cited by Moore (1962).

### IX. AMBIVALENT FAITH

1. To safeguard confidentiality, many features of Joel's case are omitted.

### X. SUMMARY TO PARTS TWO AND THREE

1. We would hypothesize that during these episodes, Electon and Mudge would have manifested some of the other indications of pervasive doubt, such as the weakening of defenses and the susceptibility therefrom to more primitive impulse and fantasy. There is clear evidence for this in the case of Electon's description of his conversion experience. In Mudge's case, it also seems reasonable to make this inference in the light of the Rorschach protocol and the hypnagogic imagery of the cross on the coffin and the fact that these sets of imagery seem to have the same source. It is reasonable to assume that this psychologically deeper source would have a more powerful and primitive effect during a period of emotional upset.

2. Pp. 184–185.

### XI. EYMAN: A PARADIGM LIBERAL

1. Eyman's fantasy itself has a strong resemblance to the phobia of "Little Hans" in Freud's famous case. Cf. Freud, 1909.

2. See discussion of Eyman's Rorschach protocol, pp. 247 f; the discussion of the turn from mastery to relationship, p. 256; and that of turning away from Father's world, p. 255 and elsewhere.

3. Freud, "Screen Memories" (1899).

### XII. STRINDGE: A LIBERAL DOUBTER

1. See Questionnaire, Appendix A, part V.

2. See Questionnaire, Appendix A, part V, items 4, 22, 24, 28, 40, and 44.

3. See Questionnaire, Appendix A, part VI, items 1, 3, 4, 5, 7, and 9.

4. See Questionnaire, Appendix A, part V, items 13, 26, and 38.

### XIV. CONCLUSION: DOUBT AND EGO SYNTHESIS IN RELIGIOUS BELIEF SYSTEMS

1. Cf. A. Angyal, *Neurosis and Treatment: A Holistic Theory* (New York: Wiley, 1965).

2. In the *Tractatus Logico-Philosophicus*, Ludwig Wittgenstein makes these interesting observations:

"6.43   If good or bad willing changes the world, it can only change the limits of the world, not the facts; not the things that can be expressed in language.

In brief, the world must thereby become quite another. It must so to speak wax or wane as a whole.

The world of the happy is quite another than that of the unhappy.

"6.431   As in death, too, the world does not change, but ceases.

"6.4311   Death is not an event of life. Death is not lived through."

3. See Erikson's discussion of George Bernard Shaw (1959, pp. 107–108). Here Erikson speaks of "elements of identity formations" and for Shaw lists "The Snob," "The Noisemaker," and "The Diabolical One."

### APPENDIX A

1. Format has been slightly changed to accommodate to book format.

2. Response categories omitted to accommodate page format.

# Index

Abandonment, feelings of: 203–204

Absoluteness, dimension of theology: 16–17

Action, moral: 228–229, 231, 246, 257, 258, 292, 313

Adolescence: 129, 136, 192, 279–280; masturbation, 187, 279–280

Aggression: 43; superego and, 44

Ambivalence: 8, 41, 52, 107, 184, 193–194, 196, 208, 213, 215, 246, 300, 312, 314–315, 317

Anal conflict: 266, 267–268, 290

Angyal, A.: 8

Anxiety: 55, 246, 256, 284–285, 316; castration, 44, 45, 132, 244, 254, 257, 258, 283, 313; death, 70, 73, 81–82, 86, 101–104, 106, 121–123, 132, 210, 270, 312–313; sexual, 151, 157–158, 161; sources of, 52–53, 81–82, 86, 312–313; tolerance of, 52, 164–165

Authority: 53–54; conflict with, 158

Baptism, and precocious identity formation: 64, 70, 73, 129–130

Baranger, W.: 53

Barth, Karl: 197, 241; concept of God, 17–18, 19, 156; on doubt, 12–13, 26

Belief systems: ambivalent, 185, 208, 215; and basic needs, 94, 153–157, 159, 167, 316; breadth, 30; defined, 10; and ego synthesis, 37–38, 46, 164–165, 308–313; family and, 42, 93–94; personality and, 4–5, 37, 86, 242–243, 257–258; as response to life, 303–305; theology as, 16

Bellah, Robert N.: 11

Brainwashing: 42, 180, 213

Briting: 214, 215, 306, 314; family life, 200–202; relationship with God, 214; relationship with mother, 206

Bruner, Emil: 156

Buber, Martin: 19, 174; I-Thou concept, 124

Bultmann, Rudolf: 93, 108

Calling, to ministry: 50, 153, 155, 218

Case method: 3–4, 58–59, 318–319; applicability, 318; categories, 56–58

Castration anxiety: 44, 45, 132, 244, 254, 257, 258, 283, 313

Certainty: 87, 159, 163, 165, 208

Chelly: 93–94, 96, 126–127, 241, 242, 303–304; baptism, 64, 70, 73; dreams, 70, 71–72, 73; father relationship, 67, 69; fear of death, 70, 73, 81–82; precocious identity formation, 63–64, 70, 76, 209; relationship with mother, 66–67, 68, 70–71, 73, 75–76, 82, 87

Cliff: 306, 314; dreams, 296; family, 297–98

Conflict: 7–8, 55; ambivalence, 8; anal, 266, 267–268, 290; developmental, 38, 57, 65, 70, 76, 130, 156, 201; ego and, 8–9, 48, 313–314; id-superego, 10; oedipal, 38, 132; religious, 124, 317; self-group, 144; sexual, 8, 65, 70–71; with tradition, 195, 290, 299–300

Consciousness: 38, 54

Conservatism: 6–7, 12–13, 17–18, 19, 20–21, 22, 24–26, 52, 54, 55, 56, 90, 128, 307; rejected, 230, 241, 254; witnessing as, 22, 120

341